George Lansbury

George Lansbury

Jonathan Schneer

Manchester University Press
Manchester and New York

Distributed exclusively in the USA and Canada by St. Martin's Press, New York

Copyright © Jonathan Schneer 1990

Published by Manchester University Press,
Oxford Road, Manchester, M13 9PL, UK
and Room 400, 175 Fifth Avenue, New York, NY 10010, USA

Distributed exclusively in the USA and Canada
by St. Martin's Press, Inc.,
175 Fifth Avenue, New York, NY 10010, USA

British Library cataloguing in publication data
Schneer, Jonathan
    George Lansbury. — (Lives of the left)
    1. Great Britain. Socialism. Lansbury, George, *1859-1940*
    I. Title   II. Series
    335.0092

Library of Congress cataloging in publication data applied for

ISBN 0 7190 2170 7 *hardback*

Set in Perpetua
by Koinonia Ltd, Manchester

Printed in Great Britain
by Biddles Limited, Guildford and King's Lynn

Contents

To Margaret Hayman

Acknowledgements

In preparing this book I have incurred many debts of both a scholarly and personal nature. First I should like to thank archivists in the U.K. and U.S. who responded to my pleas for photo copies of material which I could not view on location; and Professor John Postgate, F.R.S., who holds the copyright of George Lansbury's letters, and whose kind permission was necessary before photocopies could be sent to me. I wish to thank, too, Dr. Angela Raspin, archivist at the British Library of Political and Economic Science, Stephen Bird, archivist at Labour Party headquarters, the archivist at Dick Sheppard House, the volunteer staff at Marx Memorial Library, and archivists at the Public Record Office at Kew, without whose generous assistance my research would have been impossible.

Another kind of generous assistance was provided by Georgia State University which supported research trips to Britain and leave from teaching responsibilities so that I could write the book my research was for. When I moved to the Georgia Institute of Technology in the spring of 1989 it made similar provisions for me. I wish to thank both universities for treating me so well.

Friends and collegues who read portions, and in some cases the entirety, of my manuscript saved me from numerous infelicities of style and errors both of fact and interpretation. My grateful thanks to Bernard Bellon, Dina Copelman, Pat Hilden, David Howell, Hugh Hudson, Richard Schneer (my father), Peter Weiler and Diane Willen. Needless to say, the imperfections which remain are my responsibility alone.

Acknowledgements

Finally, my sons Ben and Seth, and my wife, Margaret, deserve more in the way of thanks than one can say or write. They sustained me, in every way, over the years during which this book was in preparation.

Abbreviations

B.L.P.E.S	British Library of Political and Economic Science
B.S.P	British Socialist Party
C.O.	Conscientious Objector
E.L.F.S.	East London Federation of Suffragettes
F.O.R.	Fellowship of Reconciliation
I.L.P.	Independent Labour Party
L.R.C	Labour Representation Committee
N.A.C.	National Administrative Council
N.C.F.	No Conscription Fellowship
N.E.C.	National Executive Committee
N.M.W.M.	No More War Movement
N.T.W.F.	National Transport Worker's Federation
N.U.R.	National Union of Railwaymen
N.U.W.S.S.	National Union of Women's Suffrage Societies
P.L.P.	Parliamentary Labour Party
P.P.U.	Peace Pledge Union
P.R.O.	Public Record Office
S.D.F.	Social Democratic Foundation
S.D.P.	Social Democratic Party
S.P.R.W.C.C.	Society for Promoting the Return of Women County Councillors
T.U.C.	Trades Union Congress
U.D.C.	Union of Democratic Control
W.L.F.	Women's Liberal Federation
W.S.P.U	Women's Social and Political Union

Introduction

If ever a man lived his life on the left it was George Lansbury. 'My sympathies are always with the left wingers and those who stand for principle,' he once wrote, and his life's story bore him out.[1] He was by turns a Radical Liberal, a Social Democrat, and a member of the I.L.P.; he devoted himself to the causes of socialism, feminism, and pacifism, among others. The men who influenced him most were Karl Marx, William Morris, Henry Hyndman, Vladimir Lenin and 'the lonely Galilean – Communist, agitator, martyr – crucified as one who stirred up the people and set class against class.'[2]

Lansbury was a robust personality, physically strong, straightforward, by all reports immensely likable. Photographs dating from the late nineteenth century, when Lansbury was in his twenties, show a brown-haired, tall man with muttonchop sideburns and a mustache. When the Russian refugee and future ambassador to England, Ivan Maisky, met him in 1914 he saw a man 'tall, broad shouldered, with a frank, open face and bright piercing eyes, [who] gave the impression of a kind-hearted bear masquerading as an English preacher.'[3] Later Lansbury's hair thinned, receded and became white, and he looked like a patriarch. There is a photograph of him presiding over the borough council at Poplar Town Hall in East London in 1921 in which, because of his height, he looks imposing, almost majestic. Only at the end, when the terrible weight of the world's troubles bore most heavily upon him, did the impression of strength and strength of purpose become overlaid by other, less happy, signals. 'There still exists a cinema news-reel,' his son-in-law, Ramond Postgate wrote in 1951, 'showing George Lansbury leading, and then speaking to, the May Day marchers to Hyde Park [in 1933]. The figure is unchanged,' Postgate continues,

> the body tall, strong, upright, if a little heavy; the step is unusually firm for a man of seventy-four. The head has the Roman grandeur which had replaced the simple geniality of 1912 – a big, Wellingtonian nose, sparse white hair blown in the wind, firm jaw; the voice is deep and full, though husky. But the eyes, as the face turns to the camera, are haggard and in deep hollows; there are deep sympathy and profound tiredness in both them and the set of the shoulders. He looks round upon the crowd as if he were solely responsible for their future and their belief, and as if the responsibility were more than his exhaustion could bear.[4]

Lansbury experienced his full share of triumphs and joys. This book shows that the sunny, optimistic, strong-willed, radical and agitator never entirely disappeared. But Lansbury lived to see, and unavailingly to oppose with all his might, the unimaginable horror of world war. So fully imbricated was he in the futile struggles to avert these calamities, and so deeply did he feel his failures, that some disillusionment was inevitable. The frontispiece of Postgate's biography of Lansbury, a photograph of Labour's leader in 1935, inspired one man who saw it, and who knew nothing of Lansbury's career, to say to me 'that is the photograph of an honest man who fell among thieves.'

The following pages do not attempt to trace chronologically the process by which the young Radical grew old. This is not a complete biography, nor even a complete political biography. On the one hand, it is not concerned with Lansbury's family life; on the other, it fails to treat his important role as editor of the *Daily Herald* from 1912–22, or the majority of his parliamentary campaigns, or his role in the Labour Government of 1929-31. Postgate's biography is an excellent source for those events and themes. This volume, one in a series entitled 'Lives of the Left,' focusses upon George Lansbury's efforts as a socialist, feminist and pacifist, the three great causes of his life and, also, three of the British left's most important preoccupations during the half century while Lansbury was politically active. If it is successful it will further illuminate some aspects of his outlook which Postgate did not examine in detail and, in so doing, add to our general store of knowledge on the history of the British left since the late Victorian period.

I hope that the three sections can stand on their own, although I have attempted to link them by referring backwards and forwards to people and themes appearing earlier or later in the text. In general the work respects the chronology of Lansbury's life: Section I concentrates mainly on his socialism in the 1880s and 1890s; Section II treats primarily his connection with the suffragettes of the Edwardian period; and Section III deals with his pacifism which only became important with the outbreak of World War I and which climaxed at the end of his life in the 1930s. There is some unavoidable overlap, however, both thematically and chronologically. Lansbury's socialism and pacifism were inextricably entwined, for example, and so Section III is really almost as much about his later understanding of socialism as it is about his pacifism. Also I discovered that it was occasionally necessary to treat various themes out of sequence. Thus Lansbury's feminism, which I treat in Section II, first surfaced before his conversion to socialism, which I treat earlier in Section I. My hope, however, is that the advantages of the thematic structuring will outweigh the drawbacks undoubtedly posed by these departures from the strict order in which events occurred.

Because this is not a biography in the conventional sense I have appended at the end a chronological listing of the main events of Lansbury's life.

1 Lansbury and socialism

Socialism has been a significant factor in British affairs since the foundation of four organizations during the 1880s and early 1890s: the Marxist Social Democratic Federation (S.D.F.), the Socialist League (although this body did not last long), the gradualist Fabian Society and the Independent Labour Party (I.L.P.). Although these were the most important, they comprised what were merely the main elements in a movement which has never lacked schismatics and iconoclasts. Since its inception the British socialist movement has been composed of diverse strands, some of which, naturally, have been stronger and more durable than others.

George Lansbury probably did as much as anyone to popularize the 'ethical,' democratic, and religious strands of British socialism and to braid them into a single rope which seemed capable, at times, of sustaining the movement as a whole. Although not a great thinker or theoretician, he was an extremely effective advocate and, (though this is not his reputation) political operator. During his lifetime Labour Party headquarters ignored Lansbury only at its peril. Even today the ghost of George Lansbury haunts Labour conferences and meetings in resolutions and motions demanding a more generous, more internationalist or, some would say, even utopian, socialist program.

Yet if Lansbury's understanding of socialism put him at odds with Labour's most influential figures, it touched a wellspring of sentiment and feeling among British workers which more astringent, dogmatic, or opportunistic politicians could never find. Thus Lansbury helped to shape, and then became the main exponent of, an enduring alternative vision of socialism which Labour's leaders have never been able to appreciate – nor yet dispatch. How Lansbury achieved his outlook and role, and what were their main features, is the subject of the present section of this study. Because he exemplified a significant, albeit minority attitude in the larger movement of which he was a part, Lansbury's experience illuminates a chapter not merely of his own biography but also of the history of modern British labor.

1

Let us begin in the mid-1880s with the young Lansbury employed at his father-in-law's saw mill and veneer works. His wage was thirty shillings a week, which was generous for the time and place. Already, however, he had six children, so that he 'lived in poverty and did so for years.' His four-room cottage, located in St. Stephen's Row, Bow, in London's East End, was a typical 'two up and two down,' with a small washhouse attached.[1]

This was the period of the nineteenth century's 'great depression,' and conditions of life and labor in East London, which had never been comfortable for the majority of its inhabitants, now were very difficult. Unemployment and underemployment were endemic. 'Sweating' was ubiquitous. Poverty and all its attendant ills were widespread. Meanwhile foreign immigrants, notably East European Jews, poured into the district in ever increasing numbers. Not surprisingly residents of more prosperous sections of the metropolis tended to treat the East End almost as if it were an alien land. Journalists like Andrew Mearns, author of a lurid but typical article 'The Bitter Cry of Outcast London' (1883) explored the district on foot in conscious imitation of Stanley and Livingstone in Africa; amateur sociologists, such as the wealthy shipowner, Charles Booth, studied it; well-intentioned reformers established settlement houses there, the most famous of which was Toynbee

Hall. Meanwhile socialist agitators proselytized relentlessly outside the gasworks in Beckton, up and down the Thames riverside where the docks and wharves were located, and on countless street corners. In 1889 their efforts were to help spark an upsurge among local workers which, when it spread throughout the country, was dubbed 'the new unionism' and contributed to the formation in 1893 of the I.L.P., forerunner of the Labour Party.[2]

In this period of his life, however, Lansbury identified not with the socialist pioneers stalking his neighborhood, but rather with the Liberals, a natural enough choice at that time for a young working-class man who was interested in politics. Historically Liberalism always had been a 'broad church' composed of diverse and even conflicting elements. Some Liberals were quite conservative, but also over the past half century Liberalism had proven to be the primary vehicle of social and political reform in Britain, and during the late 1880s the grand old reformer, William Gladstone, was still party chief. If he was resistant to the 'new Radicals' in his party who wished to base Liberal politics upon the support of urban workers, he nevertheless remained true to a time-honored vision of Liberal reform. Under his direction the Liberal Party carried the third great Reform Bill in 1884, enfranchising many male agricultural laborers and reducing the number of 'fancy franchises' which allowed wealthy men to vote more than once. In 1891, he lent support to the famous Newcastle Programme, which committed the party to Home Rule for Ireland, disestablishment of the Church in Scotland and Wales, employers' liability legislation and various measures of land reform. Such measures may have failed to satisfy the new Radicals who were demanding more sweeping measures, but at least under Gladstone the Liberal Party was open, or at any rate more open than the Conservatives, to membership and even to the parliamentary candidacies of working-class men. As a result, a handful of 'Lib-Labs,' Liberals of the laboring class, sat in the House of Commons. One, the former stone-mason Henry

Broadhurst, eventually became a junior Minister in Gladstone's third government. So, if some members of the 'broad church,' old-fashioned Whigs, for example, thought that reform had gone quite far enough, and the Newcastle Programme altogether too far, others were intent on forcing even more far-reaching reforms. These were the Radical Liberals to whom the young Lansbury was attracted. But just when he was about to involve himself in politics both the definition and aims of Liberalism were as unsettled as they had ever been.[3]

The impetus to his active participation in political affairs in Britain was his abortive attempt to escape from the great depression. In May 1884 Lansbury, then twenty-five years of age, had taken his family to Australia, only to find that conditions there were even harsher and unemployment more prevalent than at home. Returning to London a year later and settling in Bow, he was determined to make his family's difficult experience serve a useful purpose. He joined the local Liberal Party, soon becoming secretary of his ward committee. From this position he launched an agitation to expose the emigration 'swindle.' During the winter of 1885-86 he spoke almost every night at the Mile End Waste, often in freezing weather. In February 1886, he helped to organize a conference whose aim, he explained succinctly in a flyer publicizing the event, was to make known 'the true state of the case ... so that Philanthropic people may be prevented from supporting schemes that are not likely to be successful and that workers may be saved the trouble of crossing the Ocean, only to find matters as bad as they were at home.'[4] Lansbury spoke earnestly and well at this gathering, greatly impressing the Radical M.P. for Whitechapel, Samuel Montagu (later Lord Swaythling), who was one of his audience.

This first significant political effort of Lansbury's life had an unexpected result. Six months later the government was forced into a general election. Montagu, remembering the man who had organized so effectively the anti-emigration rally and spoken so convincingly at it, invited him to become his election agent in Whitechapel. Lansbury received permission from his father-in-law to leave work for three weeks, accepted Montagu's commission, and steered his candidate to victory. Then, shortly after the election, John Archibald Murray MacDonald, an 'advanced' Radical who had just become the prospective Liberal candidate for Bow and Bromley, Lansbury's home district, asked him to become his agent too. Again Lansbury accepted. Although he had returned to his daily labor at the saw mill, he was now clearly set on the path that would lead to a full-time political career.

The Bow and Bromley Radical and Liberal Association, in which Lansbury was to play an increasingly important (if relatively shortlived) role, existed 'for the purpose of uniting all sections of the progressive party in this borough,' which is to say Whigs, Gladstonians and new Radicals alike.[5] Created in 1885, its founding chairman was W.S. Robson, who lost his parliamentary seat in the general election a year later. It was Robson's seat for which Murray MacDonald stood in 1892. The Association contained four ward committees (of one of which, as we have seen, Lansbury was secretary). These committees met together in a 'Council of 400' which was governed by an executive body of twenty members. Early in 1888 Lansbury became secretary in this council and, a few months later, its chief political operative. Thus when Jane Cobden, daughter of the famous reformer Richard Cobden, stood for the London County Council as Bow and Bromley's Liberal and Radical candidate, Lansbury managed her successful campaign.[6] Two years later the Association recognized his status as the party's rising star by inviting him to become Cobden's successor in the L.C.C. Had Murray MacDonald not already occupied the position, Lansbury would probably have been asked to be its parliamentary candidate as well. As it was, both Montagu and MacDonald promised that Liberal headquarters would find him a safe constituency if he wanted one. Meanwhile, the main Radical newspaper of the metropolis, the *Star*, was lauding him as 'a remarkable man. He has not his match among the political secretaries in London.'[7] Somehow, however, Lansbury managed to withstand such blandishments and flattery. In fact, he remained a member of the Radical Association only because he had promised to act as agent for MacDonald at the next general election, which finally occurred in July 1892. He quit the Liberals immediately afterwards to found a branch of the S.D.F. At some point between 1886 and 1892, then, he had become a socialist.

This conversion represents a critical stage in Lansbury's evolution, but it had also a wider significance. First of all, when Lansbury left the Liberal and Radical Association to form the S.D.F. branch, he took with him its most active working-class members. This was a deadly blow to the political prospects of Murray MacDonald, who never won an election in Bow and Bromley again. Thus Lansbury's defection was a serious setback to East-End Radicalism as a whole and, correspondingly, an important triumph for metropolitan socialism. In addition, Lansbury partially charted the various stages of his conversion in private letters and articles for a monthly journal, *Coming Times*, which he helped to establish in June 1889. These cast some light upon the content of working-class Radicalism and socialism in East London during a critical period in the history of both, subjects of no little interest to scholars today.

Of what did Lansbury's Radicalism consist? What caused him to decide that socialism, not the new Radicalism, offered his country the better future? Why did he become convinced that labor needed an independent political party, separate from the Liberals? When did his decision to leave the Liberals occur?

George Lansbury's early Radicalism was instinctive. He wrote in his autobiography, *My Life*, that he had been interested in politics since childhood, and always had been a fervent champion of the 'bottom dog.' As a boy, for example, his sympathy went out to the Parisian Communards. A little later he opposed Disraeli's imperialist program because he pitied its African and Afghan victims. Gladstone was his hero, until the advent of Liberal coercion in Ireland in the early 1880s. After Lansbury had made the journey out to Australia and back again he participated in many of the rallies organized by the S.D.F. on behalf of the unemployed, including the famous demonstration of February 8, 1886, which degenerated into a near riot when the crowd marched from Trafalgar Square to Hyde Park, throwing stones at club windows on Pall Mall along their way.[8] He was present, too, on 'Bloody Sunday,' November 13, 1887, also at Trafalgar Square, when the police rushed a free-speech demonstration, injuring many and killing one man, Alfred Linnell. Lansbury's approach to politics, it quickly becomes apparent, was shaped by a visceral sense of identity with oppressed and exploited people whatever their nationality.

Like good souls of every time and place, he hoped to ameliorate the conditions of those who were less fortunate than himself. Deeply religious at this stage, it is not surprising that 'General' Booth's Salvation Army temporarily appealed to him. Shortly after the sojourn in Australia, when he was a Radical in Bow and Bromley, he participated actively in church-related charity work, for example, organizing Christmas dinners for children of the unemployed.[9] He became superintendent of a Sunday School. At one point he was instrumental in helping to establish a convalescent home for Christian working men.[10] Good deeds came naturally to him.

In the mid-1880s these proclivities brought him to Liberalism. He accepted the main planks of the Liberal Party: Home Rule, Disestablishment, taxing ground rents and other reforms later enunciated in the Newcastle Programme; and the Progressive platform of the new Radicals, including promises to limit the

sweating of labor, to make funds available for improved working-
class housing, to streamline and democratize municipal government, etc. Already he favored universal suffrage for both sexes.[11]
He advocated the eight-hour day. Probably he was a republican,
for in July 1889 he helped to persuade the London Liberal and
Radical Union to vote against the royal grant. 'As poorly paid
workingmen have to keep their families as best they can, the Prince
of Wales should do so also.'[12]

Above all, Lansbury sympathized and identified with the political
and social aspirations of his neighbors and friends, the workers of
East London. During the famous London dock strike of August and
September 1889, he solicited funds for the strikers. Earlier he had
aided the organizing drives of various trade unions. His letters to
Jane Cobden often included requests, which she usually honored,
to share platforms with trade unionists.[13] Similarly, he did his best
to associate MacDonald and Montagu with the labor movement.[14]
Also he was continually asking these middle-class friends for
donations to various strike funds. 'As I have no money to give the
men myself,' he once wrote to Cobden, 'I feel bound to help them
by organising help from others.'[15]

None of these activities was incompatible with the new Radicalism as understood in Bow and Bromley. On the other hand,
Lansbury's instinctive solidarity with the strivings of workers set
him apart from Cobden, Montagu and MacDonald, generous and
well intentioned though they were. One reason why many
working-class Radicals eventually abandoned the Liberal Party was
because they had come to believe that workers needed *independent*
political representation. Middle-class Liberals could not provide
that, if only by virtue of their social origins. Moreover, as Lansbury
complained in a letter to MacDonald, working-class Liberals did
not provide it either, because when their party was in power, they
feared to embarrass its leaders with radical demands.[16] So here was
a reason for him to reconsider his affiliation.

And there were others. In considering the growth of labor support for an independent political party many historians have emphasized the reluctance of local Liberal organizations to sanction Lib-Lab candidacies, Gladstone's obsession with Ireland, and a general sharpening of working-class consciousness.[17] In Lansbury's case personal antipathies and experiences may have played an equally significant role. How must the proud, ambitious, capable, young workingman have felt going so often with cap in hand to grandees like Montagu and Murray MacDonald? Then, during Cobden's campaign for the L.C.C., it was she, not her agent, who controlled the purse strings. At the height of the electoral contest a misunderstanding between them about money led Lansbury to offer her his resignation. This was a major falling out although it was resolved before Cobden's political effort suffered a serious setback.[18] Nevertheless Lansbury drew a significant conclusion. 'I would rather have two hundred men paying one penny per week than forty men paying £1 per year,' he reported afterwards to the Bow and Bromley Liberal and Radical Association.[19] So might have the party leaders, but it implied a vision of Liberalism which they did not share. 'Our attack is being made upon the citadels of wealth and of privilege,' Lansbury had gone on to say, which is not what MacDonald, perhaps, or Montagu most probably, let alone Liberal leaders such as Lord Rosebery, who eventually replaced Gladstone in the party's top position, thought they were doing.

In this regard an instructive, and possibly critical, moment occurred on December 4, 1889, during the closing moments of the National Liberal Federation's annual conference which was held in Manchester, and which Lansbury attended as a delegate from Bow and Bromley. He wished to speak in favor of a rider which Murray MacDonald had proposed attaching to Sir Wilfrid Lawson's 'omnibus' resolution. This latter was a potpourri of Radical reforms, anticipating the Newcastle Programme, but including additional measures, for example, 'mending or ending' the House of Lords. MacDonald's rider would have added the eight-hour day to this list. This was considered an extremely advanced proposal, one betraying socialist tendencies, because if adopted it would inevitably involve the government in what previously had been considered private economic matters. Here, perhaps, was the attack upon wealth and privilege which Lansbury favored; and the Liberal leadership opposed it strenuously from the classic *laissez-faire* standpoint. Lansbury thought this was inconsistent, because Gladstone was very willing to intervene in the private business affairs of Irish landlords in order to protect their tenants, for example by fixing their rents. Lansbury had pointed this out during the previous month at a meeting of the London Liberal and Radical Union which then carried an eight-hours motion nearly by acclamation.[20]

We do not know precisely what happened to Lansbury at the Manchester Conference. His son-in-law, Raymond Postgate, wrote many years later that even before the meeting was convened Liberal notables tried to dissuade him from speaking there, because they did not want 'eight hours' discussed. The young Radical, however, stood firm and when, in Manchester, MacDonald proposed the rider, Lansbury clambered onto the platform to support it. Then, according to Postgate,

> The chairman, Sir James Kitson, rang his bell with the persistence of a muffin-man. Lansbury nevertheless tried to speak: half the great audience howled at him, the other half, equally noisy, howled on his behalf. After a few minutes, on a signal from the chairman, stewards closed in upon him and removed him, gently, indeed, but unquestionably by force.[21]

The *Pall Mall Gazette*, of December 5, 1889, reported somewhat differently, however, that after MacDonald proposed his 'rider,'

> a supporter of Mr. MacDonald's [Lansbury, undoubtedly,] ascended the platform ... determinedly facing for two or three minutes the

clamour of the Conference ... At one moment it looked as if Sir James
Kitson would have to resort to extreme measures, but luckily the
delegate ultimately accepted a suggestion ... that he should forward
his suggestion to the chairman in writing.

The Times of December 5 did not mention Lansbury, but reported
with Olympian briefness only that, when MacDonald rose to speak,
'the Chairman ruled that no new question could be introduced into
the resolution.' As for the Liberal hierarchy, its own record of the
proceedings, the annual report of the National Liberal Federation,
did not carry any reference to the episode at all.

Insignificant as the matter may have seemed to what might be
called the Establishment, however, it made a large impression on
the main figure involved. He travelled back to London that evening
and, from his home in Bow, immediately penned a letter which was
printed two days later in the *Pall Mall Gazette*. Lansbury was as
staunch a democrat as ever breathed; this represents, I think, a key
to understanding his career (although precisely what he meant by
democracy was sometimes unclear). Now, what bothered him
most about his rough handling in Manchester was not the personal
slight, even if it suggested a troubling attitude on the part of Liberal
Party notables to rank-and-file delegates, but rather what he took
to be Liberalism's breach of democratic procedure, not merely in
his own case but more generally. 'No delegate has been allowed
to ask a question; no delegate has been allowed to move any
amendment to the cut-and-dried proposals of Messrs. Kitson,
Schnadhorst and Co.,' Lansbury complained. But then 'the whole
business was a huge farce.' Liberal conferences had become
'nothing more than automatic registering machines called into
being to register the decrees of the Executive Committee of the
National Liberal Federation.' Put bluntly, the Liberal Party, 'which
professes to be democratic,' was not living up to 'the principles
it professes.' This assessment of the party, according to Postgate,
proved to be the decisive factor in Lansbury's decision to quit.

Certainly the Manchester conference marked a milestone in Lansbury's growing disillusionment with Liberalism, but there were to be other disappointments equally grave. One involved the denouement to Jane Cobden's campaign for the L.C.C., an episode which is treated in detail in Section II of this volume. Suffice it to say here that although Cobden was legally elected in January 1889, in fact she was ineligible to act on the council because of her sex. It took more than a year before the courts had clarified her position, however, and in the meantime Lansbury helped her to conduct a stubborn defense of women's right to serve. Many London Radicals supported this agitation, but the Liberal hierarchy remained aloof. When, in April 1889, a Radical M.P., Frederick Channing, introduced a Bill in the House of Commons to make female participation on county councils lawful, it was quickly sidetracked. No vote took place. A month later the House of Lords defeated by 108 to 23 a Bill with the same purpose, which had been introduced by Lord Meath. Again, obviously, the Liberal leadership had failed to lead. Finally, in May 1891, the Commons *did* vote on the issue, and only fifty Liberal M.P.s supported the measure. The majority of Liberals in the House did not bother even to appear for the division. Lansbury drew his own conclusions. 'Surely those who are in earnest about the enfranchisement of women will not be content to be a mere appendage of the Liberal Party,' he wrote to the *Pall Mall Gazette* of June 1, 1891. And even more pointedly, 'Let them shake themselves free of party feeling.'

So, even without considering socialism, there were forces during the 1880s and early 1890s which might drive a working-class Radical such as Lansbury from the Liberal ranks. But Lansbury *was* considering socialism, a socialism he was learning from the everyday struggle to gain his own bread. Appalled by the poverty he saw all around him in the East End, what bothered him most was that it seemed inescapable, inherent not so much in the fallibility of individuals as in a great social and economic system, capitalism. His own employer was his father-in-law, a kindly and generous man. Nevertheless,

> a little lad of 16 ... who works with me asked me if I could understand why we were brought into the world. He said it is only work, sleep and eat. Fancy a young lad like him having such sentiments. And yet he is at work for decent people, as good and a little better, in fact, than competition will allow them to be.[22]

Here was a crucial insight, that capitalist competition forced even the best employers to drive their workers. As he had written elsewhere, thinking, perhaps, of his own situation,

> if a workman wishes to become a master-man he must first of all get some of his employer's customers, and undertake to supply them with goods at a lower price than other men, and to enable him to do so he must first grind down the wages of those who are to work for him.[23]

So it was the system which made people poor, not laziness or drunkenness or ill health or bad luck, though no doubt these played their part. Even those with steady jobs, however, suffered from arrangements which demanded competition between their employers. And Lansbury was aware that systemic problems could hardly be solved by mere charity, welcome though that might be in specific cases. 'The social problem is not a problem of the waifs and strays of society,' wrote this most charitable of men. 'Until some great scheme of national cooperation is established, there will be a Darkest England in spite of ... all the philanthropists in the world.'[24]

Socialist solutions beckoned, but he had joined the Liberals in good faith and would not leave them until convinced that they would never implement the 'great scheme' to which he had referred. Moreover he had promised to manage Murray MacDonald's campaign for Parliament at the next general election, whenever that might be. So he remained a putative Radical Liberal, if less committed to the Radical outlook with every passing day.

Doubtless his decreasing enthusiasm for the mainstream of the party was what led him to join with another socialistically inclined East End Radical, William Hoffman, to produce the monthly review, *Coming Times*, whose first number appeared in June 1889.

This shortlived journal (it suspended publication in 1891) illuminates the evolution not merely of Lansbury's outlook, but of working-class Radicalism in East London more generally. Its title suggested both the dissatisfaction of its editors with the current scene and their confidence that it would be superceded. But what would be the role of Radicalism in this process? In their first issue, Lansbury and Hoffman warned that 'We are not the advocates of party ascendency as a party, but value party only so far as it may be the advocate and possible administrator of principles conducive to the happiness of mankind.' Thus they served warning from the start. If Radical politicians did not live up to principles defined by *Coming Times*, the journal would cease to support the political party to which Radicals belonged.

But then, how far could Radical principles be stretched? In only its third month of existence *Coming Times* stretched them to the limit. 'We are moving toward an ideal of national and social life,' the editors averred, in which free, universal, education through the university level, and universal suffrage, would be the common expectation, which was unexceptional enough, and

> wherein the land of England shall be the property of the people, to be used for the national good, instead of it being used to enslave and impoverish the masses for the benefit of the few as at present... [and toward] a condition of thought and feeling when this world shall no longer be regarded as a huge money-grinding machine and human beings [as] things to make money with; but[, rather, as] a place wherein God has placed us to aid each other.

Here the influence of the American reformer, Henry George, is evident. He had gained a major following in Radical circles, following his recent tour of England, during which he had advocated land reforms as a general panacea. But even Radicals who accepted the need for nationalizing the land, a form of government intervention in the economy which went far beyond anything mentioned in the proposal for an eight-hour day, were unlikely to favor the celebration of mutuality with which the editors of *Coming Times* had concluded their predictive article. As for Lansbury, if he was not quite a socialist yet, surely he was no longer a strict Liberal either.

Five months later *Coming Times* contrasted the ideal society it had described previously with 'our *barbarous* civilisation.' This effort can only have heightened Liberal disquiet with the journal. 'At present,' the editors charged, 'we do not combine to wrest from nature or the elements the things necessary for the needs of life, but our efforts are rather to plunder or cheat each other.' The result was 'our rich and our poor, our pampered and our starved, our honoured and our despised.' Put simply, individualism and competition were producing poverty; but cooperation would end poverty. Reassuringly, the editors still preferred to term this 'the new Radicalism,' but they described it as 'a new social economy ... based upon the idea of one common humanity and not two classes, the dominating and the dominated.' And it was Karl Marx, not William Gladstone, who foretold a classless society.

The turning point for Lansbury, as for so many East End Radicals, appears to have occurred during the spring and summer of 1889, although the events and experiences of the following half decade or so would reinforce decisively the lessons learned then. During this period the East End was a veritable crucible for the socialist movement. Lansbury emerged from the melting pot transformed.

He was already very busy on the labor front. In May he joined the Gasworkers' and General Labourers' Union which the socialist, Will Thorne, was then organizing. A month later the union won a famous victory at the Beckton Gasworks, an eight-hour day, without even going on strike. In August Lansbury arranged and spoke at meetings on behalf of East End 'bass dressers, whose masters have refused to employ them *because* they have formed themselves into a Trade Union.'[25]Simultaneously he was an active member of the Bow and Bromley committee to help the striking dockers in their landmark, pathbreaking, battle with the port employers. Thus he made a new circle of friends, composed of socialists like Thorne, and the dockers' leaders, John Burns, Ben Tillett and Tom Mann. These men exerted a strong counterforce to the enticements and political exhortations of Radicals like Cobden, MacDonald and Montagu.

As a result, his socialist education progressed rapidly. Lansbury was far from being a theoretician or intellectual. 'I have been brought to see all that I think I understand now simply by experience,' he confessed at one point to Jane Cobden.[26] Nevertheless, he devoted himself to studying and understanding the theory of society which his new friends found so illuminating. 'Will Thorne and a handful of us often sat in quite small rooms listening to the gospel according to Karl Marx, taught as no other man or woman I have ever met could teach it by Eleanor Marx, the brilliant daughter of the great economist.'[27]Later, when he joined the S.D.F., he would participate in reading groups which studied the Marxist classics. Even now, however, 'I began to read more and more literature dealing with social and industrial questions rather than bothering my head about Liberalism and Toryism.'[28] He studied, among other works, Hyndman's *England for All* (1881), Morris's *News from Nowhere* (1890), Gronlund's *Cooperative Commonwealth* (1890) and Edward Bellamy's *Looking Backward* (1888). And he was listening as well as reading. 'I went to one of the meetings that [the S.D.F. leader] Hyndman addressed,' he recalled many years later. 'Soon I was tramping round London to hear Shaw and Burrows and the host of others who in that day were preaching

Socialism. I took part in all the big meetings.'[29]

His articles for *Coming Times* reflected these new influences. Although still a member of the Liberal Party, it was now clear that when Lansbury envisioned 'coming times,' he foresaw a socialist society, although he did not call it that. He had begun preaching Marxist concepts such as surplus value and production for use rather than profit, in what was ostensibly a Liberal journal, to an ostensibly Liberal readership. 'We are poor and wretched simply and solely because of the system which compels men and women to work not to produce food and clothing for their own comfort, but ... for the sole purpose of producing riches for a comparatively few men and women,' he charged in January 1891. He believed that Victorian capitalism had produced 'frightful inequalities ... aged men and women left to die of starvation or as despised paupers ... the man who wants to fatten on the industry of others and to spend in vice what others produce.' And he looked forward to a 'higher state,' which was socialism in everything but name, where

> every man and woman will have assured to them the right to work which at present is denied to a great number of people; [where] ... [c]hildren will be looked upon as precious beings whom the State must train ... [and] will be taught that labour is dignified and that only those who try to live on the toil of others are worthy of contempt ... [and] that the interests of one are the interests of all.[30]

Such predictions went well beyond the pregnant, if ambiguous, advocacy of land nationalization with which *Coming Times* had begun.

In fact although Lansbury was committed to helping Murray MacDonald at the next general election, his commitment to Liberalism had vanished. Whatever even the most 'advanced' Radicals may have believed, Lansbury now held that socialism and Liberalism were incompatible. Liberals might advocate charitable measures, but Lansbury lectured, 'if they leave the means and instruments of production in the hands of private individuals the position of the workers would remain the same as before.'[31]

Still, it seems evident that Lansbury's conversion to socialism, important as it was, represented only one of the factors which finally drove him from the Liberal Party. Equally significant was his perception gained at the Manchester conference and during the fruitless campaign on behalf of Jane Cobden's right to serve on the L.C.C. that, whatever Cobden or MacDonald may have hoped, the Liberals could not form a 'party of the people,' because they were dominated by men who wished to preserve the status quo. 'I came to the conclusion,' Lansbury wrote afterwards, 'that Liberalism would progress just so far as the great capitalist moneybags would allow it to progress, and so I took the plunge and joined the S.D.F.'[32]

This is a point which deserves emphasis. Lansbury had come to believe that the Liberal Party was closed to new people and new ideas because it was dominated by vested interests, leaders and bureaucrats who were too well entrenched to be moved by party dissidents. Better, then, to begin anew in a separate organization. The socialist movement offered scope to someone like Lansbury not merely because its goals of social and economic democracy were his goals too, but because it was still inchoate and essentially open. Lansbury joined not only because he was a socialist, then, but also because he was a democrat, seeking a party whose commitment to democratic procedure had not been ossified.

He would spend his life searching for a political organization that would live up to this lofty ideal. Invariably he was disappointed; but whatever the political body he joined, it rarely contained a stronger foe of undemocratic methods, or a more resourceful opponent of unreachable, unteachable, leaders and functionaries. His decision to leave the Liberals must be viewed within this context. When Lansbury led his contingent of Radical socialists out of the Liberal Party and into the S.D.F. (literally on the very evening of the poll that put Murray MacDonald into Parliament) it may have been the first time he sacrificed place and prospects to uphold democratic principles, but it would hardly be the last.

2

Having left the Liberals, Lansbury had entered a new political universe. What (and who) were its main stars, and where did the new recruit fit in?

The main socialist organizations of the era were mentioned at the beginning of this section. They were the Marxist S.D.F., led by Henry Hyndman, who held that socialism could only be achieved by violent revolution (but many of his followers, among them Lansbury, for instance, took a less apocalyptic view); the shortlived Socialist League, an offshoot of the S.D.F. originally led by William Morris but now dominated by anarchists; and the Fabian Society, which upheld the 'inevitability of gradualism,' and whose leaders, including Sidney and Beatrice Webb, and George Bernard Shaw among others, hoped to 'permeate' the Liberal Party with socialist ideas. In 1893 a former Scottish miners' leader, Keir Hardie, played a major part in helping to found yet another organization, the Independent Labour Party. The membership of these four groups often overlapped; and their ideologies often blurred at the edges despite the crystalline pronouncements of revolutionaries like Hyndman or gradualists like Sidney Webb. Generally speaking, however, it seems fair to say that socialists joined the I.L.P. because, often, they found the Fabians too rarefied, and the Marxism of the S.D.F. too rigid, or else its leaders too arrogant and dogmatic. Eventually Lansbury would find a congenial political home in the I.L.P., but for the moment he was a member of Hyndman's S.D.F.

It is a commonplace of British history that the aims and views of socialists of the late nineteenth century, and of the country's labor movement more generally, were derived largely from the bible and from native social critics and reformers like Ruskin, Carlyle, and Charles Dickens. These three figures were among those most frequently cited by the first group of Labour M.P.s in 1906, for example, when a Liberal newspaper editor asked who had influenced their political outlook. Actually this is not surprising since, like Lansbury, most of the early Labourites, many of whom belonged to socialist societies in 1906, had commenced as Radicals in the British tradition. Yet Lansbury never hesitated to credit the influence of Marx which, during the 1890s at any event, became evident almost whenever he spoke publicly. Perhaps he was more typical of metropolitan recruits to the S.D.F. than of the men, from all over Britain, who constituted the core of the new Parliamentary Labour Party. Or, perhaps, the impact of Marxism on the early British labor and socialist movements has been underestimated. For if Lansbury possessed extraordinary personal qualities, his political evolution thus far had followed a fairly typical pattern.

Still it is indisputable that many British socialists during this period held socialism to be a natural outgrowth of Liberalism, perhaps because they had begun forming their political opinions when they were Radicals. This was the point of view, for example, of most Fabians (notably Sidney Webb), and of Ramsay MacDonald (no relation to J.A. Murray MacDonald), who became Labour Party leader and Labour's first Prime Minister in 1924. Again, however, Lansbury's outlook was different. For him, socialism was indubitably *not* merely the logical extension of Liberalism; the break with Liberalism had been personally wrenching but philosophically necessary. He did not assert the interests of workers against the 'useless classes,' as Radicals of the mid-nineteenth century had done, but rather (as we have seen) the interests of those who could not afford to purchase the means of production against those who kept them in private hands. He did not think of socialism as one reform piled on top of another, as Ramsay MacDonald pictured it in a famous phrase.[33] Nor did he conceive of it as state intervention on behalf of the poor, which was merely Fabian 'collectivism' to his mind. Marx was not the sole influence here. Also, 'William Morris made me realise that there was something more to be thought of than Acts of Parliament, laws and State bureaucracy.'[34]

In short, Lansbury did not subscribe to the 'Labourist' outlook which historians such as John Saville have attributed to the modern British working-class movement and which is said to have been embodied in the Labour Party itself.[35] 'Labourism' was a relatively modest doctrine which, denying the inevitability of class conflict, emphasized reforms that would be supported by all people of good will and achieved through parliamentary procedures. It owed much to Fabian notions of 'the inevitability of gradualness' and to the emphasis placed by trade unionists upon 'knife and fork' issues. Although never one to slight the importance of immediate reforms, Lansbury was not greatly attracted by this rather pallid doctrine. He thought that socialism represented a new way of life, a new gospel, indeed, a new religion. 'When I was converted to Socialism,' he wrote many years later,

> life for me was entirely changed. A new vision, a new inspiration came into my life. Poverty and social misery as lived by the masses, luxury and pleasure as lived by the few, became more understandable, and in spite of my family responsibilities which were very heavy ... I took no thought of where I should find myself, but went out as a missionary on behalf of Socialism with all the reckless enthusiasm of a crusader.[36]

As he exhorted S.D.F. members, 'we must show by our daily lives that we are prepared to sacrifice all for the sake of the cause.'[37] This places him outside the Labourist tradition, but within another, the revolutionary – or, at any rate, millennarian – tradition which historians like Edward Thompson and Stephen Yeo have insisted always existed as a contrast to Labourism, not least during the late

1880s and early 1890s. In those days, they maintain, many British socialists possessed a 'transformed and transforming vision.'[38]

Certainly Lansbury did. It was based upon a series of interlocking convictions so basic as to be beyond discussion. He believed that one person was as good as another no matter their race or sex, that it was wrong to expect someone to live or labor in a manner which would be unacceptable to oneself, and that the world could be rearranged to reflect these values. This far the Labourist, and perhaps even the Radical, might have gone too, but then the Radical ascribed the failure of the world to live up to these principles to the failures of individuals rather than to the ineluctable pressures exerted upon individuals by the capitalist system, while the Labourist aspired to reform the system by stages, not to reconstitute society absolutely.

Lansbury, however, had accepted the Marxist dialectic and the stages theory of history. Just as 'the break up of feudalism' had constituted a revolutionary transformation, so the capitalist system that had replaced it would inevitably be swept away by a higher stage.[39] In the meantime, capitalism could be made more bearable as the result of reforms which, therefore, were almost always worth striving for, but it could never be reformed out of existence. The system was exploitative, and always would be, because the class interests of employers were opposed to the interests of workers; thus class conflict (between unequal forces) was inevitable, as was the immiseration of the vast majority, including the unemployed who were, Lansbury thought, 'a permanent necessity of the capitalist system.' 'I hold ... that the real causes of poverty are inherent in present-day society and that the individual is not responsible for them,' he lectured.[40]

> Labour, like every other commodity, has to be sold in the open market; it is only bought when those who buy it hope to make a profit out of doing so. There are always some men and women who are not needed, and, therefore, must be unemployed.[41]

25

Moreover, unemployment was not static, but forced by capitalist imperatives always to expand. 'The improvements in machinery ... the formation of trusts and syndicates, the competition of foreign countries ... will displace more and more labour,' he warned.[42] He believed that the main political parties represented the interests of the employing class, that they were 'engaged in a continuous conspiracy against the social welfare of the people,' and that they controlled the state apparatus, which existed merely to carry out the wishes of the ruling (in this case middle) class. Hence the need for a political party that would advocate the cause of the workers and eventually capture state power on their behalf.[43]

Lansbury, however, never focussed exclusively on the political and economic realms. Most of all he lamented that capitalist values had come to permeate British society. 'From the time when boys and girls enter school until they leave they are taught to strive to beat their classmates,' he observed in a speech delivered in 1892 at the Methodist Chapel in Bruce Road, Bromley.

> They are taught to get knowledge not for its own sake, but simply that they may be at the top...When we leave school and go out into the world to earn our living, we are told, right from the beginning that... if we would rise we must excel our neighbour, and virtually do so at his cost.[44]

Thus prevailing mores reflected 'bourgeois hegemony,' as the Italian Communist, Gramsci, was to term it thirty years later. From such observations Lansbury concluded, as would Gramsci, that the acquisition by the working class of political power alone would not put an end to capitalist rule. A more basic transformation would be necessary before each would work for all. People's values must be transformed, too.

This became the foundation of Lansbury's outlook. In the early days he described socialist values in language typical of the S.D.F. 'The only hope of social salvation for my class,' he averred in

February 1894, 'is the transformation of society from a competitive system ... to a cooperative state in which, instead of struggling against one another merely to exist, we shall work together for the common good.' This would entail 'the full control, by the whole people, over the means of creating and distributing wealth,' a state of affairs that could not be attained, or maintained for that matter, through Parliament alone.[45] Only later did the more familiar rhetoric of Christian socialism become Lansbury's trademark. This is examined in more detail in Section III. The point here is that Lansbury's essential message, whether couched in secular or religious language, was that socialism would not be achieved by Parliament alone, but only 'when each of us is content to be the servant of the other,' and this meant, so far as Lansbury was concerned, that 'what we have got to teach is a new rendering of religion.'[46]

Lansbury was not yet the Christian socialist and pacifist he would become, although during the 'new unionist' era references to Jesus Christ as a simple workingman and the original socialist, to the Sermon on the Mount as an early example of socialist teaching, and so on, were the stock-in-trade of many socialist agitators. But Lansbury, who had been brought up in the Anglican Church, and initially drawn to politics in part because he thought 'Christ came [to earth] to be an example and an inspirer of each one of us, to work on behalf of others,' lost his religion at about the same time that he found socialism.[47] The aggressively anti-religious S.D.F. played a role here, and by July 1890 its influence had become appparent. As an S.D.F. colleague wrote ten years later, Tolstoy's *What I Believe* 'helped to sweep away some of the cobwebs of religious bigotry from [Lansbury's] understanding.'[48] Perhaps more importantly Lansbury also read *Robert Elsemere* by Mrs. Humphrey Ward (1886). This is a novel about a cleric who becomes agnostic; and Lansbury, who admitted to readers of *Coming Times* that he was then 'passing through times of difficulty regarding theological

27

matters,' took the work to heart. The fictitious character became his model. 'There is no good purpose served by shutting our eyes and crying 'Peace' when there is none,' he lectured his readers and himself. 'Rather [like Robert Elsemere] let us think out these difficult matters, throw aside all that we have learned in the past, and commence to learn afresh.'

He too now became an agnostic under the influence of Dr. Stanton Coit, who founded the Ethical Culture movement. Lansbury sent his children to an Ethical Culture Sunday School. Yet he could not shed entirely the old way of doing and expressing things. If the socialist gospel he had begun to preach was new and rigorously secular, the tone of delivery and even some of the words he employed were familiar. 'It is as true today as ever that man does not live by bread alone,' he reminded readers of *Justice* on April 22, 1893. 'How many of us ... have shown by our lives ... that we had faith in our ideal?' Or, on another occasion, 'I would strongly urge that our comrades study more, and remember that those who would save others must first themselves be saved.'[49] Moreover, as will soon become apparent, Lansbury did not hesitate to borrow methods for organizing the socialist movement and for teaching its principles directly from the Christian churches. Ten years later he would rediscover Christianity and merge it with his socialism, and a decade after that he would fold in absolute pacifism as well. During the last decade of the nineteenth century, however, Lansbury forswore the theological precepts of Christianity, but not its style or methodology, for the 'transformed and transforming vision' of pure socialism which was, he thought, a religion in its own right.

3

Lansbury's visceral identification with 'the bottom dog' whatever its nationality, religion, or sex made him a democrat, in the sense that he believed with all his heart that one person was as good as another and deserved to be treated accordingly; because he was a democrat he was also a socialist. He thought that socialism would be a great leveller of economic, social and legal distinctions. Moreover, 'cooperation' and the 'common good,' watchwords of the socialist creed, could not be determined arbitrarily, but only after discussion in which everyone took part. Thus, for Lansbury, democracy was implicit in both the socialist promise and in the method of attaining it. Capitalism, on the other hand, was anti-democratic. It rewarded a few, penalized the majority, after competitive struggle between contestants who were unequally prepared to do battle.

Lansbury's democratic instincts must have played a part when he chose which socialist organization to join. He was not attracted by the anarchist-dominated Socialist League. The I.L.P. did not yet exist. As for the Fabians, he once wrote, 'I always had a feeling ... that Fabians were much too clever and superior for ordinary people like myself to be associated with.'[50] In any event the Fabians were not a political party. That left the S.D.F., although, as Lansbury confessed twenty years later, he had not been 'a Social Democrat in what Hyndman or Quelch would call the full sense of the word.'

On the other hand, Hyndman and Quelch were not exactly democrats in the manner of George Lansbury. During the 1880s and 1890s many of the socialist movement's most talented figures passed through the S.D.F., including H.H. Champion, Eleanor Marx, William Morris, Tom Mann and John Burns. Whatever had brought them to join, they almost always left for one reason: they could not get along with its dictatorial and arrogant (if also selflessly dedicated) founder and leader, Henry M. Hyndman.

According to Postgate, Hyndman may have been 'the greatest political infuence upon George Lansbury.'[51] Be that as it may, Lansbury, too, was to pass through the S.D.F., although not until he had struggled hard to make it the conspiracy of equals which he believed a socialist organization should be. Hierarchies and pecking orders always roused his instinctive distrust. One-man rule was anathema to him. 'We ought never to raise one man higher than another but all of us give whatever ability we have to the cause,' he exhorted in *Justice*, the S.D.F. newspaper, on July 29, 1893. No arbitrary rule or ruler was immune from criticism so long as he was present. For example, when he became a parliamentary candidate in 1894, the S.D.F. executive committee expected to write his election address for him, as it wrote the election addresses of all the other candidates it sponsored. Lansbury jibbed at this, composed his own address, submitted it to the committee for discussion, and when Hyndman voiced objections to certain paragraphs, refused to alter them.

Despite this display of individualism he was appointed to be the Federation's national organizer in August 1895, a position he held until March the following year when, for financial reasons, he was forced to return to the family saw-mill and veneer-works full time. For six months or so, however, his reports and recommendations, published in *Justice*, provided a revealing glimpse of conditions at the S.D.F. branch level during the mid-1890s. More importantly for our purposes, they afford unparalleled access to Lansbury's vision of the political process, underlining his special qualities as a political organizer and democrat. They also clarify his continuing debt, if not to Christianity *per se*, then to its organizational modes, and thereby they further illuminate an aspect of his conception of 'the religion of socialism.'

On October 12, Lansbury drew upon his experience as political agent for Montagu and MacDonald 'to show how our work should be organized.' He began at the most basic level.

> We should have a branch in each Parliamentary division...I lay stress
> on this because I know how hurtful it is to the party politicians to have
> continually on their flank even a small body of men determined to
> show them in their true colours.

This, of course, was a reference to the guerrilla warfare he had
conducted with other Bow and Bromley Radicals against local
Conservatives during 1886–92. But now his political activities were
invested with the near religious aura surrounding his 'conversion'
to socialism. 'The branch when formed should meet never less than
once each week....[This weekly meeting] should be the high
festival of the week, never to be missed, and should be to us what
Sunday is to the devout Christian.' Socialist propagandizing must
likewise provide a secular counterpoint to the practices of
organized Christianity, a point Lansbury attempted to drive home
in an article printed the following week. Interestingly, he turned
to the model provided by Nonconformity, although his prior
church experience had been with the Anglicans, and it was the
Church of England which he rejoined when he was 'born again'
years later. Nevertheless, as Lansbury observed on October 19,
'the Dissenters go in for what is called tract distribution, and also
the lending of small pamphlets,' and he asked his readers, 'why
should we not follow in their footsteps?' He therefore enjoined
each branch of the S.D.F.

> first of all [to] find out how many comrades will undertake to visit
> a given number of houses on Sunday between three and four, then [to]
> choose the roads you can with your available help manage, [then to]
> count up from the register the number of houses and [finally, to]
> purchase a sufficient number of pamphlets to supply [one] to each ...
> Before taking them round put them in brown paper covers stamped
> with the branch stamp and, if you can afford it, print a little appeal
> that the pamphlet should be read, and also that it will be called for

> the next Sunday. If a visitor had twenty houses, he would need twenty-one of these pamphlets ... Now it would be impossible to visit twenty men's homes every Sunday for any length of time without coming to know some of them, and I feel sure after a time we could by this means get customers for our literature and members for our branches.

Thus the Nonconformist churches turned out to be training schools of Britain's first Marxist political party.

Lansbury also thought that socialists could learn from the churches how to approach children. He believed (optimistically, or shrewdly, I am not sure which!) that children were 'more likely to listen than adults, because the[y] have no preconceived ideals to get rid of.' At any rate, in his third weekly article for *Justice* he focussed the same benign but penetrating eye upon this subject that he concentrated upon everything else.

> First then as to Sunday School. School should meet at three p.m., an opening song should be sung, then a simple reading from the life of some good man or woman; another song, then a short text from a standard work on economics could be repeated. ... After this a short address should be given ... on the life of Jesus, Luther ... or any of the religious heroes ... [This] would enable a teacher to show why it is [that] all their good work has still left the world a very bad place for innocent children. Then the men who were the prophets of Socialism, Robert Owen, Fourier, St. Simon, Lassalle, Marx and others; it could be shown how these men were real prophets, and by the failures of some of them show how the work must be done...

Lansbury had set about organizing the socialist movement as methodically and thoroughly as, previously, he had organized the East End Radicals for Samuel Montagu and Murray MacDonald. No task was too small to escape his attention. On October 19 he exhorted,

> [W]e need not only speakers [and teachers] ... we need men and women to sell literature, others to carry flag and platform and others

to help form the audience ... We also need collectors ... at least four comrades at each meeting, one for each corner and two for the center. This is the least, but if the crowd is large they should be doubled. Then we need at these meetings comrades whose business it is to look out for people who regularly attend and who appear interested.

In retrospect, Hyndman thought that Lansbury had been 'the best organiser the Federation ever had.'[52] One can see why.

For all his hard work, however, British socialist agitators of the period continued to face uphill work, a fact of life made painfully obvious to Lansbury himself on a dismal, rainy day early in February 1896. He had journeyed to Dartford, a working-class district on the outskirts of London, where the S.D.F. hoped to establish a branch. As Lansbury reported afterwards, 'At the [Dartford] station I met comrades from Erith, Bexley, Woolwich, Walworth, Deptford and other parts. At 3:15 we started in pairs to distribute handbills from house to house.' Then,

after getting rid of nearly 3,000 of these leaflets we met at East Hill to hold our meeting. Although we had asked a considerable number of people to attend only a very few put in an appearance, mainly, I suppose, because of the rain which was still falling with a persistence worthy of a better place and time. We opened by singing Carpenter's song, 'England Arise' ... Our singing brought a few more of the descendents of Wat Tyler around us, and then Barraclough of Bexley Heath opened the meeting by informing those present that we were Socialists and had come to Dartford to preach the gospel of discontent. I followed in a half hour's speech during which I vainly tried to rouse some of the spirit of revolution which we had been told lay dormant, but to little purpose. I suppose it was the rain which damped it all down. Robinson of Bexley Heath then tried another line, but so far as I could judge the natives were still unmoved, and as it was still raining and we were all hungry, it was agreed that the proceedings should be adjourned.

Not, perhaps, the most hopeful or productive of meetings. But

Lansbury closed on a characteristic note.

> What I propose now is that we bombard the place for the next two
> months with a succession of meetings and, what is more, a systematic
> distribution of literature…It is a truly working-class district and is a
> centre from which much good work can be done.[53]

Dedication, determination and optimism were always among his
distinguishing traits.

Behind them, or rather, perhaps, above them, remained the
fervent, if instinctive, commitment to democratic principles
mentioned earlier. Do not forget that Lansbury had quit the
Liberals in part because he thought they had forsaken democratic
principles. It is interesting to watch how he now attempted to
combine this commitment to democracy with an equally strong
belief in the need for organizational structure and leadership. 'Each
branch' of the S.D.F., he instructed members on October 12,

> needs a capable secretary. The stupid rule which changes the secretary
> every quarter merely for the sake of giving everyone a chance has, I
> am sure, worked untold mischief to us as an organisation. All men and
> women are not fitted for secretarial work and it is nonsensical to argue
> that they are…
>
> Each branch needs a weekly chairman. This is an office which can
> be changed, even though it is necessary to point out that all are not
> fitted to be chairmen … I am of opinion that it is a good thing to elect
> the chairman weekly and by this means train men to take the chair
> outside at public meetings.
>
> Then a librarian is needed [and] a treasurer. For this [latter] office
> I think a branch should have a comrade in whom all the members have
> complete confidence and if possible also one who is known outside
> the movement, so that when special appeals are made outsiders may
> be more likely to subscribe, and here again I am opposed to change
> merely for the sake of change.
>
> As to committees, each branch should have a general committee,
> not to do its work, but to bring suggestions. I am not in favour of

innumerable committees, as there is such a thing as too much decentralization, which only leads to chaos.

Indeed, during this period of his life, Lansbury may be found flirting with something like democratic centralism. 'We have sunk our individuality in the organization because we have recognized that no one man is the repository of all wisdom,' he explained in 1896 to those who objected when S.D.F. delegates to the Second International voted as a bloc. 'The knowledge of all must be brought together and utilised, not in each one striving against the other, but in each one contributing his or her best to the common stock.'[54] This, it must be said, is a somewhat incongruous statement given his later history. Lansbury believed in organization and, to a degree, in discipline, but his career makes evident that he believed in participatory democracy above all.

Lansbury's skills as an organizer have been forgotten, but they are critical to understanding his impact on any political body or cause with which he was associated. During the 1890s he helped to make the S.D.F. into the leading socialist body in London. On the other hand, he did not believe that salvation depended upon organization alone, or that it would ever be conferred from above. Over and over he repeated that the workers must save themselves. *That* was part of what made the socialist movement inherently democratic. 'Each man and woman has some special talent which is needed in the work of a branch and this can only be discovered by frequent meetings and members coming to thoroughly understand one another,' he explained to his readers.

Also, Lansbury really believed in fellowship, or 'fraternity' as the French revolutionaries had termed it a century earlier. If socialism was impossible without democracy (albeit a democracy whose contradictory tendencies remained unresolved in his mind), then democracy could not exist without fellowship, or so it seemed to Lansbury. This implied a vision of politics based upon neighborhoods and personal connections, upon the give and take of friendly

35

discussion among equals, upon the active involvement of masses of people (women as well as men, fraternity was not meant by Lansbury to exclude one sex) which, when it began to take root not only in East London but throughout the country, would provide the key, or one of them at any rate, to Labour's successes a few years later. Thus Lansbury's method of socialist proselytizing pointed the way forward for the movement as a whole. At the same time, perhaps it was a vision which ultimately could not be realized in a modern political system based upon parties with a mass membership. Lansbury remained confident all his life that it would be possible in a political democracy to keep party, indeed national, leaders directly accountable to the rank and file and that the rank and file could always be brought to see and do the right thing. Over the course of time, however, Labour strayed rather far from this ideal. Many local Labour parties came to be dominated by cliques; political machines proved more effective than individual activists; party conferences were dominated by undemocratic bloc votes. Most people think these developments were inevitable. Lansbury fought them at every step.

He is often held to have been a sentimental dreamer who was governed more by his heart than his head. Such charges seem most just towards the end of his career when, for example, he personally preached pacifism to Mussolini and Hitler. But are they apt at this early stage? I think not. Certainly Lansbury coupled a singularly un-dreamy appreciation of political possibilities with the principles he held so dear. He managed three campaigns for Radicals (Montagu, Cobden and MacDonald) and won them all. As organizer of the S.D.F., his attention to nuts and bolts helped to make that body into the largest and most successful socialist organization in the metropolis. There was no matter pertaining to political organization that was too insignificant for him to consider, as his articles for *Justice* reveal. At the same time his attention to detail, which might otherwise have seemed almost obsessive, was leavened by a transparent egalitarianism and good humor. In person Lansbury simply must have radiated friendliness, confidence and competence.

Thus George Lansbury at the outset of his career as a socialist agitator. He changed and modified his ideas over time, of course, but his basic approach remained constant until nearly the very end. Lansbury spent his life attempting to make British socialism better organized, more 'fraternal,' and, above all, more democratic. And, increasingly, the small circle which constituted the leadership of the movement had to include the man from Bow and Bromley in their calculations.

4

One characteristically humble and democratic aspect of Lansbury's contribution to the socialist movement was his involvement in local political affairs. He really did not aspire to cut a figure on the national stage, but only to do his bit for the common cause wherever he might be most useful. This *could* mean campaigning for Parliament and serving in it. Lansbury stood twice for Walworth in 1895, in a by-election in May and during the general election two months later, for Bow and Bromley in 1900, for Middlesbrough in 1906 (his only venture as a parliamentary candidate outside London), and for Bow and Bromley again during both general elections of 1910, finally gaining entrance to the House of Commons in December of that year. He lost his seat in 1912 as the result of a by-election of great significance (which we examine in Section II), but regained it ten years later. After 1922 he was Bow and Bromley's parliamentary representative until his death in 1940. But he really did believe that, for socialists, parliamentary elections provided first and foremost a platform for the exposition of their ideals and only secondarily an opportunity for personal advancement. Moreover, he believed that the identity of the socialist candidate was secondary, that whoever was selected to stand was merely a representative of a movement which was greater than any individual.

Perhaps this sounds too good to be true. Yet it was true. Lansbury rose to prominence not because he wished to lead, but because others wished him to. The best example of this occurred in 1931, when the Parliamentary Labour Party chose him to be its leader, a position he had never expected or sought. Whenever his principles came into conflict with the policies of an organization to which he belonged, however, he never failed to uphold his principles, no matter the importance of the organization, or the cost to his career. We saw this in his decision to quit the Liberals. We will see it in Section II below when we come to the 1912 by-election. In 1935 Lansbury relinquished leadership of the P.L.P., and thus the possibility (remote though it was), of becoming Prime Minister, for reasons to be examined in Section III.

The point, then, reverting to the 1890s, is that although briefly Lansbury had been the S.D.F.'s national organizer, he had no national or parliamentary ambitions. Rather his main field of effort was the place nearest to hand, the East End of London and, particularly, his home district of Bow and Bromley. Within days of his decision to leave the Liberals, he had established in Bow an active, high-spirited, arm of the S.D.F., 'a band of bonny fighters,' as he recalled many years later. 'Our branch activities were colossal.' Within weeks they were holding 'open-air meetings every night and two or three on Sundays.' Often Lansbury would arrive to speak at such meetings and find no audience, except 'for a dog or two and, perhaps, a stray child.' He and the comrades remained undismayed, however, and now his expertise as an organizer became apparent. 'We mapped out Bow and Bromley, [and] drew up a plan,' Lansbury remembered, 'and very soon our meetings became large and enthusiastic.'[55] This was not just nostalgic reminiscence. In April, four months after leaving the

Liberals, he was elected, as a Social Democrat, to the Poplar Board of Guardians. (Bow and Bromley sent representatives to various elective bodies in Poplar.) Eighteen months later, Bow and Bromley S.D.F. planned to run four additional candidates at the forthcoming Guardians' election in Poplar 'and expect[ed] to sweep the board.'[56] That was overly optimistic, but two Social Democrats did get in.

The acute concentration on details which Lansbury had displayed as national organizer of the S.D.F. was now manifested in the will with which he set about mastering the mundane aspects of a Guardian's duties. These were to enforce and interpret the New Poor Law of 1834 which dealt, essentially, with the treatment of paupers and their dependants. Such unfortunates often wound up in the workhouse, where conditions were supposed to be as unpleasant as was consistent with health, since it was held that otherwise an indigent might prefer living in one to actually working outside for his bread. This approach, needless to say, was utterly alien to Lansbury, who now took the trouble to learn precisely what powers the Guardians possessed. The results were startling. The New Poor Law was inhumane, no doubt, but as Lansbury soon discovered, 'the Guardians have it completely within their power to make the "House" either comfortable or wretched.' There was 'really no limit to what may be done' for children of paupers, for instance, because 'the Local Government Board encourages the Guardians to not only feed, clothe and house such children properly, but also to carefully educate and train them in useful trades.' Moreover, 'on the question of out relief [that is, relief outside the workhouse], the Guardians have a free hand for aged people and widows and orphans.'[57] 'None of us,' Lansbury had admitted three weeks after his election to the Board, 'thought that … much could be done by one man amongst eighteen.'[58] In fact, however, one guardian who knew the rules and was determined to apply them creatively, could do a great deal, as Lansbury was soon to prove.

Consider, for instance, his role on the Forest Gate schools committee which oversaw elementary education in Whitechapel, and to which he was appointed by the Poplar Guardians in 1896. As he reported back to the Bow and Bromley S.D.F., when he came onto the committee he had objected to the children wearing school uniforms, and they were abolished. Then he found that 'the tailor who taught tailoring was old, so they pensioned him off and got a better one ... They had done the same with the bootmaker ... In the carpenter's shop they had now many improvements and modern tools ... In the engineering shop the teaching was not so good as it should be ... [but] scientific dressmaking was thoroughly taught.'[59]

These were the concerns of a man determined to improve life for the multitude in the here and now, who was animated by egalitarian sentiments which made no provision for personal ambition or advance, who saw himself as 'a counter,' as he once put it, in a 'great and noble cause.' Such concerns may also seem almost prosaic for an advocate of 'the religion of socialism.' Lansbury was aware of the apparent anomaly. 'To many of us it may not seem very revolutionary or exciting to go in for the drudgery of Poor Law Administration,' he acknowledged at one point.

> All the same, the more of us who do, the better for the movement and ourselves. For if we can once let men and women understand that our proposals are practical, and in all ways better than those of our opponents, it will not be long before they give up following party hacks and quack war cries, and join with us in working, not to palliate but to sweep away commercialism with its workhouses and prisons.[60]

As he had put it several months earlier when exhorting the S.D.F. to take School Board elections more seriously, 'we are fighting first of all for better education, but also indirectly for Social Democracy pure and simple.'[61] The goal, then, remained constant whether he was attempting to rouse up a national movement or to improve the quality of children's education. Hyndman had told him that 'before long, there was no doubt, the working class would take over the control of the country, and it was the duty of himself and other workers to learn how to administer it. It was a revolutionary task to become a guardian.'[62] This, it becomes apparent, was congenial advice to a man in whom were combined the visionary attitudes of an exponent of marvelous 'coming times' with the practical talents of a local administrator, reformer, and organizer. As Lansbury asserted to readers of *Justice* on April 28, 1894, 'though we are working for the noblest ideal the world has ever known, we can still do our part here and now to use the means at our disposal for improving the daily life of those who have fallen by the way in the cut-throat race for wealth.'

Lansbury's main preoccupation as a local administrator was with the unemployed, of whom there were always many thousands in Poplar. He soon found that Guardians held important powers here too, although previously they had claimed to have none. But 'this,' Lansbury advised readers of *Justice* on December 9, 1893, 'is untrue.' Boards of Guardians could quite legally employ jobless skilled workers in the workhouses, and at union rates. As for unskilled laborers, 'For these we should start farm colonies.'[63] From the period of his brief flirtation in the early 1880s with the Salvation Army, perhaps, he had kept in mind General Booth's plan to transport the unemployed 'residuum' from urban slums to rural farms where they might be put to work. Now Lansbury asserted that Boards of Guardians had 'power ... to acquire land. Every parish could take 50 acres by purchase.' They could lease additional acreage. Already his mind was working on a variant of the scheme which would preoccupy him for the next decade and a half. He was, at present, the only socialist Guardian on the Poplar Board, but he convinced it to convene a conference of all London Boards of Guardians whose purpose would be to press the President of the

Local Government Board 'to at once use the powers vested in him' to establish farms and workshops near London in which the jobless could be employed.[64]

That the conference took place at all was testimony to Lansbury's powers of persuasion, but the assembled Guardians refused to follow his prescriptions. Lansbury, however, was determined to explore, and if possible to implement, the land-purchase scheme. Again he deployed his great skills as a political organizer. It took a few years, and the addition to the Poplar Board of several more labor and socialist members, including Will Crooks who went on to a parliamentary career for Woolwich, but eventually the Laindon Farm Colony was established. Lansbury had made a new friend during this interval, the American soap manufacturer, Joseph Fels, who like Lansbury earlier on, had been influenced by Henry George, the advocate of land nationalization. Fels now proved instrumental to Lansbury who urged him to purchase Laindon, a disused farm of 100 acres in Essex, 20 miles from London. Fels did so and leased it to Poplar Guardians 'for a pepper-corn rent.' Then two hundred of Poplar's paupers were set to work, clearing the land, and planting orchards and gardens. They even built a reservoir, damming a small river.[65]

Lansbury did not believe it would be possible to eradicate unemployment in Britain so long as capitalism survived. He viewed Laindon as 'a palliative ... [but] a palliative in the right direction.' As he put it on another occasion, 'I am fully conscious of the need for preventing the *manufacture* of the unemployed; but I hold very strongly that it is of no use saying to a hungry worker: 'wait while we reconstruct society ... ' You might as well tell him to wait until he gets to heaven when all will be well.'[66] Laindon was better than pie in the sky, Lansbury thought, but it was too small. He was determined to try something more ambitious.

His chance to do so came in 1904, when the Conservative President of the Local Government Board, Walter Long, established a committee of borough councillors, L.C.C. members, Guardians and others 'for the purpose of regularising and more efficiently organising work for the unemployed.' Long appointed Lansbury to the committee which, among other things, arranged to send unemployed workers to two farm colonies operated by private charities. At this point Lansbury persuaded Fels to write to Long, offering to buy an estate of 1,300 acres, Hollesley Bay Agricultural College, and to put it at the disposal of the newly established committee, rent free for three years. It would be, in other words, a state run farm colony.

Long agreed and the experiment went forward. Lansbury became the main force behind it. During the winter of 1905–06 he spent all his weekends at the farm, setting up classes, lectures and recreations for its inhabitants. And, to begin with, Hollesley Bay, like Laindon, was successful. Only after the general election of 1906, which returned the Liberals to power, and the former socialist, John Burns, to the Local Government Board, did this early public works program begin to languish; but more on that in a moment.

Lansbury had undertaken these activities on behalf of the unemployed with no thought except to improve their immediate conditions, but they led him, eventually, far beyond the ambit of Bow and Bromley. Already in 1895 his efforts had made so large an impression that he was called to give evidence to the Royal Commission on the Aged Poor, one of whose members was the Prince of Wales (afterwards Edward VII). The Prince thought Lansbury's evidence 'was the best that had been given from my side,' Lansbury recorded in his memoirs, but, when the heir to the throne offered him a cigar Lansbury, who objected to monarchy, felt bound to refuse it.[67] More significant than the impression he made upon the Prince, however, was the respect with which Gerald Balfour came to regard him after a visit to Laindon Farm Colony. Balfour replaced Walter Long as President of the Local Government Board in 1905, the last year of the Conservative administration. During that year the government established another Royal Commission, this one to investigate the problem of administering poor relief. At Balfour's urging, Lansbury was appointed to be one of labor's two representatives on the commission, which became famous when it divided over recommendations, finally issuing majority and minority reports. The latter, which advocated supercession of the New Poor Law with state guarantees of social security, was a milestone in the history of public attitudes towards poverty in Britain and a significant step towards the welfare state. Its authors were Sidney and Beatrice Webb. The latter had been, perhaps, the most pertinacious of the commission's dissident members. Lansbury, however, also put his name to the famous document. More self-effacing than Beatrice Webb, he nevertheless further enlarged his reputation when, after the report was published, he became its tireless advocate in the national campaign the Webbs organized to popularize its generous recommendations.[68] Thus Lansbury began to develop a national reputation as a champion of the unemployed, even while he devoted himself largely to local affairs in London's East End. His participation on both Royal Commissions was an unforeseen by-product of these local preoccupations.

Let us return to those preoccupations. They were significant, for our purposes, mainly on two accounts. First they serve to emphasize points made previously: that visionary though he was, Lansbury was also an effective local politician whose involvement in Bow and Bromley's affairs testifies to the egalitarian impulse which underlay all his activities and thinking. Lansbury believed that reforms were valuable because, pending the destruction of capitalism, they made life bearable for capitalism's victims, and because struggling to attain those reforms trained their working-class advocates in the business of running the country which, after all, was the socialist's ultimate goal. Secondly, Lansbury's local

involvements evoked a ferocious response from the vested interests which he challenged. This led to a series of confrontations
which do much to further illuminate his vision of socialism and the
way in which he thought it might be attained.

When, in 1905, the Conservative Government established the
Royal Commission on the New Poor Law, it appointed as chairman Lord George Hamilton, a former Conservative Minister, to
whom the Webbs eventually paid tribute as a model of even-
handedness. The permanent officials of the Local Government
Board, and especially the chief inspector of the Poor Law Division
of the Board, one Mr J.S. (later Sir James) Davy, however, were
determined to guide the commission to orthodox conclusions,
whatever the inclinations of its chairman or other members. Davy
wanted a reaffirmation of the principles of 1834 which, it will be
recalled, had demanded that conditions in the workhouse be kept
extremely unpleasant. He had watched with growing anger as the
Poplar Board of Guardians, at Lansbury's urging, had begun
treating paupers with something like understanding and sympathy
instead of severity and disapproval. Davy intended for the Royal
Commission to rebuke Lansbury and all others who favored his
approach to pauperism. He reckoned, however, without the
commission's dissident minority. Their report far overshadowed
the work of the majority, both at the time and historically.

Davy had, however, a second and more direct line of attack. This
was to discredit the experiments at Laindon and Hollesley Bay
specifically and to convict the socialist Guardians of Poplar of actual
malfeasance. Ironically the Conservative Government was less
receptive to his plan than the Liberal one which replaced it in 1906.
But John Burns, 'the man with the red flag,' the great leader of
the London dock strike of 1889, who had finally joined the Liberals
and become under Prime Minister Henry Campbell-Bannerman,
President of the Local Government Board, was like putty in Davy's
hands. On June 7 Burns convened a formal inquiry into Poplar's

45

practices and appointed Davy to run it!

One may easily imagine how the 'inquiry' unfolded. Descriptions of the affair read like passages from Dickens. Poplar's Guardians were not actually accused of ladling out turtle soup to workhouse inmates, but rather of providing beer to those who cleaned the sewers. Only paupers who were desperately ill were supposed ever to be given alcohol. The Guardians themselves were accused of frequent drunkenness at the taxpayers' expense. (Lansbury was teetotal all his life.) Meanwhile they were said to be corruptly paying exorbitant fees to the merchants who supplied the workhouses with foodstuffs and materials for clothing and bedding. At Laindon and Hollesley Bay the inmates were said to be terrorizing their neighbors. And so on. It did not matter that in the end most of these charges were either refuted or shown to have missed the point. They became front-page news. Poplar's new departure in the treatment of paupers had been utterly discredited.[69]

Or had it? Perhaps the readers of *Punch*, which at the height of the inquiry portrayed Lansbury and Crooks smoking cigars and ordering a fresh barrel of ratepayers' beer from the workhouse cellar, were confirmed in their low opinion of socialists and the labor movement in general. The electors of Bow and Bromley, however, were by and large beyond the reach of *Punch* cartoonists. When local elections next took place, in November, Lansbury and the other Labour Guardians were all returned triumphantly; indeed they added an additional Labour member to the Board. London's main newspapers, including *Punch*, did not bother to report this result.[70]

Here we begin to catch sight of the real importance of Lansbury's approach to local politics and to the socialist movement as a whole. When the inquiry came, he did not back down. In fact he remained entirely unabashed. 'He desired to clear their minds of cant about pauperism,' Lansbury defiantly informed a meeting in Cardiff early in 1907. 'If a poor person got 3 shillings a week he was pauperised; and when an ex-Cabinet Minister got £1,500 he was a gentleman. That was all humbug. (Loud applause.)'[71] And, later in the speech,

> he did not deny that they fed the children well, for they were aware that they could not educate a stunted or badly fed child. The child must not be robbed of the pleasures of childhood; it was a crime for the community to allow it.

Poplar Guardians, Lansbury stoutly maintained on another occasion, did not coddle the poor. Rather their reforms were mere 'temporary measures to tide over present difficulties.'[72] It was not simply that he made no attempt to soft pedal Poplar's new methods then, it was rather that he set them in a broader context. 'At Poplar,' Lansbury insisted, 'they had not socialism, only a humane administration of the Poor Law.'[73] In other words, socialists had even bigger plans than the ones which so offended Mr Davy.

In this instance Lansbury's thinking coincided with that of leading figures in the newly established Labour Party. Indeed, Labour was shortly to introduce an Unemployment Bill in the House of Commons which, in demanding that the state oversee treatment of the jobless and provide either work or generous maintenance for them, encapsulated much for which Lansbury fought in Poplar. Still, a general point may be made here. Lansbury's straightforward response to Davy's attack provided a distinct contrast to the strategy and tone which the Labour Party usually adopted. From its entrance into Parliament in 1906 Labour followed a cautious route, largely mapped out for it by Ramsay MacDonald and his allies. In part MacDonald wished to prove that 'Labour was fit to govern,' which meant demonstrating the party's responsibility and respectability, especially to middle-class voters. This, MacDonald thought, was the only way to win elections. For the foreseeable future, however, Labour was likely to remain a minority party. MacDonald hoped to maximize its impact in Parliament by minimizing the number of enemies it created there. He thought that belligerent tactics would be counter productive. As a result, few party leaders indulged in the kind of plain speaking which was Lansbury's forte.

Yet in Bow and Bromley Lansbury's approach proved electorally popular. 'Crying for Socialism is no use for the down-trodden poor,' Lansbury warned,[74] and he spent the vast portion of his time working for concrete, immediate, reforms instead; but, on the other hand, it was crucial always to situate current struggles in the larger context which a socialist analysis provided. 'The guiding principle of all our propaganda is that the toilers of the world ... have the first claim and right, not merely to a small dole, but to really enjoy the entire fruits of their daily toil.'[75] MacDonald, Philip Snowden, Arthur Henderson, three of Labour's great figures during this period, would have agreed with the first sentiment, but, as true representatives of the 'Labourist' tradition, they were always hard pressed to live up to the second.[76] George Lansbury's significance is that, without slogan mongering, he advocated a militant alternative to the cautious and seemingly pragmatic brand of politics favored by Labour's most famous leaders, an alternative, moreover, that his own experience in local government shows to have have been both popular and successful.[77]

5

This brings us to a much more famous confrontation between local government and Whitehall in which Lansbury played a crucial role. It took place in 1921 and was an episode even more fraught than the first, one that still holds implications for British politics. It makes clearer than ever that Lansbury held to a different understanding of the struggle for socialism than did most Labour Party leaders.

Fifteen years after the Davy inquiry much in Britain had changed. Sections II and III will deal with those years in more detail. Suffice it to say here merely that the political landscape had been transformed. Popular sentiment had swung to the left, in part as a result of World War I. The Liberal Party was in tatters, rent by the feud between Asquith and Lloyd George, the latter of whom now headed a Coalition Government composed mainly of Conservatives. Labour which had become officially a socialist party in 1918, although led still by pragmatic, cautious Labourists, seemed set to occupy the vacant space formerly held by the Liberals. To Labour's left was the newly founded British Communist Party.

Lansbury's role and status in this new constellation of political forces was very different from what it had been in 1906. He had been elected to Parliament in 1910, although he resigned his seat to force a celebrated by-election, which he lost two years later (and which is discussed in detail in Section II); had become the chief male champion of womens' suffrage, a cause he celebrated in a newly established newspaper, the *Daily Herald*, which became, under his direction, the chief organ of 'rebel' causes during the Edwardian era, the 'years of great unrest' as historians have dubbed them. During the war he had been one of its most vocal and effective opponents on pacifist and socialist grounds. He had become, in short, a major figure on the British left and in British politics more generally. For all that he had a national role to play, however, he maintained his interest in Bow and Bromley affairs, as a Guardian and, perhaps more importantly, as a borough councillor. In 1919 Lansbury was chosen mayor of the borough for a twelve-month stint. By 1921 Labour controlled forty-three of Poplar borough council's forty-nine seats. In both these achievements Lansbury's years of patient toil were evident at last.

Unfortunately, however, conditions in the East End during the 1920s had changed little since the 1880s. If anything, they may have worsened. After World War I Britain experienced a brief economic boom and then a severe recession. Unemployment rose nearly to two million and, until 1939, rarely fell below the one million mark. Worse, the unemployed were not spread evenly over the country as a whole, but rather tended to be grouped in regional pockets, for example the industrial north and Midlands. Even in London, while the East End suffered acutely, other neighborhoods were scarcely affected.

The attitude of the government towards unemployment only made matters worse. Joblessness was held to be primarily a regional, not a national, problem so that there was no nationally funded scheme of relief. And what was true for the nation was equally true for the nation's greatest city. In London each district was supposed to cope with its workless people as best it could, and by itself, despite the fact that no local authority could be held responsible for having *created* the unemployment problem which was due to world conditions and the dislocation which followed global war, and although some districts were better able to cope than others, either because they were wealthier or contained fewer job seekers. 'Poplarism', as it came to be called, would never have arisen if the entire metropolis had been responsible for dealing with the city's unemployed.

The borough of Poplar had to find money (of which it had little) for many unemployed, and the borough council, now dominated by socialists, was committed, as Lansbury had been committed when he first became a Poor Law Guardian in 1893, to decent treatment of paupers. This meant raising the rates of local residents to pay for poor relief, although Poplarites were less able to afford high rates than residents of better-off, West End, neighborhoods. There came a time, however, when the rates in Poplar could be borne no longer, and yet unemployment remained as widespread as before.

Probably it was Lansbury who then suggested the course Poplar decided to take. 'We should refuse to pay the London County

Council or the Metropolitan Asylums Board, or the Police precepts.'[78] ('Precepts' were sums of money.) Until the central authorities made a contribution to help solve Poplar's problem, then, Poplar would cease contributing to funds administered by the central authorities. 'This meant [a saving for Poplar of] several hundreds of thousands of pounds per year,' Lansbury recorded. Some of these would be re-routed to pay for poor-relief. At the same time Poplar could finally lower rates to something like the level in West-End boroughs. On the other hand, the course of action Lansbury recommended was patently illegal.

The sequence of events which followed may be summarized briefly.[79] When Lansbury's suggestion came to a vote on March 26, 1921, only one councillor opposed it, while thirty-six approved. Twelve others either abstained or were absent. Beginning five days later no payments would be made to the municipal bodies Lansbury had enumerated. Because this action was unlawful, most observers thought that if it was brave, it was also futile. Indeed, the L.C.C., which needed the money Poplar was refusing to send, quickly initiated legal proceedings. On July 7 the councillors were ordered to make payments in the usual way or face trial for contempt of court. They refused. On July 29 the entire Labour group of forty-three marched the 5 miles from Poplar Town Hall to the Law Courts where their trial was to be held, carrying a banner which read 'Poplar Borough Council marching to the High Court and possibly to PRISON to secure EQUALISATION OF RATES for POOR BOROUGHS.' Brass bands, contingents from the Dockers', Vehicle Workers' and General Workers' trade unions, and other supporters accompanied them. Inside the court, after a good deal of wrangling, the justices ruled that, while the councillors were not themselves liable for the money withheld, they must cease withholding it or, indeed, go to jail for contempt of court. They were given until the end of August to think matters over.

Whatever re-thinking they may have performed, however, they

would not change their policy. By the end of the first week of September the men councillors were all in Brixton Prison, and the women in Holloway. Conditions were harsh at first, but the nationwide publicity which their defiant stance had generated led to a certain loosening of the rules. Eventually all sorts of privileges were allowed them, including permission for the prisoners in Brixton to meet together as a group. In this manner they managed actually to carry out a fair amount of council business from behind bars. Meanwhile Lansbury was sending nearly daily bulletins to the newspaper of which he was now editor, the *Daily Herald*. The whole affair quickly became something of an embarrassment to the government, which began searching for a compromise solution. Prime Minister Lloyd George agreed to discuss the matter with a contingent of London's Labour mayors; various emissaries were sent to Brixton and Holloway; but on the central points of their case the councillors were immovable. Eventually, as the *Daily Herald* of October 13 reported, they agreed only 'to express our profound regret that our action has involved us in disobedience to the order of the Court and further to disclaim any wish to treat the Court otherwise than with the respect due to it'. Other minor regrets were then enunciated, but the councillors refused absolutely even to consider paying the money. They had not, then, 'purged their contempt', and yet, on October 12, they were discharged from prison. Five days later a meeting of London municipal authorities chaired by the Minister of Health, Sir Alfred Mond, met Poplar's main demand. The cost of outdoor relief for the unemployed would be met by a fund to which all London boroughs contributed equally. 'Poplarism' had triumphed, against all the odds.

This is an episode in Labour's history which repays examination and, in fact, a fine study of it has been written by Noreen Branson. But we may focus on it from a single angle in order to better understand George Lansbury's approach to politics and socialism.

It is necessary first to remember that Britain after World War I was passing through an extremely tumultuous phase of its history. Many soldiers and workers who had been promised 'homes fit for heroes' and other wonderful things in return for supporting the war, now faced unemployment and poverty. Throughout the country demonstrations by the unemployed were common and often violent. The daily newspapers of the period give an idea of how widespread, frequent and rough these disturbances were. And yet the government did not expand social services to meet the emergency, but rather reduced them. It was under these circumstances that Lansbury began to devise the strategy which led, eventually, to 'Poplarism'. He thought the unemployed should 'Go to the Guardians', and demand 'Work or Maintenance', since it was the duty of Guardians to provide them. It soon became evident, however, that many Boards had not the resources, or in some cases the inclination, to do their duty. In the latter cases Lansbury advised the unemployed actually to *occupy* the workhouses. This was legal since Guardians were obligated to treat paupers in their districts. In the cases where Boards wished to do their duty, but could not because they were too poor, Lansbury advised the unemployed, and the Boards, to demand equalization of the rates, as Poplar did. But given the obduracy of central authorities, the next step (which was illegal), withholding money normally sent to various central bodies and using it instead to provide a decent standard of poor relief, was inevitable. Lansbury calculated, rightly as it turned out, that the national government would itself move to resolve the problem, rather than allow local councils to flout the law.

Lansbury's calculation was risky, however, because it assumed the willingness of Labour-dominated borough councils in impoverished districts to do as the Boards of Guardians bid them, and withhold the precepts. Publicly breaking the law is rarely a politically viable path for politicians to take, especially as a group. It requires uncommon unity, strength of purpose, and discipline among the law breakers themselves. It requires the understanding and support of an aroused population. It requires, if not the support, at least the neutrality, of their party leaders.

With regard to the first of these requirements, Poplar was ideally suited. Socialist borough councillors outnumbered non-socialists by forty-three to six. So long as the majority were united no local opponents could say them nay. And although the Poplar Labour group was hardly homogeneous with regard to sex, age, occupation, experience or even political outlook, its elan rested upon a long tradition of socialist and labor unity in the borough which was itself the product, in part, of Lansbury's continual strivings. He had helped to build the old S.D.F. in the early days, as we have already seen. When he left the S.D.F. for the I.L.P. early in the twentieth century, he maintained friendly relations with his old comrades. From 1911 the Social Democrats were the dominant element in the British Socialist Party. The latter body affiliated to Labour in 1916, but subsequently provided the largest constituent of the Communist Party. Lansbury hoped that the breach between Labour and the Communists would be temporary. Certainly in Poplar Labourites, I.L.P.ers and Communists were on close terms. To give a few examples: Lansbury's own son, Edgar, and daughter-in-law, Minnie, who were both borough councillors, were members of the Communist Party. Lansbury's old friend, John Scurr, who was an alderman, had been a member of the S.D.F. and B.S.P., a supporter of the suffragette movement, a pacifist during the war and belonged now, to the I.L.P. Socialist unity in Poplar was not a phrase or aspiration, but a reality. Many socialists in local government were linked by shared experiences which extended back over three decades. Their solidarity was unshakeable. During the nearly seven months between the original decision to withhold the money and Poplar's eventual triumph, only one socialist councillor backed down.

This solidarity reflected a shared understanding of the causes and nature of the crisis. A common objection to local authorities having responsibility for their own unemployed was that it meant the poor having to pay for the poor, since rich boroughs rarely suffered from serious unemployment. On the most basic level this was unfair, and many Labour authorities and national leaders said so. In the long run even the government was brought to acknowledge the elemental justice of this complaint. Lansbury saw it too, of course. As he put it in a typical passage, 'Our protest is against a system which allows the rich to shift their responsibilities onto the backs of the poor. Rates and taxes should be levied equitably on shoulders able to bear them.'[80] But this was only part of his argument. He also objected to 'the system' on another, deeper, level; and it was his great accomplishment to explain this more profound objection in such a way that it came to undergird Poplarism as a whole.

Under Lansbury's direction the entire affair became a vehicle for the dissemination of socialist teachings. Of course, under capitalism, the poor paid for the poor, Lansbury lectured time and again. They paid for the rich, too. Labor was the source of all value. The rich were rich precisely because the poor were poor, that is to say because the system made it possible for the rich to extract surplus value from those who worked for them. Thus Poplarism was not merely a movement demanding a more progressive tax structure. Forcing the rich help to pay for the poor, rather than vice versa as at present, was part of the struggle to stand the system on its head. As Lansbury put it, 'Labour administration means something different from Capitalist administration ... [It] means diverting wealth from the wealthy ratepayers to the poor. Those who pretend that a sound Labour policy can be pursued either nationally or locally without making the rich poorer should find another party.'[81]

The struggle to equalize the rates enabled Lansbury to reiterate other basic socialist principles too, for example, production for use rather than production for profit. As we have seen, he had been preaching this particular sermon for many years, but never, perhaps, so pointedly as now. 'Look where you will,' he directed his readers in the *Daily Herald,*

> there are needs which cannot be supplied, and why not? Simply because no one can make money out of the job. Surely the ordinary person should now be able to understand that unemployment and poverty and want all arise because we have not yet discovered how to use man-power for the service of mankind.[82]

Current miseries stemmed from this central failing of 'competitive commercialism.' 'Unemployment, underemployment, sweating and low wages are all a necessary part of the capitalist system,' Lansbury insisted. 'The war has made matters worse, but the war is not the root cause of our trouble.'

At the same time, he deftly connected the present crisis to the national and international scene in order to make another socialist argument, that government policies reflected the needs of British capitalism. Referring back to Churchill's attempt to 'strangle Bolshevism in the cradle' at the end of World War I, Lansbury wrote,

> Russia, three years ago, would have helped us all to re-start our social and industrial life, but Churchill acting for and on behalf of his capitalist masters and employers made secret and open war on the Socialist Republic ... We are reaping the harvest of our crimes against [the] Russia[ns] ... We cannot now either send our goods to them or receive food from them.[83]

As Churchill had been the agent of British capitalism in foreign affairs, so Sir Alfred Mond, the Minister of Health who was responsible for framing policy with regard to the Poor Law, was now 'the tool – a pliant, willing tool, no doubt – in the hands of the governing classes for driving the workers down and down below the standards which prevailed in 1914'. This, however, was only to be expected under current arrangements. 'Politicians and governments exist only to maintain the present social order, which rests on wage slavery and exploitation.'[84] As for the legal system, under capitalism it performed a like service. Lansbury wrote,

> It is well that organised Labour should understand that in the Courts of law all the scales are weighted against us because all the judges administer class-made laws which are expressly enacted not to do justice but to preserve the present social order.[85]

Lansbury hammered at these themes throughout the crisis, as did other Poplar borough councillors whose similar pronouncements may be found in the pages of the *Daily Herald* and local press. Their point was to situate the immediate struggle in a much larger context. But this, of course, was what Lansbury had been doing in local government for years. As he now put it, in a statement with which all the embattled councillors would have agreed, 'Our going to prison is an incident in the working-class movement – in the only fight that matters, that towards a world organised on the basis of common service for the common good. (Loud applause.)'[86]

Because Poplar's councillors viewed the struggle in this light they were prepared to take measures which might not appear responsible or respectable to some. To quote Lansbury yet again, 'Ultimately it was a question of two kinds of contempt, contempt of court or contempt of the people. For his part, and he was sure the majority of the council were with him, he would choose the former rather than the latter.'[87] This was more than simple determination to act in what Lansbury judged to be principled fashion, however. It was a conscious rejection of the authority of the state. 'If the majority will not move until the minority breaks a bad law,' Lansbury declaimed, 'then the minority must do so.'[88]

Just how far this might have brought him remains an open question. Certainly Lansbury envisioned some pretty grave steps if Poplar's initial defiance did not gain its immediate object. For a time it seemed that the government might not only imprison the councillors but also appoint more tractable replacements who would collect the rates and send them to the L.C.C. and other bodies as they were supposed to. Lansbury devised a counter-strategy. Rent and rates were collected in one payment. Very well, then, Lansbury reasoned, if necessary Poplar residents could withhold rents, in order to continue withholding the rates. 'I want to tell you,' Lansbury informed an enthusiastic crowd several nights before he and the others went to jail, 'they cannot send you to prison for not paying your rent. All they can do is throw your furniture in the street. But, well, if three hundred of you have your furniture in the road at once, that street will be blocked.'[89] A Tenants' Defence League was quickly established to organize the rent and rate strike should one became necessary. During the six weeks Poplar councillors spent in jail, the League grew by leaps and bounds, organizing rallies and distributing placards to members who then displayed them in their windows as signs of willingness to withhold rent and rates and suffer the consequences. Poplar was venturing, now, into deep waters indeed. The English revolution of the seventeenth century began, in part, as a protest against the collection of unpopular taxes, Ship Money. The American Revolution started with patriots dumping tea into Boston Harbor because they objected to the heavy taxes levied on it. Even the origins of the great French Revolution of 1789 may be traced in part to a tax revolt by the Third Estate. When, in late September, the borough councils of Bethnal Green and Stepney both voted to withhold money as Poplar had done, and two new Tenants' Defence Leagues immediately sprang up, observers might be forgiven for drawing apocalyptic conclusions. At one of the League rallies the speaker, R.L. Outhwaite, a former Liberal M.P.(!), thought 'the final fight for the overthrow of wage slavery ... was near at hand.'[90]

Lansbury may have thought so, too, and here it becomes important to situate his views and Poplarism not merely within the postwar economic context of unemployment and government cutbacks as we did above, but within the history of the Labour Party itself.

In 1921 a bitter struggle was being waged in the British labor and socialist movements between advocates of 'direct action' and advocates of 'constitutional' methods. To return to concepts introduced earlier, the battle was between labourists who insisted upon the primacy of the parliamentary and 'constitutional' road to socialism, and militants who favored utilizing, or at any rate threatening to use, labor's economic weapons, above all the strike, to achieve political ends. On one side were Labour's cautious leaders, J. R. Clynes, who was temporarily the head of the P.L.P., J. H. Thomas, leader of the N.U.R., and the prewar trinity, Arthur Henderson, Ramsay MacDonald, and Philip Snowden; on the other side was an assortment of less well-known figures affiliated with the Communist Party and the I.L.P., or, like Lansbury, belonging to Labour but holding more 'advanced' views than the party leaders.

During 1918-21 Great Britain experienced more strikes than during any other three-year period in her history. Labourists did not object to strikes *per se*, of course, but only to strikes that were carried out for political, as opposed to economic, objectives. They had plenty to object to during those three years, but once, in 1920, they broke their own policy. The labor movement had organized strikes through 'Councils of Action' to oppose Britain helping Poland in the war against Russia, and the Labour Party supported this 'unconstitutional' strategy. At the time many thought this was one reason why Lloyd George changed the government's policy.[91]

A year later, however, Labourists faced a graver crisis and re-verted to constitutionalism. It seemed as though a general strike would break out, led by the Triple Alliance of Miners, Railway-men and Transport Workers. It would be called on behalf of a political object: to keep the mines, which had been taken over by the government during the war, in public hands rather than return them to their former, private, owners. On 'Black Friday,' April 15, 1921, however, the leaders of the N.U.R. and N.T.W.F. backed down leaving the miners to strike alone. The Triple Alliance broke up into its constituent parts and, eventually the miners were defeated. From now on the advocates of parliamentarism and constitutionalism in the Labour Party and affiliated trade unions would have things pretty much their own way.

Except for Poplarism and George Lansbury. For nearly thirty years Lansbury had been 'convinced that there must and will be a social revolution in this country.'[92] He did not think it would be a violent one. 'Great Britain is the one country in the world within which it is possible to change fundamentally the existing social and industrial order without the horrors of a "bloody revolution,"' he wrote shortly after 'Poplarism' had won its victory.

> Our reasons for this faith are: our people have won elementary education, manhood suffrage, a limited franchise for women; in addition tens of thousands of working people, men and women, ... have served long terms of service in the great tasks connected with the administration of affairs. We have established huge friendly societies, cooperative societies and trade unions. In no other country in the world has the working class taken so large a part in the affairs of the nation as here.[93]

How Lansbury thought the great change might take place we will come to in a moment. He was a pacifist, as Section III shows, and so 'would not assist in establishing Socialism by brute force even if [he] had the chance.'[94] On the other hand, this did not automatically mean that he was aligned with the constitutionalists. While he was always willing to acknowledge the plausibility of the 'constitutional' or parliamentary road to socialism in a country with Britain's political traditions and practices, he did not believe that it was the only road. During 1918-22, when the House of Commons contained a Conservative majority that manifestly did not represent popular opinion, he did not even think the parliamentary road to socialism was the best one.

Lansbury believed that 'the power of standing still doing nothing is the greatest weapon in the hands of [British] Labour. Used by all for all it can, and will, remove all mountains of difficulty.'[95] This was the old syndicalist panacea, the 'general strike' as the key phase in the struggle to vanquish capitalism. Lansbury claimed, however, that the general strike was a form of passive resistance. It was a 'pacific weapon,'[96] representing the best alternative to violent revolution, and parliamentarism alike. It was, in fact, 'the reasonable way out of our difficulties.'[97]

Considered against this backdrop the meaning of Poplarism emerges. It was a political strike carried out by politicians. Thus it challenged Labourism, insurrectionism *and* capitalism. 'The only possible course open to us is that of determined passive resistance,' said one of the rebel councillors, when asked why Poplar was not following Labourist prescriptions.[98] 'We cannot go in for violence even if we had the means, because most of us do not agree with killing or destruction,' Lansbury explained on the eve of his departure for jail, 'so we adopt what, to us, is the more excellent way – we fold our arms and refuse to levy the rate.'[99] 'I know that we are not going to end Capitalism by Poplar methods. It is for the workers through their national organisations to put an end to the system of wage-slavery and exploitation,' Lansbury acknowledged some months later. But, as an earnest of intent, Poplarism was important. 'Are we going to attempt to carry out what we say on the platform, or are we to be misled and sidetracked by considerations of "statesmanship"?' Lansbury asked rhetorically.[100] The stand of the Poplar councillors, although not perhaps what militant communists would have recommended, was nevertheless a last, defiant, example of the militant spirit which had created the Councils of Action in 1920, and like them it hinted at what a more resolute Labour leadership might have accomplished during the early postwar years.

A word here about Lansbury's leadership during this crisis. Still at the height of his powers he remained as canny a political operator as the labor movement possessed. Poplarism was impeccably organized and stage-managed from beginning to end. So overwhelming was the support which Lansbury mobilized in East London for his borough council's illegal action that few Labourists dared condemn him openly. Henderson sent a telegram of support. The T.U.C. met while the councillors were in prison and recorded its appreciation of the 'real national service' they had rendered. For the moment it was possible to condemn 'direct action' only obliquely, for example by upholding less risky organizing methods instead, as J.R. Clynes did at the T.U.C., when he suggested that the best way to support Poplar's councillors was to elect a Labour majority at the next general election.

The key to Lansbury's success as an organizer in 1921 remained what it had been thirty-five years earlier. Poplarism was organized not merely with painstaking thoroughness but also along thoroughly democratic lines; no movement of which Lansbury was a leader could have been otherwise. The embattled councillors made sure to carry Poplar's residents with them by explaining their course of action at every step of the way. The very day that they voted to withhold payments, they also voted for Lansbury and two others 'to draw up a statement explaining the reasons for the policy.' This was to 'be delivered to every house and lodger in the borough.' Should this not suffice, regular 'town's meetings to explain the policy to the ratepayers' were also mandated by the council.[101] As the date for their court hearing approached, and then as the date for entering prison drew nigh, such consultations between councillors and electors became more frequent. A dozen 'town's meetings' were held during August 17-31 alone.[102]

This kind of interaction between Poplar's residents and their elected representatives had the desired effect. Rallies and demonstrations which were held on significant occasions, for example the day the councillors went to court, the day they went to jail, the evening of their last formal meeting in the Town Hall, and so on, appear always to have been well attended and enthusiastic. Even making allowance for the bias of reporters sent by the *Daily Herald* to cover them, the popular engagement and commitment they recorded seem beyond question. 'Extraordinary scenes were witnessed last night when the Council held its meeting,' one reporter wrote on July 29. 'The gallery was packed with people and the whole of the back of the chamber was filled to overflowing. The enthusiasm of the public was wonderful.' Or, on August 24, 'They were terrific in the intensity of feeling shown,' a reporter wrote of 'two enthusiastic meetings' held the previous evening. Perhaps the climactic rally occurred on September 1, the day the Court issued writs for jailing the rebel councillors.

> Long before the Labour Members had reached the Town Hall from their final business meeting in the Municipal Chambers, the big building was crowded until it was literally impossible for another person to obtain admission. In the hall every alley-way was packed and those lucky enough to obtain seats were almost swamped by the subsequent onrush of enthusiasts ... Crowds even gathered on the windowsills and on the balcony.
>
> Impressive as was the crowd within the hall, it dwindled into insignificance when compared with the huge overflow concourse outside, which was unable to obtain admission. Every vantage was seized. Men clung to railings and every foothold on adjoining buildings was eagerly utilized. The size of the crowd was only limited by the carrying-power of the speakers' voices.

When the councillors finally went to jail, sympathizers regularly serenaded them from outside their barred windows. On September 8, 8,000 demonstrators gathered outside Holloway Prison. Outside the Brixton Prison that day, 'the Hoxton Boys' Band struck up a revolutionary tune. The "Red Flag" was sung again and again.'

63

Back in Poplar, 'Ye Old English Fayre' was raising funds for the families of imprisoned councillors. Other funds were raised to send councillors' children to the country for summer holidays. The establishment and growth of the Tenants' Defence League also testified to the support local people felt for the cause.

It may be objected that such evidence of mass backing for the illegal actions of Poplar Council is impressionistic, or reflected the sentiments of only an active minority. But there is harder evidence too. Quite simply, more people voted in Poplar local elections than voted in other borough elections, and they voted overwhelmingly for Labour. In March 1922, London went to the polls to elect the County Council. Labour did not do very well as a whole, raising its total representation by one, from sixteen to seventeen. In Poplar, however, the Labour group maintained an absolute monopoly over the four seats accorded the district (and sent two additional Poplarites to the L.C.C. for Battersea and Whitechapel). A month later London voted for Boards of Guardians. Of eligible voters, 23 percent participated in greater London; 43.2 percent participated in Poplar, however, the highest rate in the metropolis. And although Labour as a whole actually lost ground this time, in Poplar Labour increased its representation on the Board of Guardians from sixteen to twenty-one, out of twenty-four members altogether. Then in November 1922, borough council elections took place. This time London Labour did very badly, losing over three hundred seats. In Poplar, however, Labour lost only three seats, which still left it with four times the representation of all anti-Labourites combined. And whereas in London as a whole 36.4. percent of eligible voters cast ballots, in Poplar the figure was 51.5 percent. Also, in 1922 both of Poplar's parliamentary seats went to Labour. Poplar had become as 'safe' a constituency as Labour had in the country.

There is some evidence, however, that Labour's leaders were not comfortable with this situation. Behind the scenes they worked to bring Poplar's revolt to an end as quickly as possible. They agreed with Lansbury's goal, equalization of the rates and government responsibility for the unemployed, but as Labourists they abhorred his illegal tactics. The main Labour figure in London was the Mayor of Hackney, the young Herbert Morrison. It was Morrison who tried hardest to find a quick end to the affair. In search of a compromise he led the contingent of London Labour mayors to confer with Lloyd George in Gairloch, Scotland, whence the Prime Minister had retired to nurse a toothache. He arranged various meetings and conferences back in London which were designed to resolve matters one way or another. Morrison opposed 'direct action' because he was confident that eventually Labour would attain success at the polls. He opposed Poplarism specifically because however popular the rebel councillors might be in their own borough, he thought their choice of tactics would hurt Labour's electoral chances in the metropolis as a whole.

Morrison's goal was to organize Labour in the localities. Municipal power would be the springboard to a national Labour government. This entire strategy depended upon Labour participation in democratic elections. On one level it would be absurd to charge its creator with holding anti-democratic sentiments. On the other hand, however, Morrison did not believe in participatory democracy. He was often accused of wanting to establish for Labour in London an equivalent of Tammany Hall, the Democratic Party's political machine in New York City. (His emphasis upon efficiency rather than democracy is unambiguously evident in the great schemes of nationalization which he prepared for Labour during the 1930s and 1940s. No provision for worker control of industry appeared in these.) In 1921 Morrison was impressed by the electoral machine Lansbury had helped to build in Poplar, but he had little appreciation of its democratic basis which was, in fact, the precondition of its success. He thought it would be possible to arrange a deal between Poplar council and the government, a compromise worked out between the principals, as it were, and then announced to a largely passive public. His plan was that the rebel councillors should delegate a few representatives to attend a conference at which equalization of rates and other relevant matters would be discussed. They would be let out of jail for this purpose. In fact, however, nothing could have been better calculated to arouse Lansbury's wrath, or to put him more on guard. Morrison's strategy threatened the democratic foundation of Poplarism. In a sense it represented the antithesis of everything for which Poplarism stood. 'No neutral person, no good offices are needed,' Lansbury warned in the *Daily Herald* on September 26. 'Poplar is governed by democrats ... we do not intend handing over our future to a few selected delegates or to our friends.' A little later he wrote even more pointedly, 'the claim to leadership, the claim to act on behalf of others, can only be accepted in a democratic organization after consultation with members.'[103]

Thus two conceptions of democracy in the labor movement, two contrasting approaches to Labour's struggle for socialism, came into conflict in 1921, and the concept grounded in fraternity, fellowship and participatory democracy, in short the concept encapsulating the ideals which originally had brought Lansbury out of the Liberal Party and to the 'religion of socialism,' emerged triumphant. Morrison was forced to abandon his scheme. The Poplar councillors held out until they could all attend the meeting in question and together they reaped the reward to which their solidarity entitled them.

But their great victory set no national precedent. The East End was no microcosm but only Lansbury's home ground. He had spent a lifetime there building not only his own reputation but also a basis of understanding for the views he held. The rest of Britain proved a tougher nut to crack. Moreover, in Herbert Morrison, Lansbury confronted not merely a representative of the Labourism he had been opposing since entering the British socialist movement thirty years before, but a member of the generation which would bring Labourism to its fullest flowering a quarter-century later in the governments led by Clement Attlee. In 1921 Morrison lost a battle, but the campaign to define the Labour Party was far from finished. Lansbury would eventually have to deal with other representatives of this new generation of Labourists, and in the end they would defeat him.

2 Lansbury and feminism

As we have seen, George Lansbury did not seek national recognition and yet, even during the first part of his career, he found it to a degree, as a Poor Law Guardian whose efforts on behalf of paupers prompted the Davy Inquiry of 1906. Within half a decade of that trial, however, and despite his genuine humility, he had become indubitably famous – or, rather, notorious – according to some. He had earned this reputation by his fierce support of the women's suffrage movement, the subject of the present section, and by his public friendship with the militant suffragettes, Emmeline Pankhurst and her daughters, Christabel and Sylvia.

When Lansbury took up a cause, he did so with all his might. Almost inevitably then, given the historic circumstances, his commitment to 'Votes for Women' during the 'years of great unrest' led to a stint in jail and to his forcing the famous by-election of 1912 which resulted in his losing the parliamentary seat he had won only two years before. It led, even, to his renouncing membership of the National Administrative Council of the Independent Labour Party and of the Labour Party itself. On a more positive note it made him for a time, more even than Keir Hardie, the chief and most visible male supporter of the feminist movement in Britain. Clearly Lansbury's experiences shed fresh light on the relationship between socialists and suffragettes during the Edwardian era. Yet, until now, they have never been examined in detail.

To understand Lansbury's conception of feminism and the depth of his commitment to the women's suffrage movement, however, we must briefly abandon the Edwardian era, and return to the 'Outcast London' of the 1880s and 1890s. During that early period Lansbury did not define himself in terms of the women's movement, as he would twenty years later, but he played an active role in a pioneering women's suffrage campaign, Jane Cobden's effort to gain election to the London County Council. It is to that campaign that we must turn first.

1

Let us begin not in Lansbury's Bow and Bromley where the campaign was conducted, however, but rather in Bloomsbury, at 11 Endsleigh Gardens. This was 'a well known rallying place of all good work,' according to the *Pall Mall Gazette* of November 19, 1888, and the home of Mary Hyett Lidgett Bunting and her husband, Percy, who was editor of the *Contemporary Review* and a Liberal activist. Two days earlier 'a meeting of the kind reporters call "small but influential,"' had been convened there to consider the implications for female suffrage of a law recently passed by Parliament. Among those present at the gathering were 'many of ... those familiar as being to the front in every effort for the economical or political advancement of women ... Ladies, of course, were in the majority,' but speakers included the well-known barrister and future Liberal M.P., Corrie Grant, the solicitor and co-founder of Toynbee Hall who was to become prominent on the London County Council, Frederick Costello, the host of the meeting, Percy Bunting, 'and other gentlemen.' Lady Aberdeen, a future president of the Women's Liberal Federation, was in the chair.[1]

The situation which this socially august gathering had to consider was as follows: despite an agitation that dated from the 1850s, women continued to be denied the parliamentary franchise and the right to sit in either House of Parliament. Yet they could vote in local elections and serve on some locally elected bodies, provided that they satisfied existing property qualifications. Now Parliament had just restructured English local government, establishing county councils and scheduling elections for them early in the following year. Women who already possessed the franchise would be allowed to vote in them. But Parliament remained silent on two related and important issues: could women legally stand for election to these councils and could they serve if elected?

After speeches and discussion, the gathering determined to test the new law. It established a Society for Promoting the Return of Women as County Councillors and promised to raise £400 for up to four female candidates. 'Great anxiety was shown,' the *Pall Mall Gazette* reported, 'to avoid crossing the issues with those of party,' but in the end the S.P.R.W.C.C. sponsored only two candidates, both of whom belonged to the Radical wing of Liberalism. These were Lady Margaret Sandhurst, the elderly widow of an Indian Army officer and a prominent member of the Women's Liberal Federation, and Jane Cobden, who was likewise a W.L.F. activist, and the daughter of the famous Liberal politician and reformer, Richard Cobden.

Given contemporary political alignments perhaps such a political tilt was inevitable. In 1888 although the Conservative leader, Prime Minister Lord Salisbury, favored the admission of propertied women to the franchise (because he hoped to counteract Gladstone's Reform Bill of 1884 which had given many male rural workers the vote), most Conservatives opposed extending the franchise to women of any class. On the other hand, many Liberals and Radicals, if not their party leaders, favored some measure of enfranchisement for women.[2]

Most socialists also believed in adult suffrage as a basic principle of democracy, but apparently they had no representatives at the Bloomsbury gathering. And yet there may have been some indirect socialist influence at work there, for when the time came to choose which constituencies to contest, the S.P.W.R.C.C. arranged not only for Lady Margaret to stand in Brixton in South London but also for Cobden to stand in Bow and Bromley in the East End. The latter was one of the capital's most proletarian districts. Possibly, then, members of the S.P.W.R.C.C. thought they could build upon the successes of the socialist, Annie Besant, who had just been elected to the London School Board for Tower Hamlets, and who had led the famous 'Match Girls' Strike' there during the previous autumn.[3] These events may have suggested to the gathering in Bloomsbury that 'Outcast London's' working-class women would welcome the benevolent attentions of their middle-class sisters, especially if they held advanced views.

On the other hand, a more prosaic reason for choosing Bow and Bromley, at any rate, probably existed. Lansbury was general secretary of the Liberal and Radical Association there and, as we have seen, although still a comparative unknown, had already begun to impress metropolitan Radical circles. He may already have been known to Frederick Costello, through Toynbee Hall, or to Corrie Grant who was later to become a staunch and generous friend. When the S.P.R.W.C.C. asked Jane Cobden to stand in Bow and Bromley, it must have known that Lansbury would manage her campaign.

In the late 1880s, as we have seen, Lansbury's politics were essentially Radical. He believed implicitly that women should vote on equal terms with men. When he learned of the decision at 11 Endsleigh Gardens to make the contest in his constituency, he was delighted. He must have been consulted about prospects early on, since even before the executive of his local Liberal and Radical Association had met to discuss Cobden's candidacy he was already coaching her on the pending interview. 'It would be well,' he advised, 'if you could get some authoritative statement ... [on] the legality of your election if returned. I mean some well known lawyer's opinion on the matter so as to be able to quote it.'[5] Three days later, he took 'great pleasure' in reporting to the candidate that the executive had voted fourteen to three to support her. He was also aware of the campaign's historic significance. 'May I say how proud I am to have been able to help in your return?' he wrote her after her victory at the polls had been announced some weeks later. And, significantly, given what we know of his later political evolution, 'I am so glad to think that it was people of my own class who rallied to your support.'[6]

Lansbury's approach to the campaign revealed much about the late Victorian suffragist movement. For all that he believed in equal political rights for men and women, he rarely mentioned women's rights during the campaign. Rather he stressed other long-standing Liberal and Radical goals. He thought that Cobden could best 'rouse enthusiasm' in Bow and Bromley 'by going straight for social reform.' He wanted her to emphasize 'the housing of the Poor, ending [?] the letting of contracts to sweaters, equalisation of poor rate, [thirty-two years before Poplarism!] right to outdoor meetings, control of the police ... payment of Members [of Parliament].'[7] These, as we have seen, were standard themes of advanced Radicalism in the metropolis at the time. Despite his enthusiasm for the pioneering aspect of Cobden's campaign, then, he saw it mainly as a vehicle for social reform, and more particularly as part of an assault which London Radicals had launched upon the capital's local government, hitherto something of a Tory preserve.

Cobden's most important supporters saw it in the same light. The *Star* and *Pall Mall Gazette* newspapers, for example, endorsed her for her Radical, not her suffragist, views. 'It is felt that Miss Cobden in her address, has struck the right keynote,' the *Star* reported on December 22. *Reynolds's Newspaper* endorsed her on January 13 as 'a tried friend of the masses.' The Bow Branch of the Irish National League backed her in part because she was 'the daughter of England's greatest reformer.'[8] And the candidate herself followed this line. Her election address faithfully repeated

Lansbury's suggested program. Meanwhile in Brixton, Lady Sandhurst had chosen a similar tack. As she explained to the *Pall Mall Gazette* on January 25, she was a Liberal first and a suffragist afterwards. 'I prefer by means of the Women's Liberal Federation doing what I can to arouse the interest of women in politics, and at the same time educate them in Liberal principles.' The S.P.R.W.C.C. never deviated from this basic strategy, either during the campaign or in its controversial aftermath.

This is not to say that feminist ideology played no part in the campaign, far from it. But feminism in 1888 was very different from feminism a quarter-century later. Cobden, Lansbury and their allies rarely, if ever, explicitly contested prevailing concepts of gender roles, as the suffragettes were to do during the Edwardian era. Rather they believed, along with most Victorian feminists, that 'the weaker sex' should enter the political arena not to break down the separate sphere which women were thought naturally to inhabit, but in order to extend it. The campaign for representation on county councils grew from this outlook because the councils had been designed expressly to deal with those aspects of life most in need of the kinds of reform which, it was held, only the maternal, nurturing touch of a woman could provide. For instance, 'There was every reason why women should be on the County Council,' Cobden's supporter, Eva McLaren, lectured a meeting of female electors. 'One was that the Council would have the control of Paupers and Lunatic Asylums and ... it needed a woman to see that things went straight [for the unfortunate inhabitants of such places].'[9] Or, as the *Pall Mall Gazette* of October 22 put it,

> Like a good housewife the Council has to keep the house and the staff of servants in order: to see that the floors are swept (or rather the roads mended), that the menage is without waste and disorder, that the children don't run wild (reformatories & etc.), that the charities are administered without cheating or pinching, that the plant, the furniture ... are kept in repair ... What are all these but the very things in which women have always had their fingers?

Here was 'domestic feminism,' as historians term it, with a vengeance. If it seems condescending or patronizing to modern sensibilities, nevertheless its essential message, and the essential message of Cobden's campaign, was quite radical in several important respects. After all, domestic feminism provided a rationale for democratizing Britain's political system. More, it provided Radicals, like Lansbury, with a partial answer to the 'social question.' Domestic feminists held that poverty affected the human family, not just a number of unfortunate, isolated, individuals, and that women were naturally best suited to care for family members. Domestic feminism thus demanded the empowerment of women in order to combat poverty. 'Women ought to have not only a vote but a voice in all questions affecting the Housing of the Poor,' Cobden asserted in the only reference she made to women's rights in her election address.[10]

And, in George Lansbury, Cobden had discovered a political agent who might have been expressly designed for the S.P.R.W.C.C. campaign. As an organizer he was tireless, imaginative and effective. His letters to her were filled with references to the posters, bills and leaflets he was having printed and distributed on her behalf, the rallies and meetings he had arranged for her, and the influential speakers he hoped to bring to her support. His detailed knowledge of local conditions was a valuable asset to the campaign. 'I hope you will be able to live here for the election. It will never do to have to rush off for a train,' he counselled Cobden at one point. 'You see the people don't leave work till late and then if the meetings are got over early they don't learn half they would do, and in the case of a good speaker they don't like him cut short.'[11]

More than political acuity which was rare enough in itself, no doubt, Lansbury possessed a benevolent understanding and sympathy for the residents of his district, which in turn somehow enabled him to grasp the centrality of the family and of the domestic economy to the S.P.R.W.C.C.'s domestic feminist vision. 'I ought to tell you not to be disappointed if the meetings are not very large tomorrow,' he warned the candidate on another occasion.

> It is very near Christmas and Christmas only comes once a year in the East End and every father and mother has to take the children to see the shops, and Friday is payday for some of the men and it will be chosen for this purpose.

Few Liberal Party operatives can have placed family preoccupations at the heart of their political practice. Yet that was precisely what was required of a campaign based upon both the Radicalism and the domestic feminism of the late Victorian era.

This rare combination of acumen and empathy proved fruitful. Even the Conservative *East London Observer* conceded on polling day, January 19, 1889, that 'wherever Miss Cobden was seen she was at once recognized and enthusiastically greeted.' She finished second in the division with 2,054 votes, only fifty-five behind the leader W. Hunter, a justice of the peace and civil engineer, and ahead of E. Rider Cook, a soap maker and fellow Radical who had gained 1,722 votes, and J.H. Howard, a timber merchant who, with 1,060 votes, finished last. Since Bow and Bromley returned two representatives to the L.C.C., she had won. Her victory, and Lady Margaret's in Brixton, contributed to a radical sweep which saw 'Progressives' win 73 of the 118 seats contested in the L.C.C.'s first general election. Moreover, the L.C.C.'s first item of business was to elect nineteen aldermen who would sit on the council with them, serving for a term of six years. (Councillors sat only for three years.) Naturally, the Progessives were determined to choose political sympathizers. One, Emma Cons, who later founded the Old Vic theater, was female. So there were now three woman members of London's first county council.

This triumph, however, did not mark the end of the story but only its first stage. The aftermath of the election proved more significant than the campaign itself for what it revealed about attitudes towards female suffrage and gender in late Victorian Britain.

Once elected Cobden, Cons and Lady Sandhurst could proceed in one of two ways, depending upon their reading of the relevant laws. Either they could carry on with the normal activities of a county councillor, thereby courting a challenge to their right to serve; or they could hope to avoid such a test for a year, and then argue for their right to serve on the basis of a statute which declared that any election not questioned for twelve months should be deemed valid. If taking this latter route, Cobden's lawyers advised, it might be expedient for the women to arrange with male allies on the council to represent their views, and meanwhile to refrain from speaking or voting at council meetings so as not to be held to have acted illegally.

In the event, Lady Sandhurst did not have the luxury of choosing which tactic to pursue. No sooner had the results of the Brixton election been posted than her male runner-up, the barrister, L.T. Beresford Hope, applied to court for an order declaring her election void and himself elected. His argument was that women were excluded from sitting on county councils because the Act which had created the councils did not specifically state that women *could* sit on them. 'It is understood,' the *Pall Mall Gazette* hinted darkly, 'that Mr. Beresford Hope is being supplied with the sinews of war by Conservative friends, who thus hope to regain one of the seats won by the Progressives.' In response the S.P.R.W.C.C. promised to cover Lady Sandhurst's costs.[13]

While the case was pending, the L.C.C. agreed to debate it. The three women members chose Cobden to represent their views and she did so by reiterating the domestic feminist arguments employed during the campaign. 'There were many special reasons why women should be allowed to sit' on county councils, she argued.

They had to look after the housing of the poor, the female inmates of lunatic asylums, and industrial schools. Lady Sandhurst had under charge no fewer than 23 baby farms. Now might she ask whether the chairman, the deputy chairman or the vice-chairman would undertake the arduous duty of visiting these interesting establishments in case Lady Sandhurst's election was declared void?[14]

It seemed self-evident to Cobden and her supporters that women were better suited than men to visit them. Extending the woman's sphere into the political realm was, for them, merely a natural acknowledgement of women's special capabilities. Or could it be that by embracing the Victorian understanding of gender with such enthusiasm that she hoped to assuage those who feared any expansion of woman's sphere? On this occasion the L.C.C. voted forty-eight to twenty-two (and on other occasions by similar margins) in favor of women's right to serve. But the courts could not be thus reassured. Lady Sandhurst's case was heard by Sir James Fitzjames Stephen (uncle of Virginia Woolf) in early April and resulted in victory for the plaintiff. The defendant immediately appealed, but judgement again was given against her. On May 22, 1889, Beresford Hope replaced Lady Sandhurst on the L.C.C.

Jane Cobden, therefore, chose the second tactic: silence for a year in hopes that no one like Beresford Hope would challenge the validity of her election. At first, Lansbury opposed this course since, while perhaps safeguarding Cobden's position on the L.C.C., it would fail to establish the principle that women should be able to serve by right. The results of Lady Sandhurst's day in court, however, gave him and Cobden pause. So, too, did 'expressions of public opinion' which originally Lansbury had predicted would favor Cobden. By nearly a five-to-one margin the House of Lords rejected arguments in favor of women being allowed to sit as county councillors. The *Nineteenth Century* chose this moment to print Mrs. Humphrey Ward's famous women's appeal against female suffrage signed by, among others, Beatrice Potter (soon to

77

marry Sidney Webb); and *The Times*, while acknowledging that there might be some grounds for admitting women to county councils, 'and drawing the line at that point,' went on to laud Parliament for resisting even that: 'But there is no need for legislating in a hurry, as though there were an obvious grievance to be redressed or a palpable oversight to be corrected.'[15] So Cobden chose to delay the legal test for a year. She and Cons attended L.C.C. meetings, but neither voted nor spoke at them.

Lansbury now agreed that this was the proper strategy to pursue. Yet if the lawyers were to be avoided, the law itself needed changing, and for this, he well knew, a political campaign would be necessary. Throughout his career, Lansbury remained confident that the common people of East London, Britain, indeed the world, were sensible, peaceable, and democratic. Consequently, whenever he became involved in a political battle, his first instinct was to appeal to democracy. He never believed in making arrangements with other politicians in smoke-filled backrooms. The courts, *The Times*, the Lords and some prominent women might oppose female suffrage, but the people had yet to speak. Lansbury wanted Cobden to go to the people, on behalf of women's rights and to defend democratic principles. 'If we once rouse the people down here so that they realise that they are not to be permitted to choose who they like as members for the County Council, we shall not lack either energy or enthusiasm,' he assured her shortly after the decision against Lady Sandhurst had become known.[16] She should explain her situation first to the executive of the Bow and Bromley Liberal and Radical Association, then to the 400 members who composed its council, and then to 'a big public meeting' to which 'all classes' would be invited. 'You would then have the whole weight not only of the Association but also of the Electorate behind you,' he predicted confidently, 'and could afford to tire your opponents out by the simple process of doing nothing [on the L.C.C.].'[17]

Cobden followed Lansbury's advice – and more. Not only did she address the explanatory meetings he had recommended, but also a host of others designed to cement the affections of local voters. At Lansbury's urging she spoke to 'a meeting [which was noted in Section I] in support of the men called Bass dressers whose masters have refused to employ them *because* they have formed themselves into a Trade Union;'[18] a rally for East End shop assistants whose employers made them keep very late hours; a demonstration to support striking bargebuilders. Of course, when Radical and feminist causes merged, so much the better. Lansbury wrote to Cobden on another occasion,

> Tonight a woman called on me and asked if I could get you to help the women of Bow by attending a meeting it is proposed to hold down here for the purpose of getting women to join the new union. I told her that you would do all that it was possible for you to do in that way.[19]

Mainly, however, as during the election campaign the focus was on Radical, not feminist, goals; or, rather, the feminism was implicit in Cobden's leadership role at political events which previously had usually been dominated by men. Cobden's supporters, Lansbury included, still viewed Cobden mainly as a Radical reformer who happened to be a woman. Indeed, she saw herself in the same light. They all agreed, however that certain reforms could best be carried by women. This was the distinguishing mark of the late Victorian feminist movement.

When the year had elapsed and Cobden prepared to resume an active role on the L.C.C., Lansbury was convinced that her Radical activities had assured her hold upon local affections. He thought she now 'might rely on the undivided support of the men and women' of the constituency.[20] Unfortunately, however, she had still to reckon with the minority on the L.C.C. who opposed her right to serve. As soon as the twelve months following her election had elapsed, and Cobden (and Cons) dared to vote at L.C.C. meetings (on February 18 and 25, 1890), Sir Walter De Souza, the L.C.C. member for Westminster, sued to prevent either woman from doing so again. As De Souza was a Conservative, and the notice of his intention to bring action against Cobden and Cons was handed them (on the steps of the L.C.C. meeting hall) by the lawyer for Beresford Hope, the Conservative councillor who had sued Lady Sandhurst the previous year, it is likely that the two actions were coordinated.[21] On the other hand, it seems clear that the motivation was more misogynistic than political, since the result of unseating Cobden would have been to replace her with her Radical runner-up, the soap maker, E. Rider Cook, and not with another Conservative.

Once again Cobden consulted her legal advisers, and Lansbury. His response was so characteristic and revealing that it deserves to be quoted at length. 'I have been thinking about what you ought to do if the Judges decide against you,' he wrote to Cobden on March 14, 1890,

> and I have come to the conclusion that you ought *not* to resign, but go to prison and let the Council back you up by refusing to declare your seat vacant, and no other power so far as I know can issue the writ for an Election but them ... and I am certain the people down here will [support you also] especially if you have to suffer any inconvenience in maintaining your position. I hope you will not think me very hardhearted in telling you to go to Holloway, but if it were possible I should willingly go myself, so convinced am I that it is the right thing to do. I often think of Danton's words during the French Revolution. He said that what the people of France had to do was 'To Dare and Dare and yet again To Dare.' And if you and Miss Cons show a firm front to the Beresford Hopes and De Souzas, I am sure that public opinion will not allow you to remain in prison very long.

Do we discern here a parallel manifestation of the spirit which propelled the dockers, gasworkers and other 'unskilled' laborers during the 'new unionist' upsurge, or even a portent of the tactics employed by the militant suffragettes during the Edwardian era? Perhaps it is worth noting in this context that Lansbury's militant advice was not so uncommon as one might think. On March 13 the *Pall Mall Gazette* recommended an identical course. And the following day it printed a letter written and posted from the House of Commons by 'M.P.' who had heard Cobden advising Irish peasants 'to stand firm to their organizations and to each other' at a time when the Irish National League had been proclaimed under a Coercion Act. 'As she was the first Englishwoman to give this advice after any personal risk attached to the giving of it,' 'M.P.' concluded admiringly, 'she would, I think, be the last to shrink from any of the consequences of doing her duty as she understands it, on either side of the Channel.'

There were also less risky methods of carrying on the campaign and, as might have been expected, already Lansbury was demonstrating his mastery of them. The Earl of Meath, who had sponsored the Bill in the House of Lords on behalf of lady county councillors the previous year, wished to bring it up again. Lansbury planned a meeting at the Bow and Bromley Institute supporting his efforts. 'If you could get Earl Meath to come,' he exhorted Cobden, 'and, if possible, John Burns [who was then a county councillor] ... we could get 12 or 16 hundred people in easily.' Annie Besant, and Lady Dilke, the working-women's champion, were other figures he hoped to bring to the gathering which duly took place on May 19.[22] He was also pressing London M.P.s to introduce a resolution like Meath's in the House of Commons.[23] These efforts bore fruit in a Bill sponsored by a London Radical with ties to Gladstone, Professor James Stuart, M.P. Lansbury was determined to increase its chance of passage in the House. This required circularising 'all the clubs and associations in and around London,' a task he was 'most willing to see to,' and which resulted in the London Liberal and Radical Union twice endorsing Professor

Stuart's Bill, and in 'nearly all' the London Liberal and Radical associations and clubs sending delegates to a deputation which waited upon the leader of the Liberal Lords, the Earl Granville, asking him to support Lord Meath's Bill.[24] Nor was this the extent of Lansbury's energy and commitment to the cause. As the day approached when the House would consider Stuart's Bill, he redoubled his efforts. 'I have written twelve' letters, he reported to Cobden,

> and have sent them to MPs Buxton, [illegible], Crilly, Montagu, Bryce, Arnold Morley, Rowntree, J.H. Wilson, H.C. Lawson, R.K. Causton and T.W. Channing. I did not write to more London M.P.s as I am sure [Professor] Stuart himself will be able to secure their attendance if they are in town … I have sent over 200 petitions and besides sending them to the political Clubs and Associations have also got them sent to all the 60 branches of the Gas Workers and General Labourers Union.[25]

Lansbury concluded, 'One thing is quite sure, people will know we are still alive and in earnest.'

Yet his efforts were in vain. As the Lord Chief Justice put it when the case finally came before him in April 1891, ' Miss Cobden must … be deemed to be validly elected [but] … Miss Cobden cannot act as a member of the County Council because [being female] she is not duly qualified.'[26] The result of this judgment was that Cobden (and, by extension, Cons) could continue to attend L.C.C. meetings, but could not take part in them. Or, as the *Pall Mall Gazette* disgustedly put it on April 17, 'As little girls at school are taught, they may be seen but not heard.' One month later, when the House of Commons finally considered Professor Stuart's Bill, only fifty Members could be found to support it. The crusade to enable women to sit as county councillors, embarked upon at 11 Endsleigh Gardens three years before, had been defeated, at least for the moment. It would not be until 1907 that women would gain the right to sit as county councillors.[27]

Thus this pioneering women's suffrage campaign had accomplished little. But it provided Lansbury with rather more experience of the women's movement than most other male socialists could draw upon twenty years later when the suffrage crusade was revived. And it provides his biographer with a window into Lansbury's early views on 'the Woman Question' as it was then called, and perhaps into the views of other working-class male Radicals of 'Outcast London,' substantial numbers of whom, after all, must have supported Cobden with their ballots.

We have seen that Lansbury's feminism complemented but, nevertheless, was subordinated to his Radicalism. He believed, as a Radical, that the rights to vote, stand for office, and serve if elected, were fundamental to democratic practices and, therefore, that women as well as men should enjoy them; not merely because all adults should be able to participate in the political process, but also because voters should be able to choose anyone they pleased to represent them. 'Anything short of that,' Lansbury asserted in one of his many letters to Cobden, 'is simply a fraud.'[28]

Lansbury believed, too, that the vote was a crucial weapon in the struggle for reform and that, therefore, women should wield it as well as men. But this was not simply a democratic argument. It was, also, a domestic feminist argument which stemmed from the perception that women were better suited than men to care for society's unfortunates: the poor, the homeless, the aged, the infirm, the children. Domestic feminists condemned the masculine world view which placed so little emphasis upon the needs and disabilities of such people. They condemned the England which men had made. That is why their natural supporters came mainly from the left of the political spectrum.

And it is one reason why Lansbury shared their critique. 'Women as well as men must solve the social problem,' he wrote to Cobden. Throughout this period he expressed himself in terms which were characteristic of domestic feminism but which hinted at something even more radical. He thought the woman's sphere as currently defined was too constraining. He certainly did not accept that finding a husband and raising a family were the only worthwhile goals a woman might have. 'If the women will in future do much more in the way of training their daughters to look on life as something besides being married they will do a good deal to help on social reform,' he lectured Cobden (unnecessarily, one presumes).[29] He understood, too, that Victorian England afforded women few options *except* marriage, so that many had to sell themselves to a man for security, so that marriage itself was for them a form of bondage. And he believed that this was the worst 'of all the tragedies in life,' especially if the wife was 'tied to a man who is a brute or a drunkard.'[30]

Many years later Lansbury told a news reporter who asked about the roots of his feminism that

> There were certain things I always felt. I felt how hard the working woman's life was, spent in unending labour, cooped up in a little brick house in an interminable street of similar brick houses. I saw too that if the boy went out to work he could have his evenings to himself for play or study, but the girls, however hard their work, must also work in the house and wait on the men and boys. This always seemed to me grossly unfair.[31]

These sentiments and the perceptions revealed in his letters to Cobden, seemed almost to presage the stage of feminist thinking which superceded domestic feminism, and which the miltant suffragettes of the Edwardian era proclaimed: that women were exploited, both at home by their husbands and at the workplace by their employers, because they were women; that power, or the lack of it, was rooted in sex as well as in class. Lansbury had been brought by Cobden's campaign and by his instinctive response to the issues it raised, to the brink of making this conceptual leap. Cobden's final defeat in the courts and the ending of the agitation on her behalf meant that the leap was deferred, but twenty years later he actually made it, as we will see below. By 1912, Lansbury was supporting the militant suffragettes with all his power and energy. The vast majority of the Labour Party, however, were then advocating the domestic feminism with which he had begun. Arguably they are still advocating it. In Lansbury's earliest views on the 'woman question' we may see the outlines of a vision still potent in the British labor movement.

Lansbury's experience with Jane Cobden may cast some light upon another aspect of Labour Party history, its origins. He was disgusted by the failure of Liberal leaders to work harder for women's rights, so disgusted in fact that he contemplated quitting the party. 'We in Bow and Bromley shall take every opportunity of letting the public know what they may expect from the Liberal leaders,' he warned in an angry letter which the *Daily News* declined to print, but which found an outlet on June 1, 1891, in the faithful *Pall Mall Gazette*.

> Surely those who are in earnest about the enfranchisement of women will not be content to be a mere appendage of the Liberal Party. Let them shake themselves free of party feeling and throw the energy and ability which they are now wasting on minor questions into the broader and more important one of securing ... the full rights of citizenship to every woman in the land.

A few months later he followed his own advice, leaving the Liberals for the S.D.F. which also had offered, unsuccessfully, a woman candidate ('Miss Varley'), in the L.C.C. election. He brought with him a cadre of talented, dedicated, local working-class activists who set about building socialism in Poplar with results already examined. Their defection from the Bow and Bromley Radical and Liberal Association in 1892 proved to be one of the first real nails in the coffin of East-End Liberalism.

Of course their disenchantment with the Liberals did not stem only from this single experience. On the other hand there can be no doubting that the failure of Liberal Party leaders to more enthusiastically support Jane Cobden was a major factor in the decision of Lansbury and his comrades to leave them. Have we, then, come across an ingredient in working-class disillusionment with Liberalism and the appeal of socialism and independent-labor politics which historians have not taken with sufficient seriousness? I think so. While William Gladstone, John Morley and even Lansbury's friend, J. A. Murray MacDonald, were turning their backs on the women's movement, the S.D.F., following a directive of the Second International in 1893, was making universal suffrage its major rallying cry for that year. It seems only logical that the socialist position attracted, while the Liberal stance repelled, the kind of people who had supported Jane Cobden's pioneering suffragist effort. Sandra Holton has recently demonstrated the extent to which women's suffrage societies emancipated themselves from the Liberal Party and formed close links with Labour during the Edwardian era. What we have seen above suggests that a varient of this process had begun some twenty years earlier.[32]

For Lansbury, then, and perhaps for many other East End Radicals, the failures of Liberalism, the wrongs done to women, and the attractions of socialism, were all related. 'Thousand of our fellow creatures, men and women like us, don't know how to make ends meet, in fact don't know how to live,' he wrote in one of his final letters to Cobden. 'Our economic conditions seem to compel a large number of women to be mere slaves.'[33] It is a commonplace of British history that the East End provided a well-spring of support for the new unionism, but perhaps it offered something more. For a man of Lansbury's sensibilities there could have been no better breeding ground of a socialist and *feminist* outlook than 'Outcast London'.

2

The fifteen years which followed Jane Cobden's fruitless campaign saw Lansbury's conversion from Liberalism to socialism and then his passage from the S.D.F. to the I.L.P. and Labour Party. Of course he did not abandon the women's cause during this period, but his efforts in its behalf were now largely subsumed within his agitation for the unemployed, as a guardian and borough councillor. It was within this context, for instance, that he organized a march of unemployed women to the House of Commons in 1905.[34]

Meanwhile the women's movement, as such, experienced an interlude of relative quiescence – until 1906, when it re-emerged with, if anything, increased vigor and determination. The swath it cut in British politics after that year was a wide one; and it could be only a matter of time before its path and Lansbury's intersected again.

In order to understand that intersection, and the electric shock then delivered to the labor and suffragette movements, it is necessary to examine briefly certain aspects of the evolution of the suffragette agitation, and of the history of the I.L.P. and Labour Party. Lansbury had joined both political bodies in the early years of the new century.

The Labour Party, as much as the Liberal Party, was a 'broad church'. Even during the pre-1914 period it contained ex-Radicals and Liberals like Lansbury (but only some of whom had converted to socialism), non-socialist trade unionists, Fabians, 'ethical socialists', and Marxists. To a lesser extent the same was true of the I.L.P., as a comparison of the disparate views of (say) MacDonald and Keir Hardie, or of J. Bruce Glasier and Victor Grayson would attest. Such broadness was the result of many a compromise between conflicting elements within each party, and generally has been considered a characteristic strength of the British working-class movement. Yet there were always party members who opposed the compromises and even the notion that it was good for Labour to be so broad a church, on the grounds that the party's basic commitments were being weakened. For example, many socialists in the I.L.P. opposed the adhesion to Labour of trade unionists who did not accept even the most rudimentary collectivist principles. These socialist militants resented those who, they believed, were reaping the benefits of their earlier hard work, and literally stealing the party from them. But the issue which divided Labour most in the years before World War I, and which assumed great importance in Lansbury's career, becoming the point of departure for his next great effort on behalf of women's suffrage, turned upon the relationship between Labour and the Liberal Governments of 1906-14.[35]

The Labour Party, as is now well known, first secured a significant parliamentary presence in 1906 as the result of a secret agreement with the Liberals not to stand against each other in a number of carefully selected constituencies. Arguably, some such agreement was the prerequisite to such electoral success as Labour enjoyed before 1914, and yet it directly contradicted the party's original reason for being, namely *independent* working-class representation in Parliament; and of course it would also have been an anathema to those socialists who, rejecting Fabian notions of the 'inevitability of gradualism', opposed any compromise with capitalism or the organizations they considered to be its political agents. Yet many Labour supporters became increasingly suspicious that such a pact must exist, not merely because three-cornered election fights were so often discouraged by their party leaders after 1906, but even more because the Parliamentary Labour Party so rarely opposed the Liberal Government in the House of Commons. And if opposition to the government had been rare between 1906 and 1910, when the Liberals enjoyed a vast parliamentary majority so that Labour could vote its conscience without worrying about consequences, it was practically non-existent after the general elections of January and December 1910, when the Liberal majority was wiped out, and the government had to depend upon the support of Irish Nationalist and Labour M.P.s to pass legislation. In these circumstances any government defeat in the House could mean its defeat as a whole and replacement by the Conservatives. Labour, under the pragmatic leadership of Ramsay MacDonald, preferred to keep the Conservatives out, even if that meant voting consistently for Liberal Bills which had nothing to do with socialism. This further raised suspicions of some sort of deal between the two parties, particularly among rank-and-file members of the I.L.P., who considered themselves a sort of socialist conscience to the Labour Party, but whose leaders, Keir Hardie and Ramsay MacDonald, were the architects of the secret pact and who were often, MacDonald especially often, found with other members of the P.L.P., defending Liberal policies, and sustaining the Liberal Government in the House with their votes.

Within the I.L.P. there were sporadic attempts to challenge Labour's cautious political practices. In 1907, in a by-election in the Colne Valley, the young Victor Grayson stood successfully as an Independent Socialist. Once in Parliament he scornfully refused to sign Labour's constitution or to accept Labour whips. Rather he put himself at the head of the militants within the I.L.P. who sought 'socialist unity' with the S.D.F. and an end to Labour's political compromising. Grayson was undisciplined and, as it transpired, lacking in stamina: his rise was meteoric but shortlived; his downfall was equally sudden and much more permanent. Yet the unrest and suspicions he had helped to focus within the I.L.P. survived his brief career. More determined efforts to redirect and re-energize the Labour Party would soon be taken.

In fact, the next significant challenge came from within the I.L.P.'s National Administrative Council itself. This body, like the rest of the socialist movement, was divided over what to do about Labour's seeming softness for the Liberals. Even the I.L.P.'s leading figures, Bruce Glasier, Ramsay MacDonald, Philip Snowden and Keir Hardie, did not present a united front, Hardie (despite his knowledge of the secret Lib–Lab pact) calling often, Snowden somewhat less regularly, for a more militant and socialist line, Glasier and MacDonald defending the existing strategy. Yet whenever their own paramountcy within the I.L.P. was challenged, the 'Big Four' invariably rallied to defend it. This is what happened during the years of Grayson's effectiveness, as it was when, in 1910, four militants on the N.A.C., Leonard Hall, J.M. MacLachan, J.H. Belcher and C.T. Douthwaite, issued a pamphlet (which was called the *Green Manifesto* because that was the color of its cover) questioning in biting terms the value of the I.L.P.'s membership in the Labour Party, demanding socialist unity and that the party follow a more resolute socialist program. Meanwhile a second, only slightly less militant line was being advocated by another member of the N.A.C., Fred Jowett of Bradford, who wanted Labour to vote in the House on the merits of each Bill, without taking into account what the effect would be upon the Liberal Government. The Big Four opposed this position too.

Lansbury was not yet at the center of these events, but he soon would be, and even in 1910 he was much more than a simple observer. A member of the I.L.P. since early in the century, his popularity and reputation within it had undergone a steady if unspectacular rise, so that by 1909 he had been elected to its N.A.C., a position he kept until his resignation from the Council in 1912. He was neither a supporter of the Big Four, although he had worked with Hardie previously on behalf of the unemployed, nor (yet) of the militants who charged the leaders with betraying socialism in order to maintain the Liberal Government. For example, despite Big Four skepticism, he successfully moved the N.A.C. resolution accepting an S.D.P. (formerly the S.D.F.) invitation to discuss socialist unity; on the other hand, at the behest of the Big Four he and I.L.P. chairman, W.C. Anderson, composed the N.A.C.'s condemnation of the *Green Manifesto*. At an important provincial I.L.P. conference ('Division 9, Cheshire, N. Wales, etc.', which, actually, was Douthwaite's division) it was Lansbury who explained N.A.C. opposition to Jowett's demand that the P.L.P. vote only 'on the merits' of Liberal legislation.

What brought Lansbury from careful neutrality between the conflicting wings of the I.L.P. to passionate militancy was his election to Parliament in December 1910 and his reaction to MacDonald's leadership of the P.L.P. He was astonished, and deeply troubled, by what he took to be Labour's lack of fighting spirit in the House of Commons. Within a matter of weeks of his election, he was observing, in the *Forward* of March 4, 1911, that Labour in the House 'must adopt a very much more determined attitude.' As he explained in an interview for the *Labour Leader* of March 24,

> There is a great danger that if the Government once imagine that in the Labour Party they may count on 42 safe votes ... they will see us to Heaven or Hades before they will trouble about the unemployed, the destititute and the women's question ... I am bound to acknowledge that I don't know where Labour comes in ... Nothing very effective will be accomplished in the House of Commons until the fear of turning the Government out of office has been overcome.

Lansbury saved his most prophetic and, from the point of view of Labour's leaders, most troubling words for the end of the interview: 'I am going to refuse to vote according to the bidding of those who look at politics more or less from the Liberal standpoint,' he warned. 'It is an intolerable position and I, for one, could not stand it for forty-eight hours.' Fred Jowett, and all socialists who advocated 'voting on the merits' had gained a powerful ally.

Just how powerful an advocate Lansbury could now be was revealed at the annual conference of the I.L.P. held in late April 1911. There, in the words of the young Fenner Brockway, who covered the conference for the *Labour Leader* of April 21, he delivered a 'burning oration' on behalf of Jowett's position.

> I am in the House of Commons with the picture before me of those men and women who night after night toiled in the slums of Bow and Bromley to send me there. They worked for me because they thought I was different from the Liberals and Tories. They did not work for me and would not have worked for me out of consideration for the Government. They sent me to face the question of poverty, poverty, poverty.

When Lansbury had concluded, according to Brockway, 'the delegates rose and cheered again and again. The speech stirred them as no utterance has done at recent conferences.' Aside from Keir Hardie, another observer asserted, Lansbury was now the most popular figure in the I.L.P.[36] Certainly he had become the leading, and most effective, advocate of Jowett's line. In this regard he had replaced even Jowett.

It is at this point, with Lansbury in something approaching revolt against the 'tame' policies of the P.L.P., that we must bring the women's suffrage movement back into the story, for its history and Lansbury's were about to coincide with remarkable effect.

Very briefly, there were, during the Edwardian era, two main bodies actively seeking extension of the franchise to women. The National Union of Women's Suffrage Societies (N.U.W.S.S.) had been established first, in the mid-nineteenth century, and was now led by Millicent Fawcett, the widow of one of Gladstone's Cabinet Ministers and mother of the famous Philippa (who was senior wrangler in the maths tripos in Cambridge in the 1890s, even though the university would not let her hold the title). Of more recent origin but equal significance was the Women's Social and Political Union (W.S.P.U.), founded in 1903 and led by Emmeline Pankhurst and her daughters, Sylvia and Christabel. (There were, actually, several other women's and adult suffrage societies during this period, but for the sake of simplicity they are not considered in detail here.) In the past, scholars have emphasized a distinction between the 'constitutional' N.U.W.S.S. and the 'militant' W.S.P.U., but recent work suggests that the two organizations were less at odds than has been supposed. At any rate, both groups faced the same problem when, in 1906, the Liberals finally attained office. Although many, and possibly most, Liberal backbenchers favored some measure of female suffrage, the government did not. Thus, in the years before 1911, despite various backbench efforts to pass a women's suffrage Bill, none was successful. Prime Minister Asquith always found reason to oppose, or to postpone, positive action.

The suffragettes, who originally had thought a Liberal administration would sympathize with their movement and approve their goal, were greatly disappointed and driven to re-think their strategy. Hence 'militancy' which, in the first instance, generally took the form of interrupting Liberal politicians in mid-speech with demands of 'Votes for Women,' but which eventually came to include violent demonstrations, destruction of property, and even pitched battles with police. During the terms of imprisonment which followed such confrontations, some suffragettes went on hunger strike. This led, in turn, to forcible feeding and, when severe injury (leading to death in one instance) resulted, to the infamous 'Cat and Mouse Act'. After April 1913, starving suffragettes could be let out of jail and then re-imprisoned when they had recovered their health.

In 1910 a 'Conciliation Bill' passed its second reading in the House by a comfortable majority. Cobbled together by representatives of the three main political parties, this measure proposed the enfranchisement of women who independently occupied property. By the summer of 1911, the Bill had been redrafted to admit amendments which would increase its scope. It had an important, if finally unreliable, supporter in Chancellor of the

Exchequer, Lloyd George, and virtually unanimous support in the P.L.P., which believed that the majority of women enfranchised by the Bill would be of the working class. The N.U.W.S.S. gave the Bill wholehearted support; the W.S.P.U. called off its militant campaign while the Bill was pending. At its second reading the Bill received another massive demonstration of support. Only eighty-eight Members opposed it.

It seemed as though passage of some measure of women's enfranchisement was pending. Asquith, however, refused to provide further time for consideration of the Conciliation Bill. Instead he promised that the government would offer, in the next session, a Manhood Suffrage Bill which could be amended to include women. The question of Labour's attitude now arose. Possibly Asquith's Bill could be transformed into an adult suffrage Bill. This was Labour's stated goal. Suppose, however, Labour amendments to widen the scope of the Bill to include women were defeated? Should the party then oppose a measure which finally enfranchised the entire male working class? On this question MacDonald, and not only MacDonald, might have doubts. Labour seemed to promise that it would oppose the Manhood Suffrage Bill if it was not suitably amended, but the language was ambiguous. Despite wishful thinking on the part of many suffragettes, the question remained open.

From his newly won position as Member for Bow and Bromley, Lansbury viewed these tergiversations with growing anger. He was already a more committed proponent of 'Votes for Women' than the majority of his colleagues. There had been, as we have already seen, his early work on behalf of Jane Cobden. In addition, during an unsuccessful parliamentary campaign in Middlesbrough in 1906, he had become friends with a leading light in the local I.L.P., Marion Coates Hansen. This woman, as her correspondence with Lansbury reveals, was a forceful, articulate, feminist. 'I was *quite* satisfied with you,' she once wrote to him after he had delivered a (post-election) speech at Middlesbrough.

Don't dare to think to think me presumptuous. I don't mean to be. I'm not always satisfied with you men. I'm as old as any of you – and have a right to stand as judge once in a while. My sex has been judged unheard and undefended for centuries. These centuries of experience and injustice make some of us very, very, old.[37]

Coates Hansen, whose name is rarely even mentioned in the standard histories of the suffragette movement, was responsible for bringing into it one of its most important male recruits. 'You failed in your duty that you were not in Trafalgar Square on Saturday,' at a 'Votes for Women' rally, she admonished Lansbury late in 1906.

No one associates your name with the women's cause – hence you won't 'get asked.' Look at your beautiful wife and daughters and ask to speak. We were short of speakers on Saturday and Mrs. Pankhurst said to me that they could not think of another soul to ask. Even *I* did not think of you.

Lansbury, who must have been stung, wrote immediately to the W.S.P.U. contributing money and volunteering his services. 'You can help us immensely,' Emmeline Pethick Lawrence, one of the W.S.P.U. leaders, replied prophetically.[38]

To his standard speeches on labor and socialism Lansbury, who was then stumping the country on behalf of the I.L.P., added a section endorsing the women's movement. He became, with Keir Hardie and Philip Snowden, one of its most constant and prominent socialist supporters. When Lansbury entered Parliament he did not cease to back the suffragettes; and, of course, the P.L.P. as a whole gave nominal support to women's suffrage. Yet, Lansbury soon formed a low opinion of his fellow Labour back-benchers. 'They are a weak, flabby lot,' he confided to Beatrice Webb who had long since come to regret signing Mrs. Humphrey Ward's anti-suffrage petition in 1888.[39] And, as the Liberal Government prevaricated over the issue of women's suffrage, and

95

George Lansbury

the P.L.P., under MacDonald's leadership, continued to support the Liberals in order to keep the Conservatives out, Lansbury's patience wore thin.

This, then, is the background to his dramatic intervention on behalf of women's rights in the years before World War I. When he began demanding that Labour in the House support the women regardless of Liberal policy, as he did after the summer of 1911, it represented the culmination of a process of disenchantment with Labour policy whose roots were located in Victor Grayson's rebellion, the *Green Manifesto* and, above all, in Jowett's demand that the P.L.P. emancipate itself from the Liberal Government by voting on the merits of each bill rather than on the consequences for Asquith's hold on power. Moreover, Lansbury's disillusionment with Liberalism's attitude towards women's suffrage was rooted in Jane Cobden's experiences during 1888–92, and probably went deeper than with other members of the P.L.P.

It is hard to tell which enraged Lansbury more during the late Edwardian era, Asquith's fertile ability to discover ever more creative reasons for postponing action, or MacDonald's invariable support of Asquith. Characteristically, Lansbury wanted plain language and plain deeds. He knew well, as he told a W.S.P.U. audience at the London Pavilion, that 'words spoken by the Prime Minister and by Mr. Lloyd George did not always mean what ordinary people thought.'[40] Labour should cease to parley with such slippery customers, and rather, as he told the *Edinburgh Evening News* on October 9, 1911, 'put [its] men forward wherever [it] thinks it policy to do so.' In Bradford a week later he was warning that, 'The humbug about Liberalism and Labour had got to be brought to a head.'[41]

Asquith's promise of a Manhood Suffrage Bill only stiffened Lansbury's resolve. Responding to the Liberal offer in a column for the *Labour Leader* of November 17, 1911, he metaphorically threw down the gauntlet to Labour moderates. 'Let us forget we are

Parliamentarians – a word invented, I am sure, by the King of Lies,'
he exhorted,

> and let us remember that one of the chief principles we hold and
> advocate is that women have the same right to citizenship as men. Let
> us tell our leaders, whether in the Labour movement or Socialist
> movement, that on this question we will have no compromise of any
> sort or kind, but that we will, if necessary, go down fighting.

Lansbury feared, correctly as it turned out, that the P.L.P. would
vote for the Liberal measure even if it had not been broadened into
an Adult Suffrage Bill.

Meanwhile, as MacDonald picked his way delicately through the
minefield that militancy represented to most politicians, Lansbury
was celebrating its accomplishments. He was careful, at this stage,
to distinguish between the militant goal, which he shared, and
militant methods which he would not condemn but did not
approve. 'No one, least of all myself, wishes to see women set fire
to theatres or do anything violent,' he assured an interviewer from
the *Daily Herald* for August 9, 1912. But, on the other hand,
'nobody bothers about the poor except when the poor commence
to kick.' And what was true for striking workers applied equally
to the suffragettes. 'They would not have even had the question
discussed, or any talk of the Manhood Suffrage Bill, if it had not been
for the six or seven years of definite militant action.'[43] As he told
one of the W.S.P.U.'s regular meetings at the London Pavilion,
'if people can create enough the impression that they will fight, they
will get their way. It is clear as daylight.'[44]

He was conducting the battle on two fronts now: in Parliament
where at question time he was the government's regular interlocu-
tor, as pesky a backbench opponent, in fact, as it had to face; and
within the Labour Party, particularly within the I.L.P., whose
leaders now must have felt about him pretty much the way the
Liberal hierarchy did. On May 26 Lansbury submitted to the

N.A.C. of the I.L.P. a resolution which he wanted brought before the party's annual conference, scheduled to meet in four days' time:

> That this Conference strongly condemns the refusal of the Government to concede the demand formulated by the Labour Party for a measure enfranchising all adult men and women. The Conference claims that as the Government has brought forward proposals applying only to men and affording no guarantee that women will secure the vote, the support of the Parliamentary Labour Party should be immediately and entirely withdrawn from the Government, and calls upon the Labour Members to institute a policy of sleepless and relentless opposition to the Government with the object of driving them from office.[45]

So 'voting on the merits' had been replaced by 'sleepless and relentless opposition' to the Liberals. This was, at least for the moment, however, a non-starter, even among Lansbury's allies on the N.A.C. For it was one thing to consider proposed Liberal legislation against Labour's longstanding goals, and to vote against those Bills which failed to measure up; but it was quite another to set out deliberately to defeat the Liberals by voting (with Conservatives) against *all* legislation, including Bills which, otherwise, might be deemed eminently deserving of Labour support. Lansbury's resolution received only one positive vote from the N.A.C., and that was his own.

Lansbury's isolation on the N.A.C. was not, however, a true indication of his standing within the I.L.P. as a whole. A better measure was provided as a result of his decision to challenge the party's sitting chairman, W.C. Anderson, an invariable supporter of MacDonald. 'I am going to the poll whatever the result may be,' he informed Hardie somewhat pessimistically. And then, more brightly, 'A good many branches asked me to stand.'[46]

Lansbury was now the chief spokesman for the wing of the I.L.P. which, some years earlier, had looked to Victor Grayson for leadership, and which had greeted the *Green Manifesto* as its own. During the years before World War I this was not an inconsiderable force in the party. Lansbury was defeated by Anderson for the chairmanship but only by 185 votes to 112. This was a respectable result. As Fenner Brockway diplomatically put it for the *Labour Leader* of May 31: 'The fact that Mr. Lansbury polled as many as 112 votes proves how eager the Party is to pursue a militant policy for it has never been served by a better chairman than Mr. Anderson.'

For Lansbury these political campaigns were invested with a deeper meaning than ambitious politicians usually feel. The women's and workers' movements were hardly mere stepping stones for his career as, perhaps, they were for some of his parliamentary colleagues. Just how profound were the emotions now influencing his political behaviour was soon to become very evident.

The suffragettes had taken up militancy again with a vengeance. Arson, stone throwing, and confrontation with the police were common. The number of suffragettes in jail rose dramatically. And there was a double standard to consider. The imprisoned leaders of the suffragette movement were placed within the 'first division' of the jail, with certain privileges, but rank-and-file suffragettes were put into the 'second division,' and denied privileges. Given the determination shown by suffragettes in the past, the authorities cannot have been too surprised when both 'first' and 'second' division prisoners hunger struck in protest at such unequal treatment. By now the horrors of forcible feeding had become well known. Lansbury was appalled by the stories of suffering which daily issued from Holloway Prison. Incredibly, however, some parliamentarians found the stories amusing. On July 25, amidst guffaws, the Under Home Secretary, Mr. Ellis Griffiths, joked in the House that one suffragette who had attempted to hurl herself from a prison tier obviously had not intended suicide, 'or she would have chosen a higher drop.' The Prime Minister added that any suffragette could go free immediately, and spare herself future sufferings from forcible feeding, if she would only renounce militancy. For Lansbury this proved to be the last straw.

What followed was one of parliamentary history's great scenes. 'You know they cannot!' Lansbury cried in a voice of thunder when Asquith suggested that the women make promises of good behavior. 'You know it is perfectly dishonourable to ask them to give such an undertaking. I call it perfectly disgraceful.' He had left his seat and was striding up the floor of the House towards the front bench. 'You are beneath contempt,' he told the startled Prime Minister, who was unused to breaches of parliamentary etiquette. 'You will go down in history as the man who tortured innocent women ... You ought to be driven out of public life.' And to Members opposite, previously jeering, now strangely, uneasily, quiet: 'You call yourselves men. You talk about principles ... You do not know what principle is. The women are showing you what principle is and instead of laughing at them you ought to honour them.'

By now the Speaker had risen and was directing Lansbury to leave the House: 'I ask the Honourable Member to withdraw.' But Lansbury refused, returning instead to his seat by the gangway. MacDonald and Snowden hurried over, advising him to obey the Speaker. And so, at last, Lansbury went. He was white and trembling with a combination of rage and mortification. The House sat in stunned silence. Like the Prime Minister it was not used to displays of genuine emotion.[47]

And this had been only a portent. Lansbury was on a collision course with the entire constellation of forces which, together, were holding up action on women's suffrage. These included, of course, the Conservative and Liberal Parties, but also and more importantly, the Labour Party itself; for by now MacDonald had made plain not merely that the P.L.P. would continue voting for Liberal

legislation (which might include an unamended Manhood Suffrage
Bill) but also that it would keep its distance from the suffragette
militants; while Lansbury was more convinced than ever that
unceasing opposition to the Liberals in the House, and militancy
outside, were the only effective strategies to pursue.

He took few pains to hide his growing estrangement from his
party leader and parliamentary colleagues. To the *Observer* of
August 4, he expressed the hope that MacDonald would step down.
'I think there are men in the party such as Mr. Philip Snowden who
are quite capable of taking the leadership and doing the work well
and efficiently.' On August 23, in *Votes for Women*, he warned that
Labour Members and their leader were not to be trusted, and
advised his party's rank and file to compel their parliamentary
represesentatives to reject an unamended Manhood Suffrage Bill,

> even if it means another General Election ... There have been many
> statements made on the platform and many attempts made to prove
> that the Labour Party is pledged to do this, but I speak what I know
> when I say that the Parliamentary Labour Party – the men who in this
> matter really count – have not up to the present decided the matter
> one way or the other.'

Meanwhile he had revived the proposal which he had placed
before the N.A.C. of the I.L.P. in May, that the P.L.P. be
instructed to oppose the Liberals in the House at every opportunity. He sent, on his own initiative and responsibility, a letter to
every labor and socialist organisation in the country asking it to
support this position by signing a resolution which said:

> The — Branch of the —, being determined that the political
> enfranchisement of the women workers shall be granted without
> delay, condemns the Government for introducing a Franchise Bill for
> men only, repudiates the sham pledges by which the Government are
> trying to trick the advocates of Votes for Women, protests against the
> Government which is guilty of such a policy being kept in power by

and of Labour votes – and finally calls upon the Labour Members of Parliament to vote constantly and relentlessly against the Government from now onwards until they have either driven them from office or compelled them to carry a proposal giving votes to women on equal terms with men.[48]

Militant suffragettes, many of whom were members of local I.L.P.s supported him. I.L.P.s in Barnet, Byker and Heaton, Cambridge, Dudley, Erdington (Birmingham), Eastwood and Langley Mill, Heanor and Codnor, Gravesend and Northfleet, Shaw and Crompton, and Sunderland endorsed Lansbury's appeal within the week.[49] But, in the *Votes for Women* of October 4 and October 18, Christabel Pankhurst inadvertently revealed where Lansbury's campaign inevitably was headed – and why a majority of Labourites could never follow him to its logical end. 'What if they [the P.L.P.] prefer to keep the government in office without demanding and securing women's enfranchisement in return?' Pankhurst demanded. And she answered herself, 'Well then, they become indistinguishable from the government whose allies they are, and for whose existence and policy they are responsible.' But this could only mean, as she wrote two weeks later, that 'the next election contest in which a Labour candidate is nominated will see the W.S.P.U. striving to prevent that Labour candidate's return.' Pankhurst ended with a distinction which Lansbury might have appreciated, but which party leaders like MacDonald would have thought absurd. 'It should be understood that the W.S.P.U. attack is not made upon Labour and Socialist principles ... The attack is upon the official Labour policy.'

By now the confrontation between suffragettes and Labourites was fast approaching. During the second week of October, I.L.P. chairman, W.C. Anderson was heckled by the W.S.P.U. at a 'War Against Poverty' meeting. Previously such treatment had been reserved for Liberals and Tories. 'If affairs follow their natural course,' the *Daily Herald* parliamentary correspondent remarked on

October 14, 'the Labour Party and the suffragettes will be at each other's throats before the winter.' Lansbury would have to choose between them.

When the moment came, he scarcely hesitated. On October 16, the P.L.P. met with Labour's National Executive to discuss their line on the Manhood Suffrage Bill and Lansbury's circular letter. 'We were told,' Lansbury recalled afterwards, 'that ... it was our duty to attend regularly and on no account risk the defeat of the Government.'[50] This was precisely the policy to which he objected and, not surprisingly, he came in for some harsh words. As the party's number-two man, Arthur Henderson, put it, Lansbury had been elected with the aid of the Labour Party and, therefore, owed it his loyalty. One of the miners' M.P.s was even more blunt. 'Men [like Lansbury] who could not accept the view of the majority [of the P.L.P] ought either to remain quiet or get out.' Lansbury alone demanded 'relentless' opposition to the Liberals if they failed to amend their bill. This argument was defeated at a second meeting that evening (which, owing to previous obligations Lansbury could not even attend). The P.L.P. pledged to try to amend the Manhood Suffrage Bill, but pledged, too, to maintain the Government against the Conservatives.[51]

It finally had become clear to him that membership of a party so opposed to his position on so critical an issue was meaningless. He consulted friends, but his mind was made up already. As he told yet another W.S.P.U. rally in the Albert Hall on October 19,

> he refused to support any party which did not stand for justice to women; so although the Labour Party had taken up this attitude [to vote in favor of an unamended Manhood Suffrage Bill] he would consider himself free, after consulting his electors, to adopt an independent policy.[52]

But what did he mean by 'consulting his electors?' The rumors flew. 'A certain morning newspaper has been hearing, in the way morning newspapers do hear things, that Mr. George Lansbury, M.P. is contemplating resigning his seat in Parliament,' reported the *Daily Herald* of October 30.

> [But] the morning newspaper in question has not got hold of the right end of the stick. Mr. Lansbury certainly is contemplating resigning, but it is from the Labour Party and not from Parliament that he contemplates resignation.

The *Daily Herald* had it wrong too. 'Make your protest the strongest and straightest possible and have a mandate from your constituents that can't be gainsaid,' advised an old friend, Walter Coates (brother of Marion Coates Hansen). Lansbury agreed. He would resign from both party *and* parliament, taking the Chiltern Hundreds, to force a by-election. Then he would present himself to voters as Victor Grayson had done five years before, not as a Labour candidate, but as an independent socialist. He would campaign specifically on the issue of Votes for Women.

3

So began Lansbury's second electoral effort on behalf of women's rights. But where, twenty years earlier he had played a supporting role (as political agent to Jane Cobden), now he was a principal actor in the drama. His vocal support of the suffragettes, his confrontation with Asquith in the House of Commons, his circular letter demanding 'relentless' opposition to the Liberals, and finally his decision to force the by-election, had made him, for the moment, virtually the spearhead of the suffragette movement in Britain. Thus the Bow and Bromley by-election of 1912 represents a more significant engagement than Cobden's earlier battle in the war of attrition which women and their allies were forced to fight for full citizenship. More than any other single political event in British history, the looming contest in London's East End would focus the problematic, complicated, interaction between the feminist, socialist and labor movements.

On November 11, Lansbury made his plan public. Significantly, he did so before a meeting of the W.S.P.U. at the London Pavilion, and not to a Labour or I.L.P. audience. Nor (and afterwards this would be held against him) had he consulted in advance any of his colleagues on the N.A.C. of the I.L.P. since, 'rightly or wrongly, the past two years have convinced me that whatever I might advocate would receive no attention and very little discussion at the hands of ... that body.'[53] Later that evening he met with the executive of his local party in Bow and Bromley which unanimously endorsed his course of action.

From the start, offers of assistance poured in. Lansbury must have known that wealthy supporters of the W.S.P.U. would make available to him 'the sinews of war' for which Mrs. Pankhurst, at the London Pavilion, appealed immediately after he announced his intention to take the Chiltern Hundreds. But he could not have anticipated that, in addition to the W.S.P.U., help would be forthcoming from the Votes for Women Fellowship, the N.U.W.S.S., the Women's Freedom League, the Men's Political Union, the Men's League, and the New Constitutional Society (all women's suffrage societies), that fifteen Radical M.P.s, 'while differing from Mr. George Lansbury on many political questions and methods,' would urge the electors to vote for him and offer to speak from his platforms, and that important Labour M.P.s, Keir Hardie, Philip Snowden, Will Thorne and James O'Grady, would break party ranks to support him. Writers G.K. Chesterton and Hilaire Belloc likewise offered aid. (They may not have agreed with his views on women's suffrage but they supported anyone fighting 'the Servile State' as they called it.) Ben Tillett, the militant, idiosyncratic, leader of the Dockers' Union endorsed Lansbury's campaign in the following terms: 'So robust and so direct is his alert mind that he breaks the orthodox bonds and strictures and has the courage to face the soothsayers and charlatans, with a resentment ablaze; and a live brain to strike at the enemies of Labour.'[54] Endorsements of his circular letter also continued to arrive: from scores of I.L.P. branches across the country, from trades councils, Labour Representation Committees, branches of trade unions, even local branches of the B.S.P. (British Socialist Party, an amalgam of dissident branches of the I.L.P. and smaller socialist bodies and the old S.D.F.). Meanwhile, volunteer canvassers from outside Bow and Bromley had begun flocking to his committee rooms at 150 Bow Road East. There were 10,858 voters in the district and Lansbury's campaign manager, Charlie Banks, was determined that a canvasser contact each of them personally. With so many willing workers this did not seem impossible. Little wonder, then, that Lansbury soon was predicting confidently 'we are going to win with a big thumping majority,'[55] and that the *Daily Herald* found it necessary, on November 20, to warn that 'overconfidence on our side will be one of the most dangerous weapons in the hands of the enemy.'

In fact, however, the obstacles confronting Lansbury's re-election were significant. In the first place, quite naturally, both the Labour Party and the I.L.P. refused to endorse him. On November 14, the organ of the latter body, the *Labour Leader*, tartly reminded readers that Lansbury had 'resigned an I.L.P. seat without forewarning the responsible executive of the body under whose auspices he stood [in 1910]. Such actions seriously strain party relationships and make cooperation exceedingly difficult.'

Secondly, there was the attitude of official Liberalism to consider. In December 1910, Lloyd George had endorsed his 'good friend, George Lansbury,' while the local Bow and Bromley Liberal and Radical Association had declined to field a candidate against him, advising local electors to plump for Labour. Now, however, it directed its members to abstain from voting. Radicalism in Bow and Bromley was still relatively strong (indeed, as we know,

Lansbury had done much to build its strength in the years before his conversion to socialism). Twenty years later, he faced a problem partially of his own making: if local Radicals remained true to the party machine which he himself had helped to build, then inevitably he would forfeit a significant number of votes.

There was also the Tory candidate to consider. Reginald Blair was not, himself, particularly formidable. 'A young man, dark and slender and immaculately well groomed ... trim, but totally undistinguished ... he looked the perfect undergraduate.'[56] Like so many 'gentlemen' of the Edwardian era, he favored tariff reform while opposing Home Rule for Ireland. He was against payment of M.P.s, because 'the independence of individual members has been seriously affected.'[57] He opposed socialism because it 'offers no reward for thrift and destroys liberty.'[58] But, more dangerously, just as Lansbury's campaign was a magnet for all the forces in Britain which favored women's enfranchisement, so Blair's attracted the anti-suffragists. His campaign slogan, 'No Petticoat Government!' was borrowed from the Anti-Suffrage League, which, like the numerous suffrage societies, had rented premises in Bow and Bromley for the duration of the campaign. This organization decorated the doorway to its East End office with depictions of 'The Suffragette's Home,' showing a slatternly looking woman with an untouched pile of mending before her and with holes in her stockings. It brought supporters into the district to speak for Blair – possibly as many as were brought in for Lansbury. 'There were six meetings [on the Roman Road alone!] the other night,' Sylvia Pankhurst reported for the *Daily Herald* of November 22. 'At three of these women speakers supported Mr. Lansbury, and at the three others men speakers opposed him.'

Over and above all these obstacles to re-election loomed a great contradiction at the very heart of Lansbury's campaign. As one of his constituents warned, many local electors were saying that they sent you to the House to advocate the interests of the workers – and not to advocate 'votes for women' who were rich, well-placed individuals who were quite capable of getting what they wanted without you helping them – and so neglecting the interests of the workers – your constituents – who sent you to the House.'[59]

This was a graver problem than Lansbury or his supporters were prepared to admit, especially in class-conscious, proletarian Bow and Bromley, where the parliamentary franchise was restricted entirely to men, many of whom might resent middle-class, not necessarily socialist, female, outsiders advising them how to vote. It became, in fact, the crux of the campaign.

It was apparent to Lansbury that the socialist and suffragette movements were complementary. 'The women's cause is of fundamental importance to the future of the Socialist movement,' he told a reporter from the *Daily Herald* on the evening of his resignation from Parliament. But this was not so obvious to Bow and Bromley voters or even to some of his most fervent supporters in both the socialist and suffragette movements. Banks, his campaign manager, actively resented Lansbury's connection with the women's movement, for instance. Others, who shared his platforms, and spoke on his behalf, while believing in 'Votes for Women,' believed even more strongly in the labor and socialist movements or in Lansbury's fight for independence from political bossism. They aided him, as Ben Tillett put it, 'because it was imperative that the people should have one fearless and honest mouthpiece in that place of thievery and corruption,' the House of Commons.[60] These sentiments (though, perhaps, not the actual words) could have been uttered by the fifteen Radical M.P.s who endorsed his candidacy. But what would they, or more importantly, what would some middle-class members of the W.S.P.U., have thought of the following declaration, delivered by Keir Hardie, at another Bow Baths meeting on Lansbury's behalf? 'The working class were called upon to defend the country. Where was the country they had to defend? They talked about their native land. What had their native land done for them? Nothing!'[61]

If Lansbury's Labour and socialist allies spoke a language unfamiliar or even disagreeable to some of his Radical and suffragette friends, the latter might speak in terms highly unfamiliar to a Bow and Bromley audience. 'A man who gets 30s. a week and brings home 27s. 6d. to his wife ...' began one W.S.P.U. speaker, only to be interrupted with derisive laughter at such ignorance of working-class life.[62] One cannot escape the sense that some, at least, among the suffragettes approached the campaign with the attitude of Lady Bountiful. For example, one evening towards the close of the campaign, the novelist and suffragette Beatrice Harraden arrived a bit early in Bow and Bromley with a W.S.P.U. member who was to speak for Lansbury. 'So we thought we would pass the time by having something to eat in that little corner shop.' In revealing lines Harraden then described her repaste: the onion, biscuit, cheese,

> and a mouthful of that pickled red cabbage for which one searches in vain in so-called 'civilised centres'. And whilst we were enjoying this rash meal, in came little boys and girls carrying bottles and the shopkeeper did a brisk trade in farthingsworths of milk or vinegar. I regained my long-lost respect for that annoying coin, the farthing, and realised as I had never done before its purchasing capabilities. The halfpenny, too, went up in my estimation when I saw what the factory girls who dashed in with cups received in exchange from that resourceful shop.[63]

Could such people help mount the kind of campaign which would be necessary for Lansbury to win in Bow and Bromley? Or would their *de haute en bas* attitudes alienate as many voters as they attracted? Moreover, even if one grants that Beatrice Harraden approached the by-election with the best will in the world, there is evidence that other suffragettes did not. 'It does not help,' one volunteer canvasser wrote to Lansbury after the poll,

> when some [suffragettes] go round saying that they do not agree with
> your socialism, but are supporting you on the suffrage question – in
> fact, frankly that they are using you as a tool. My wife, and I and my
> son found a lot of that when we were canvassing for you.[64]

If this report is true, such conduct and the contradictions within
Lansbury's camp to which it pointed, raised an obstacle which
probably no candidate could have overcome.

Moreover, Lansbury was associated in the public mind not
merely with the crusade for women's rights, but with a particular
wing of the movement, and more specifically, with a single organization, the W.S.P.U. This body inspired profound commitment
among many of its members, but not among a mass of outsiders
who viewed its militant tactics with distaste. This, too, boded ill
for Lansbury's campaign and requires further comment.

Lansbury steadfastly refused to distance himself from the
W.S.P.U., in part from strong feelings of personal loyalty. These
stemmed from his connection with Marion Coates Hansen, at
whose behest he had joined the W.S.P.U. in the first place, and
who, herself, belonged to the militant organization. He was also
on close terms with Sylvia Pankhurst who was then living in the
East End. In fact, his connection with the Pankhursts was already
nearly two decades old. In 1895 he had stood, in forlorn isolation,
as the S.D.F. parliamentary candidate for Walworth. He had been
resoundingly defeated, but

> two of the people who came up to help me and who worked just like
> modern Trojans were Mrs. Pankhurst and her husband [who died
> shortly thereafter]. They took me by the hand, a man comparatively
> unknown ... It was the enthusiasm in Mrs. Pankhurst's face ... that
> tied me to [her] from that day to this.[65]

Lansbury, who did not consult the Labour Party or I.L.P. when
he decided upon the by-election, did hold conversations with the
Pankhursts. It is even possible that the main proponent of the

course he eventually took was Christabel.

Another reason for Lansbury's continuing link with the unpopular W.S.P.U. was also personal, but in a different sense. Throughout his life, Lansbury felt deep sympathy for victims of injustice. This attitude went to the core of his being. In 1912, militant suffragettes were being subjected to veritable torture for actions which 'respectable' opinion deemed acceptable when committed by Protestant men in Ireland, or by Poles and Russians in their own countries, or by Englishmen who had demanded the franchise in years past. This double standard was as unacceptable to Lansbury as was torture itself, and helped drive him into the camp of its victims. Finally, Lansbury was never averse to taking strong measures for a goal in which he believed. Equally he never would advise others to do what he, himself, would not do. Originally he had avoided endorsing militant methods, while applauding their results. But by the time of his campaign he had come to believe that militant measures on behalf of women's suffrage were justified. For all these reasons, then, Lansbury identified with the militant suffragettes of the W.S.P.U.

In retrospect the mutual incomprehension among his supporters, his connection with the W.S.P.U., and the opposition that organization inspired, seem more daunting obstacles to victory than Lansbury recognized at the time. Yet the campaign he mounted nearly overcame them all. It was characterized by plain speaking and straight dealing. He made no concessions to political tacticians, if there were any among his circle, who advised soft-pedalling his differences with the Labour leadership or his links to the W.S.P.U. His election address was a lucid, accurate, report of his two-year stint in Parliament. 'I find myself,' he confessed to the electors, 'in complete disagreement with my party on a question which is to me of fundamental importance, namely the enfranchisement of women.' And he asked to be returned to the House so that he might 'fight, irrespective of the convenience either of Government or parties, for the principles you have supported' in the past. These, he made clear, were socialism and women's suffrage.

But how to link the two? We are back to the crucial problem of the campaign. Time and again Lansbury strove to drive home the central meaning of the by-election he had forced. As he put it to the *Daily Herald* of November 12, on the very evening of his resignation from Parliament,

> The people down here in this constituency, women as well as men, are suffering intolerable destitution and misery. Only when the women and the men are able to stand side by side to fight in the common fight can we really hope to accomplish economic and social emancipation.

And in his election address: 'We men have wanted to use our votes to improve our social condition. I want that our mothers, our wives and our sisters shall be allowed to join us in the fight.' And in the first speech of the campaign, delivered at the Bow Baths packed to overflowing with his supporters, and with several hundred more in the street outside straining for a glimpse of him: 'He believed that the political emancipation of women must be achieved before any complete economic freedom could be won for the whole of the people.' And a dozen times more as the campaign progressed. But it was Mrs. Pankhurst who, perhaps, most vividly drove home the lesson Lansbury wished to teach. At one campaign meeting, she was asked, 'Why does Lansbury stand up for the women instead of for the poor?' She answered with a counter-question: '"Who are the people who are working for a penny and for a halfpenny an hour?" Women in the audience cried out "Me! Me!"'[66] It was not for nothing that Mrs. Pankhurst had served her political apprenticeship helping to build the early I.L.P.

'Votes for Women and ... the cause of the common people.' These were Lansbury's goals, as they had been in 1888. But his thinking had evolved since then. Now the political empowerment of women was more than an elementary democratic right in which he implicitly believed. It was more, even, than the necessary first step which Great Britain must take towards a more just and humane society. Still believing deeply in these truths, he believed, too, that women were exploited and oppressed because of their sex, that power, or the lack of it, derived from gender as well as class. As he put it to the *Daily Herald*, 'Women are fleeced and robbed and sweated because they are women,'[67] and to the W.S.P.U.,

> Every working man who has thought at all, every man who has considered the position of his own wife, knows that the denial of the right of citizenship marks the inferiority in the eyes of the law of his wife as against every man in the land.[68]

Thus Lansbury had changed his mind since 1888. He now believed that the socialist and the women's movements impinged upon each other in important ways, but were distinct. The demand for female rights complemented, but was not subsumed within, the demand for workers' rights.

In bringing this unfamiliar message to Bow and Bromley Lansbury could count, at least, upon a sympathetic hearing. By 1912, he had devoted more than a quarter-century to easing the conditions of the poor in his district. As a result, he was a well-known and, in certain quarters, a well-loved figure. Reports of his popularity were common during the campaign. For example, a reporter for the *Suffragette* of November 29 described how,

> when [Lansbury] walked onto the platform ... the cheers that went up ... were of a different kind altogether [from those which other speakers had received]; there was no doubt about their implication. There was in that welcome such a friendly feeling of intimate sympathy and high hope, so much promise of better things to be.

Sylvia Pankhurst witnessed something similar at one of the many gatherings Lansbury addressed during the campaign.

As he enters there are cries of 'Good old George!' and cheers and waving of hands. Then all the people sit as quietly as they can in order to save, as far as possible, his big voice that has grown so hoarse during these strenuous days. By their earnest faces and deep sighs of assent you know how thoroughly they are at one with him, how absolutely they believe that he will always fight against poverty, disease and all evils of misgovernment for them. When he has finished and goes on to the next meeting they leap to their feet again, cheering.

The children of Bow and Bromley followed Lansbury as though he were the Pied Piper. 'Our George', they called him, imitating their parents. They tramped the streets of the district singing,

> We'll all vote for Lansbury.
> He's for all the workers,
> He's against the shirkers,
> We'll all vote for Lansbury,
> That's the one and only plan.
> All the whole collection,
> We'll make no exception,
> We'll think of the women and the children,
> Lansbury, you're the man.

Characteristically, Lansbury opposed such hero worship. '"Now look here,"' he is reported telling 'a little mission hall packed to overflowing with boys and girls who had just come out of school. "I don't want you to sing for me unless you know why you're doing it."' And then, patiently, without condescension, he explained the basis of his campaign.

'Now your mother does a good chunk of the work at home and sometimes gets a bit tired, doesn't she? Are there any boys here who sometimes help their mothers?' (Virtuous show of hands.) 'Of course there are! Same thing with your sisters. You've got to think your sister is a very valuable person at home.' (Great, though mute, satisfaction evident among the girls.) 'You mustn't let her do all the work for you; I should like to see the boys clean their sisters' boots for them.' (Slight decline of political enthusiasm among the boys.) 'You must remember that when your sister gets to be 21 she is to have a vote as well as you; she is just as good as you are and when she gets the vote she will set to work to make conditions of life better for all of you, boys as well as girls.' (Spirits of the boys in the audience rising rapidly.) 'If you sing songs to help me you must do it because I want to help your mothers and sisters.'[69]

'It is like no election contest that I have ever seen,' Sylvia Pankhurst commented, with some justification, for the *Daily Herald* of November 25.

But it was more than a children's crusade. It was a hectic, eclectic, battle royal between Lansbury's supporters and those whom he described as 'Anti-Socialists, Anti-Suffragists, Anti-Home Rulers, anti-everything that is of any real worth.' 'The place is covered with [them],' Lansbury warned.[70] It was not just the Roman Road on which soap-box orators could be found. 'There is one at every busy street corner,' *Votes for Women* reported on November 22. In addition, as the *Daily Herald* of the same date had discovered, 'All the available halls are taken every night by the various parties and are filled to overflowing by their most enthusiastic supporters.' The W.S.P.U., for example, had booked in advance two halls for meetings every night of the campaign.

On the eve of the poll, all the suffrage societies, except, significantly enough, the N.U.W.S.S. which declined an invitation to participate, mounted a final, impressive, demonstration in Lansbury's honor. Thousands of marchers assembled at Bow Church where lanterns and torches were distributed. At 8.00 p.m. the procession set out, 'down Fairfield road, into the shop-lit thoroughfare of Roman road, then via St. Stephen's road and Coburn road into Bow road and eastward till the starting point was regained.' It was a striking affair: all 'colour and light and motion,' according to one description; 'and in the middle,' wrote someone else, 'there walked, or rather, danced, a shouting, singing, multitude of girls and boys.' According to the *Daily Herald* of November 26, 'the route was lined by several thousands of the general public and there was considerable excitement.' Adding to the general din was a brass band playing the 'Marseillaise,' 'John Brown's Body,' and the 'Woman's March.'[71]

But organizations unaffiliated with the suffrage campaign did not take part in this procession and, as noted, the N.U.W.S.S. refused to participate. As the suffragettes and their supporters wound their way through the East End streets, these organizations were separately continuing to hold their own open-air meetings on Lansbury's behalf. The candidate had been unable to heal the breach between suffragettes and Labourites, or even between 'constitutionalists' of the N.U.W.S.S. and militants of the W.S.P.U. In fact, according to Sylvia Pankhurst's bitter account, 'the most ridiculous episodes of the campaign' were still to come.[72]

These occurred the next day – polling day – when it rained continually. Wealthy supporters of the W.S.P.U. had donated carriages to transport voters to the poll, but the W.S.P.U. organizer refused to send the vehicles to Lansbury's headquarters on the grounds that 'Mrs. Pankhurst would never allow the Union to work under the men!' The campaign manager, Banks, could have sent lists of voters needing transport to the women with the carriages. He refused. Eventually Emmeline Pankhurst settled this foolish dispute to Banks's satisfaction, but precious time had been lost. More than time, an election had been lost. Having failed to build a bridge between the women's and socialist movements, having failed to establish the central message of his campaign, Lansbury went down to defeat.

With the polls closed and night fallen, the rains continued. Nevertheless, 'the streets ... were filled from end to end and side to side by great seething crowds, who waved hats and flags and shouted themselves hoarse in frenzies of delight or disappointment.'[73] After 8.00 p.m. a multitude assembled in front of the

Bromley Public Hall, where the result was to be declared. Directly opposite were the Tory, Blair's, committee rooms, before which his supporters attempted to maintain spirits with a fireworks display. But the majority of the crowd were partisans of Lansbury; so much so, that when the result was finally announced, that Blair had prevailed by more than 700 votes (the precise tally was 4,042 to 3,291) 'the working-class populace outside the hall refused to believe it and stoutly maintained that Lansbury had won.' According to the *Daily Herald* of November 27, 'No result could have come as a more staggering surprise to both parties.' At any rate, once the bad news finally had been digested, the crowd, 'in a great irresistible wave ... swept round the corner to the Obelisk, where Lansbury spoke to them in his blunt way.' There, and to an interviewer from the *Daily Herald* next day, he maintained doggedly that 'he did not regret his resignation and would act in a similar way under similar circumstances.'[74] He emphasized two further points: first, that 'neither Liberals, nor Tories nor the Labour Party, nor the Church, nor God in Heaven could save the people – they must save themselves,'[75] and secondly, that 'We in Bow and Bromley now know that the Liberals in the constituency prefer a Tory reactionary to represent them instead of a Socialist.' But these had been costly lessons to teach. Lansbury was out of Parliament, out of the Labour Party, off the N.A.C. of the I.L.P. Surely he had reason to ask himself whether these sacrifices had been justified by the result, and whether the lessons to which he referred had even been learned.

4

It remains to trace briefly Lansbury's further efforts in behalf of the women's movement in the year and a half left before the outbreak of World War I, and to offer conclusions on the nature and significance of his feminism.

Lansbury had lost the Bow and Bromley by-election, but aside from his entrance into the political wilderness little had changed. As he had predicted would happen, the Liberal Government rejected amendments designed to broaden the Male Suffrage Bill; the Labour Party did not promise to vote against the unamended measure; and militancy scaled new heights. Lansbury's grown children, Daisy and Edgar, were involved now. Towards the end of the year they both received two-month terms of imprisonment with hard labor for destruction of property. In late February 1913 came a spectacular suffragette demonstration, the firebombing of Lloyd George's country home. Mrs. Pankhurst was charged with 'Procuring Damage to a House,' and was jailed when she refused to give assurances. Immediately she hunger struck and was released. When her trial came up in April she was sentenced to three years' penal servitude. Jailed again, she again refused all food and was sent home. But the Cat and Mouse Act meant that she could be re-imprisoned at any time.

These were only among the most sensational events in the continuing suffrage campaign. They drew Lansbury further into the women's movement. He was 'more certain than ever,' as he reported in the *Suffragette* of April 4, 1913, 'that [he had been] right in resigning [his] seat, more certain than ever that the way to get anything is to fight for it, and equally certain that Women's Suffrage will only be made possible by the policy and work of the W.S.P.U.'

But men could not become members of that organization. On the evening of April 10 in the Albert Hall, where the W.S.P.U. was holding a meeting to support Mrs. Pankhurst after her most recent hunger strike and release from prison, Lansbury suggested a decisive change of tactics. 'I have come to this conclusion,' he explained during his speech, 'that men who are interested in this business have got also to make sacrifices ... I want to see set on foot a league of militant men ... who are not going to sit down and allow their sisters to be coerced in this brutal and disgusting manner.' Such a league would inevitably lead to confrontations with authority, but Lansbury did not flinch. 'You have a right to rebel,' he assured his audience,

> when you are tricked and deceived, it is the only course open to you. I will ask all of you here to stand shoulder to shoulder with the militant women. Back them up in the fight they are waging. Burn and destroy property or anything you like ... Let us teach that make-believe Liberal Government that this is a holy war ... a war in which we will do our best to preserve human life, but a war in which we will have no regard for property of any kind ... Every window that is broken, every golf course that is attacked, every race-course stand that is burned down worries them.[76]

The Liberal Government was worried enough to attempt silencing Lansbury. On the evening of April 15, as he was leaving a meeting he had been addressing at the Canning Town Public Hall, he was served with a summons. Like so many supporters of women's suffrage before him, he was accused of inciting criminal acts. And, like most of those predecessors, he remained defiant in the face of the law. His case was heard on May 3. Affirming to the judge that at the Albert Hall meeting he had 'appealed to the audience to stand by the women who were breaking the law ... [and to the men present] to organise themselves into a militant league to defend the women from brutal and outrageous conduct,' he nevertheless declined to find sureties of £1,000 'because I consider that the Government have prosecuted me as a political opponent.'[77] Friends found his bail; he lodged an appeal which, inevitably, failed; and on July 29 he trod the familiar path from the Bow Street police station to the windowless van which brought him to Pentonville jail.

Lansbury was probably even more troublesome to the Liberal Government in prison than he had been outside. 'I am going to hunger strike,' he had warned when a jail term first began to seem likely, and he did. While refusing food, he was not inactive, however. His first move was to compose a letter to the Home Secretary, Reginald McKenna, protesting conditions in Pentonville; his second was to write an article for the *Bow and Bromley Worker* of August 1913 linking his current efforts with the failed by-election, and his efforts on behalf of the women with his efforts on behalf of the poor: 'I go to prison for you whoever you are, who are poor and destitute. You are heavy laden and afflicted. I am in public life for you. All my career has been spent on your behalf.'

Meanwhile, in Bow and Bromley, according to the *Daily Herald* of August 1, 'immense meetings were [being] held attended by thousands of residents' demanding Lansbury's release. The Poplar Trades Council planned a series of demonstrations which would wind up with 'a monster procession to Pentonville Prison.' Frank Smith, Keir Hardie's friend and secretary, booked Trafalgar Square for an even larger rally. This all anticipates the campaign on behalf of Poplar's Labour councillors in 1921, and it had the same result. The government backed down. Lansbury was released after three days. As with Mrs. Pankhurst, the Cat and Mouse Act meant that he could be re-imprisoned at any moment, but, in fact, he remained at liberty.

Lansbury was determined to help the suffragettes create the mass movement which would lead to victory. Inevitably this brought him into further conflict with the Labour Party, of which seemingly he had despaired. 'How can any woman or any man back these men [of the P.L.P.] any longer?' he had asked the Albert Hall meeting on April 10. They were 'broken reeds' who 'had no notion of endangering what they are pleased to call their political careers' for women's rights. But, if not the Labour Party, then which organization would provide the necessary base for the movement Lansbury hoped to build?

Probably not the I.L.P.: although he had resigned from its N.A.C., Lansbury remained a rank-and-file member of the party.

He still considered men like Hardie and Jowett political allies. But there is no evidence that, in the months remaining before the outbreak of World War I, he had very much to do with them. His attention was focussed elsewhere.

It certainly would not be the W.S.P.U. Ironically, despite his longstanding affection for the Pankhursts, and the fact that he had gone to jail for advocating that men back them up, it was also inevitable that Lansbury develop doubts about them. After all, his emphasis upon socialist feminism was increasingly at odds with Christabel's evolving outlook, which had been much influenced by her study of rape and the spread of venereal disease in Britain. Christabel now was demanding 'Votes for Women and Chastity for Men.' She had come to dominate the W.S.P.U., by dint of her forceful personality and, in part, because her mother was harried by the Cat and Mouse Act, and exhausted from hunger striking so many times. Christabel ruthlessly expelled from the W.S.P.U. all other possible rivals, including the Pethick Lawrences, who had helped to found the organization and to bankroll it, and even her sister, Sylvia, whose proletarian connections in East London were increasingly suspect in Christabel's eyes. Despite having sacrificed his political career for the W.S.P.U., then, Lansbury found both its style and ideology increasingly distasteful. Like the Pethick Lawrences and Sylvia Pankhurst, he hesitated to publicize his differences with it. But sometime after his term in jail, that is to say after the summer of 1913, he joined the United Suffragists, which the Pethick Lawrences had set up when Christabel purged them. In addition, he remained close to Sylvia who also had founded a small suffragist group, the East London Federation of Suffragettes. Like the United Suffragists, the E.L.F.S. combined feminist and socialist goals.

Many believed that Lansbury had committed political suicide. He had given up his seat in Parliament and membership of the Labour Party to support the W.S.P.U., and now that organization had taken a line he could not accept. He was reduced to membership of splinter organizations. He had been relegated, had relegated himself, to the periphery of British politics. Or had he? Here the conclusion depends upon one's reading of political possibilities during the last years before World War I. One influential interpretation of the era claims that the 'rebel' tendency exemplified by the *Daily Herald* was Edwardian England's animating force.[78] Now that Lansbury was out of Parliament, the *Herald* had become a primary outlet for his energy. Also, he was very busy helping to establish 'Herald Leagues' across the country. These were bodies of 'rebel' activists as much as support groups for the newspaper, and, significantly, they often linked up with local branches of the United Suffragists. Meanwhile, back in London, in addition to his labors for the *Daily Herald*, Lansbury was working closely with Sylvia Pankhurst and the E.L.F.S. Their activities were hardly marginal to the main political currents sweeping Britain. It was an E.L.F.S. delegation led by Sylvia Pankhurst to which Asquith declared in June 1914 that, 'If the change has to come, we must face it boldy and make it thoroughgoing and democratic in its basis.' Historians have usually taken this as a sign that the Prime Minister was finally preparing to legislate 'Votes for Women.'[79] Moreover, when shortly after Asquith's meeting with the E.L.F.S. delegation, the government opened negotiations with the women's movement, it was Sylvia Pankhurst and George Lansbury whom it contacted. Lansbury later claimed that these discussions were fruitful but short-circuited by a variety of causes. Far from being on the margins of political life in the last months before the outbreak of war, then, Lansbury's activities as a United Suffragist, organizer of the 'Herald Leagues' and fellow traveller of E.L.F.S., appear to have placed him, at least during certain strategic moments, at their center.

From this position he preached unity on the Left. 'We shall never cease to declare,' he wrote in a 1914 'New Year's Message' to *Daily Herald* readers, 'that Syndicalists and Socialists, Suffragists and Labourites, have better work to do than waging war upon each other.' It was Lansbury who organized the famous Albert Hall rally of November 1, 1913, where Sylvia Pankhurst, Frederick Pethick Lawrence, the Irish revolutionary James Connelly, the British syndicalist Robert Williams, the Fabian George Bernard Shaw, the trade unionist Ben Tillett and many others shared a platform. If this was isolation, it was a very splendid isolation indeed. But of course it was precisely the opposite of isolation. Lansbury was 'binding all rebels together to fight for the things that matter,' as he put it.[80] Of these, 'Votes for Women' was most pressing. He was, then, attempting to assemble the building blocks of a mass socialist feminist movement. Such a coalition had been his aim since he first became involved with the suffragettes. It proved to be unattainable. But then, he was seeking to recast the British left – a project for the ages – and he had only a few months before the outbreak of World War I put an end to all such efforts.

5

Lansbury's attitude towards women's rights evolved significantly during the quarter-century which began with his entry into politics and ended with the outbreak of World War I. As a Radical Liberal he had seen Jane Cobden's right to serve on the L.C.C. as an end in itself. He had supported her campaign mainly on the democratic grounds that women and men should enjoy the same legal rights, and that voters should be able to elect whomever they wished to represent them. He also believed that the more democratic the suffrage, the more Radical the electorate was likely to be. Twenty-five years later he still believed that possession of the franchise was an elemental democratic right which women must have, but his thinking had advanced considerably.

During the intervening quarter-century he had embraced social-ism; while feminism had been transformed. Now the advocates of

'Votes for Women' wanted to abolish the concept of separate spheres altogether, not, as Jane Cobden's supporters had wished, to extend the woman's sphere into the political realm. Lansbury's views on this issue likewise had evolved. In 1889, he had agreed with Cobden herself that women were better suited than men for certain tasks the L.C.C. would be handling, and that this was one important reason why she should be permitted to become, and then to remain, a member of the council. He had thought that the woman's sphere was too constraining but never, quite, that separate spheres should be abolished. As late as 1899, Lansbury could still be found positively endorsing them. He was sympathetic, he said, to women who were 'tied down to the drudgery of housework,' which he thought more onerous than labor in a factory or workshop. 'If toil is to be rewarded at its true value, no workingman can really pay his wife anything like an equivalent for the work she does for him.' But it did not occur to him that the wife should cease to 'work for' the husband and that the two should share housework and other domestic chores more equally. Rather he wanted the husband to share more equally with the wife – his wage. 'I want a man to consider that his wife as much earns the money she is paid [by the husband] on Saturday as he does himself, and that the spending of that money should be a joint business.'[81] This was helpful, well intentioned and goodhearted. But it hardly questioned the notion that housework was the woman's sphere, and factory work the man's. Indeed Lansbury's implicit acceptance of the family wage in this lecture could only buttress the separate spheres ideology. Even the title of the talk indicated the extent to which he still accepted prevailing mores. It was called 'Our Wives,' as though it could be delivered only to an audience of working-class men, as though only men should compose the audience for political speakers.

Even as late as 1909 Lansbury was repeating the domestic feminist arguments of his early adulthood. If a married woman was 'to rear healthy, vigorous children,' he warned, 'surely she must be removed from such work as machine-minding, matchbox making in filthy slums, and the drudgery of factory life. In this respect let us join with the anti-Socialist in his cry for the preservation or rather the restoration of the home, where our women shall be queens not drudges.'[82] He still believed, that is to say, in the woman's sphere.

But the campaign of the militant suffragettes educated him so that, by 1912, his outlook had undergone a revolution. His wife, Bessie, had 'had very little chance,' he wrote to Marion Coates Hansen,

> and mainly because of the sort of lines of conduct that she and I were brought up to believe in. If we started our lives over again, happy as we have been, we should have been still happier, because she would have understood, and I would have understood, that the most perfect kind of life would be that not merely should *I* think, but she should have the opportunity of thinking and doing too ... She might have had, and ought to have had, a much fuller kind of existence than has been possible.[83]

So much for Victorian gender roles! Women were 'human beings who want to be recognized as comrades, not merely as women,' he had written, in 'A Call to Socialists' for the *Labour Leader* of November 17, 1911. 'It is our women whom we need most to have by our side, thinking with us, working with us for the salvation of the race.' As he wrote in an early edition of the *Daily Herald*, 'We base all our theory of life and conduct on this: that the average man or woman is of equal value in the community.'[84]

Once accept this idea and no issue could be exempt from re-interpretation. When the House of Commons refused to find time to debate a Criminal Amendment Bill Lansbury was incensed because, 'with all that we know of the White Slave Traffic, and the social conditions of our land, especially as regards young girls ...

it really means that a girl is not of so much value, in the eyes of society, as a boy.' His message to Bow and Bromley school children during the by-election of 1912 had been the same. 'You've got to think your sister is a very valuable person,' Lansbury told the boys. It was precisely this thought which was so subversive of the separate spheres ideology. Lansbury was arguing for a transformation of attitudes not merely in the Parliament but in the home as well.

He brought these feminist insights to his political practice. Thus, during the Bow and Bromley by-election campaign, his closest political advisers included the Pankhurst women; and his wife played a visible role for the first time. She spoke for her husband from public platforms and wrote on his behalf in the feminist press. 'I feel very keenly how necessary it is for men and women to work side by side,' she explained in the *Votes for Women* of November 22.

And he brought the feminist insights to his socialism as well. Since the early 1890s he had believed that capitalism forced workers to sell themselves, through their labor power, to employers. But now he also believed that capitalist mechanisms of exploitation were brought to bear upon women workers because they were women. That, in addition of course to all the arguments about fairness, is why it was so important to enfranchise them. Gaining the suffrage, Lansbury wrote, would be 'the first step that women will take for asserting their right to own themselves.'[85] The vote was an essential weapon in the struggle against capitalism *and* sexism, against sweated labor *and* separate spheres. Thus, for Lansbury, socialism that was not feminist and feminism that was not also socialist, were incomplete.

It is fascinating to see how rare this position was, even among his supporters, during the Bow and Bromley by-election which, after all, he had forced in order to demonstrate the complementarity of the two movements. It appears to have been beyond the comprehension, even, of his most natural supporters on the extreme left wing of the political spectrum. 'I am not opposed to the enfranchisement of women,' Victor Grayson almost grudgingly conceded in the *Daily Herald* of November 28, immediately after Lansbury's defeat,

> but I do feel there are questions of more immediate importance ... Does the ex-Member for Bow and Bromley really think that the demand for Women's Suffrage (as at present stated) is of more importance than the demand for the Right to Work Bill?

Even that veteran crusader for social justice, the redoubtable Herbert Burrows, failed to understand Lansbury's point of view. 'Frankly,' he wrote in a letter of condolence to the defeated candidate, 'I did not agree with you in making the woman suffrage the one supreme question. I don't believe it is. To me the question of the children, the unemployed and housing are more important still.'[86] This was entirely to ignore the instrumentality of the vote and to undervalue a political right which Burrows would have considered paramount if it had been denied to men. More to the point, however, it was to insist upon a division between the suffragette and socialist movements which Lansbury was attempting, through his by-election campaign and other political efforts, to deny.

Among many suffragettes, as we have seen, comprehension of the worker's quest for social change, was equally rare. During the by-election of 1912, whose success depended upon Lansbury's ability to bring the two movements together, they never coalesced, but rather spoke past each other, like the proverbial ships passing in the night. In London, unlike northern England as depicted by Liddington and Norris in their classic study, it seems that most suffragette leaders were middle class and had little understanding of working-class life or sympathy for socialism. Sylvia Pankhurst was less typical in this latter respect than, say, Beatrice Harradean.[87]

The by-election showed how difficult it was to assemble and mesh together the constituent parts of the coalition Lansbury was

127

striving to build. Yet afterwards he may have been more successful. In the United Suffragists and E.L.F.S. on the one hand, in the
Herald Leagues on the other, perhaps we discern the nucleus of
a socialist, feminist, British left. But the war smashed that one, as
it smashed so many projects of construction.

It is helpful to view Lansbury's efforts within the context established and refined by historians of the suffragette and socialist
movements. His views on feminism and socialism place him
squarely in the European social democratic tradition. He employed, consciously or not, the language of the Socialist International. In Britain this placed him within the camp of 'democratic
suffragists' as Sandra Holton has called them, who whether
affiliated with N.U.W.S.S. or W.S.P.U., emphasized 'Votes for
Women' as part of the wider movement for democratic and social
reform. These figures came most often, however, from the
working-class towns of the north, and generally were suspicious of
militancy as practiced by the W.S.P.U., not because they opposed
violence in all circumstances, but rather because the militancy
practiced by the W.S.P.U. seemed tactically counterproductive,
and because it was overshadowing the main goal. Eventually
Lansbury agreed. The evil of the present position,' he wrote in *Votes
for Women* of June 26, 1914, after he had left the W.S.P.U., 'is that
people are discussing everything but Women's Suffrage itself.'
This, undoubtedly is why he finally quit the organization despite
longstanding personal ties to many of its leaders.

Lansbury's experience also suggests a new way of regarding the
battle within the Labour Party, to keep it independent from
Liberalism, more democratic, less bureaucratic. Historians as
diverse as Stanley Pierson and David Howell have charted that
struggle, without linking it to the campaign for women's rights.[88]
Sandra Holton has linked the suffragettes with Labour, but not with
the Labour dissidents. Surely, however, Lansbury's own course
suggests how inextricably linked the two reform movements were.

'Voting on the merits' of Liberal legislation was more principled, truer to Labour's original aspirations than the cautious course advocated by MacDonald; it was also the precondition to suffragette success. Or, consider the demand for 'Socialist unity,' a watchword on the left wing of the I.L.P., but a bogey for I.L.P. and Labour Party leaders. For Lansbury, as we have seen, it was the suffragettes' best hope.

Lansbury emerges, then, as a critical figure in the history of the Edwardian left. Three-quarters of a century ago he attempted not merely to synthesize socialist and feminist ideals, but to create a mass political movement on their behalf. Years later Lansbury was disposed to minimize the attempt. He claimed to have learned a simple lesson from the Bow and Bromley by-election, 'Never Resign!' From a further vantage point, however, one recognizes that the resignation marked a singular moment in the history of Edwardian Britain. The decision to force the by-election made possible, as was Lansbury's intention at the time, a unique confluence of the women's and socialist movements. The moment was fraught with possibilities that never crystallized. It seems less remarkable that the fusion Lansbury sought did not take place than that it almost did, that he fell short in Bow and Bromley by only seven hundred votes, that his campaign was as pointed and honest as it was, that afterwards, nothing daunted by electoral defeat, he began assembling the building blocks of a socialist feminist movement whose goal, nearly prefigured in the by-election campaign, was to recast first the British left and eventually his country's political and social institutions.

3 Lansbury and pacifism

The outbreak of World War I shattered the British feminist movement by confronting its activists with even more pressing issues than 'Votes for Women.' Some supported, others opposed, the war effort. In any event, they suspended their suffrage campaign for the duration – and never resumed it in its prewar intensity. Nevertheless, in 1918 the government finally enfranchised women over thirty years of age. Ten years later it accorded women the vote on equal terms with men.

The war faced Lansbury, too, with a new situation. Not to put too fine a point on it, World War I changed his life. Essentially it led him from one great cause, feminism, to another, pacifism. If he had been a thorn in the side of the Labour Party leadership during the Edwardian era, he was, during part of the inter-war period (1931-35), himself leader of the Labour Party, and a thorn in the side of the British Government. By the end of the 1930s, although no longer Labour's leader, Lansbury was playing for the highest stakes imaginable. His search for a pacifist answer to the rise of fascism had led him into personal meetings with Franklin Roosevelt, Benito Mussolini and Adolf Hitler. So far had the radical reformer from 'Outcast London' traveled in the course of his remarkable life.

In this last, doomed, effort Lansbury was to reveal a doggedness in the face of adversity, and a willingness, even eagerness, to risk all for a deeply held principle (whatever the impact on former allies who now disagreed with him) that was astonishing in a man approaching his eightieth year. These were characteristics that already had distinguished him from other public figures, but now they seemed almost to define his identity. The last phase of his career, then, reveals an exaggerated Lansbury, a heightened Lansbury, perhaps, even, the essential Lansbury. But its importance is not merely biographical. This chapter shows that Lansbury's pacifism during the 1930s was more significant, politically, than has been recognized generally. Moreover, it was significant histori-cally. 'If I were the Prime Minister, backed by a majority in the House of Commons,' Lansbury told a gathering of pacifists in September 1935, while he was still the Labour Party leader, 'I would go myself to the Assembly of the League of Nations and say, "Our nation, once and for all, renounces armaments and war, and is prepared at once, to disarm and invites all other nations to follow our lead."'[1] In campaigning for unilateral disarmament, Lansbury, perhaps more than any other individual, bequeathed to Labour a legacy which has troubled it ever since.

1

As an old man, Lansbury was frequently to remark that he had been a pacifist all his life. This was not strictly accurate, although it was true that during his lifetime he never supported any war in which Great Britain engaged.

In his early days, Lansbury's opposition to war was rooted in his Radical politics and, specifically, in his instinctive sympathy for the 'bottom dog.' Like many Radicals, he withheld support from British military ventures in Africa and Afghanistan, not because he opposed the use of force in all circumstances (indeed, at some point during this early period he tried to learn boxing), but because he shared Gladstone's moral sympathy for 'subject peoples struggling to be free.' 'Let us look on other nations as having the same right to exist as we have,' he had exhorted the Bromley Methodist Chapel, in words that were reminiscent of Gladstone's attacks upon Beaconsfieldism. 'Let us refuse (either as individuals or as a nation) to sanction the increase of wealth at the expense of others be they white, yellow, red or black men.'[2]

Lansbury's conversion to socialism did not so much alter this aspect of his outlook as confirm it. He read Marx, but as we saw in Section I, was never one to concentrate upon inexorable, indivertible, and impersonal forces as many Marxists of the period did. He believed too firmly in the positive, or negative, role individuals might play in history. Capitalism was reprehensible at least in part, he now believed, precisely because of its impact on the individual. 'We are taught from the beginning,' he had lectured Bromley's Methodists, 'that if we would rise we must excel our neighbour, and virtually do so at his cost.' The ramifications of such teachings were grave.

> This individual striving one against the other has, I am sure, as much to do with wars as anything possibly can have … [Because, similarly,] the struggle amongst nations is for the best markets, irrespective of the interests or rights of others.

As a socialist, then, Lansbury condemned capitalism for inculcating among individual men and women competitive values which led, inevitably, to international conflicts. But he also opposed Britain's wars for a second, complementary, reason. He now believed that capitalism was responsible for the poverty he saw all around him. And since 'I have no portion of the country, I am really not going to fight [for it].'[3] Eight years later he condemned the Boer War from this perspective. As he declared to the electors of Bow and Bromley, the British working class had nothing to gain from a conflict which had been 'got up like the Jameson Raid, in the interests solely of gold and diamond mineowners and millionaires.'[4]

Such an outlook might lead, eventually, to pacifism, but in 1900 Lansbury still was not condemning violence *qua* violence. 'As for supporting the [Boer] war because it was our country's war,' he informed a meeting in Battersea, 'he did not believe in backing your friends if they were wrong.'[5] If one's friends were *right*, then, if they were fighting against imperialism for example, perhaps a man of Lansbury's opinions would have lent them support. At the age of forty-one, Lansbury, who probably is remembered best as a pacifist, still seemed able to imagine a 'just' war whose prosecution he could endorse.

Ten years later he was mainly preoccupied with the battle to emancipate Labour from Liberalism and to win equal political rights for women. Yet he shared with many the haunting fear of a violent clash between the greatest powers of the era, Britain and Germany. Among British socialists there were two main responses to this fear. Some, like Henry Hyndman of the B.S.P. and Robert Blatchford editor of the *Clarion* newspaper, argued that their country should arm to deter German aggression. Others, Lansbury among them, had an ill-founded confidence in the power of the international socialist organization, the Second International, to avert, or at least to contain, the looming confrontation. Lansbury did not play a prominent part in the 'peace campaign' launched by Keir Hardie to raise support for this internationalist answer to Hyndman and Blatchford, but he supported it. In 1910, at an I.L.P. conference, he introduced a resolution which called upon the Second International

   to formulate a practical and effective scheme of international action
   on the part of the workers for the preservation of peace, and to secure
   a concerted preventive policy by the Labour and Socialist parties in
   each country in the event of war being declared.[6]

Obviously Lansbury had in mind here the international general strike, which many socialists of the day viewed as a panacea. After all, if the workers of belligerent nations downed tools when international conflict threatened, how could a war be fought? Lansbury had been a member of the I.L.P.'s two-man commission to study the feasibility of such action, and believed implicitly, if mistakenly, in the existence of the international working-class solidarity which was the precondition for its success.

Lansbury's views on the causes, prospects and means of avoiding wars between nations up until 1914 were thus an amalgam of Radicalism and Marxism typical of the left wing of the British socialist movement of the era. They were not strictly pacifist.

Nor was his approach to class relations strictly pacifist either. Although Lansbury later often claimed to have advocated only what the old Chartists had termed methods of 'moral suasion' throughout his career, in fact during his stint with the S.D.F. he was prepared occasionally to qualify this stance. As he had put it in his election address of 1895, 'The work of Social Democrats ... is to bring about, *by peaceful means if possible*, the transformation of society' (My emphasis). He took part regularly in S.D.F.-sponsored commemorative dinners celebrating the Paris Commune, which had not exactly carried on the class war with pacifist methods. Given sufficient provocation, Lansbury himself may have been prepared to act like a communard. During the dock strikes of 1912, for example, he witnessed

> the starvation of women and children. Over and over again I wished to kill, and when, one day in Liverpool, and another in London, I saw police and soldiers, horse and foot, charging and batoning my unarmed brothers and sisters my whole being rose in rebellion.[7]

This was only two years before the outbreak of World War I and his conversion to absolute pacifism.

Clearly, then, the experience of World War I was critical. An anti-war socialist with pacifist tendencies before it broke out, he became afterwards an absolute pacifist who was also a socialist. From 1914 until his death in 1940, depending upon political conditions, he would emphasize the one aspect of his total outlook or the other. But since, aside from a brief period during the mid and late 1920s, war or the prospect of war was almost a constant concern, the pacifism, not the socialism, often predominated. This was to have grave consequences for the Labour Party of which Lansbury was leader during his pacifist period and, therefore, for British politics during the 1930s. It is, then, to the watershed years of World War I that we must now turn.

2

Before examining the evolution of Lansbury's outlook during World War I a few preliminary remarks are necessary to set it in context. First, of course, his opposition to the conflict placed him among a tiny, beleaguered, minority. The vast majority of his countrymen and women rallied round the flag when the time came. Secondly, and as we might have expected, Lansbury was not intimidated by his isolation. If anything it drove him to greater efforts for the causes in which he believed. This hard work had significant repercussions. By 1918, when the war was distinctly less popular than it had been originally, he had cemented his reputation with the right as a revolutionary firebrand and, with the center and parts of the left, as a sentimental and difficult character. To many on the left, however, he had become the embodiment of principle, goodheartedness, generosity and courage. Thus the war had a decisive impact not only upon Lansbury's outlook, but upon his public image and career as well.

July 1914 was the last moment when he sought to avert conflict as an international socialist rather than absolute pacifist. As he reported in despair and amazement to Keir Hardie, 'I tried day after day to get others to move ... No one could or would.'[8] It was Lansbury who, through the *Daily Herald*, finally organized the famous anti-war demonstration in Trafalgar Square on August 2, at which Hardie, Hyndman, Tillett, Thorne, Henderson, Cunninghame Graham and other labor and socialist luminaries agreed to

speak. This was the last great manifestation of socialist internation-
alism and solidarity in Britain before the war blasted it to
smithereens, but already the parting of ways was discernible.
Beatrice Webb who walked past Trafalgar Square that day, for
example, referred contemptuously to the gathering there as 'an
undignified and futile exhibition.'[9] Lansbury, however, spoke out
direct as usual, appealing to the Triple Alliance of Miners,
Railwaymen and Transport Workers to 'refuse to produce coal,
run trains or transport materials,' in other words, to make British
participation in the war impossible by declaring the general strike
broached by the I.L.P. Not only did his speech give no hint of the
pacifism which soon would become his trademark, it breathed
socialist defiance of the 'capitalist warmongers' whom he held
responsible for the impending disaster.

> Wars are only in favour of the possessing classes. The workers of all
> countries have no quarrel. They are all sweated, robbed, exploited in
> times of peace and sent out to be massacred in times of war ... Go
> back to your homes and let the Government know that you, the
> workers, will fight to the death against this atrocity.[10]

He was to maintain this interpretation of 'the war to end all wars'
throughout, unlike the other speakers at Trafalgar Square, most of
whom wound up supporting the Allies.

Yet Lansbury's views were to evolve, too, if in a different
direction from those with whom he shared the platform on August
2. Men like Tillett, Thorne and Cunninghame Graham became
exhalted by the martial spirit now moving Britain, and by the
spectacle of workers volunteering for military service in droves. So
did their counterparts in all the belligerent nations. By contrast,
Lansbury grew deeply depressed. His dream of international
working-class solidarity had gone up in smoke. 'The workers all
round might well put on sack cloth and ashes,' he lamented in the
Daily Herald of August 10. And to a new friend, Charles Trevelyan,

a junior member of the Liberal Government who had resigned his position in protest of the war, Lansbury may be found lamenting the 'dark and gloomy days' of August 1914. That was the month which patriots the world over found so exhilarating.[11]

Lansbury was too resilient a personality, however, to allow depression to overwhelm him as, apparently, it overwhelmed Keir Hardie who died in 1915 broken hearted as a result of the war. A few adamantine souls stood out against the nationalist tide sweeping Britain, and Lansbury stood with them. Trevelyan, for example, helped to organize the Union of Democratic Control (U.D.C.) to study the causes of war and press for an early and just peace. Lansbury rallied the Management Committee of the *Daily Herald* behind this effort. John Burns, the former socialist and Liberal Cabinet Minister who had sanctioned the Davy Inquiry into Hollesley Bay and Laindon Farm Colony, now resigned his post as President of the Local Government Board, because he opposed Britain's entry into the war. Lansbury, who was always prepared to let bygones be bygones, sent 'sincere and hearty congratulations,' and tried to interest him in an interview with a reporter from his newspaper. '"Only John Burns Resigned." It would be of tremendous interest to our readers,' Lansbury urged, forgetting for the moment that the old Radical John Morley had resigned from the Cabinet also. In any event, however, Burns refused to be drawn.[12]

Of course these early efforts lacked impact. There was little that the few, isolated, dissidents could do at this early stage of the war. It is not surprising, then, that Lansbury sought 'the strength that comes from fellowship' with Trevelyan and other friends. Perhaps equally natural for a man of his temperament, he now rediscovered an even more important source of solace and inspiration in religion.

Although he had returned to the Anglican Church early in the twentieth century, there is no evidence that religion dominated George Lansbury's life before 1914 to the extent that it did afterwards. At no time could he have been accused of sectarianism. 'My mind is such that though my own view is strongly held, it always seems to me the other person's opinion or argument may also be true, or at least has some piece of truth which is different from mine,' he once wrote.[13] Even at his most devout he refused to place Christianity above 'the various Churches of the East.' The words of a Hindu philosopher could still deeply move him, as he wrote to Violet Markham in the spring of 1916,[14] and he continued to honor his many friends who did 'without the inspiration which comes from faith in the supernatural and the goodness of God.'[15] But Lansbury had experienced an epiphany. 'Some years ago,' he confided on December 1, 1917, to readers of the *Herald* (which had become a weekly owing to war shortages), 'after spending some time away from church, I returned as suddenly as I had stayed away.' Lansbury's 'rebirth' as a Christian had occurred early in the century. As he remembered it,

> In the midst of the first service I attended, a hymn was sung in which these words occur: 'Our hearts were filled with sadness. And we had lost our way. But morn has brought us gladness. And songs at break of day.' My whole heart and soul responded to the words of that hymn; it seemed to have been written and sung for me. From that day till now I have never really lost my faith and hope in the eternal truth that outside me and around me there is a power stronger, mightier, than all of us, by which, if we will but cease our vain striving, our reliance on selfishness, and accept the teaching, and pattern our lives on the life of Him who came to the world that Christmas Day 2000 years ago, the whole of mankind will soon find itself truly sanctified and redeemed.

Lansbury had employed the vocabulary of 'the religion of socialism' long before 1914. He had always stressed that socialism was derived as much from the teachings of Christ as from Marx, except for his period of association with the S.D.F., and even then his speeches and writings frequently damnned materialism and self-seeking, while calling upon 'born again' socialists to dedicate themselves to a life of self-sacrificing service for an ideal. But when he returned to the Anglican Church, his socialist exhortations became more explicitly Christian.[16] Finally, with the advent of World War I the language became overtly, even primarily, religious. For example, as he urged his Bow and Bromley neighbors in a Christmas message during the first year of the war, 'We must never forget, however evil the days may seem to be, however dark and gloomy the outlook, God's message to man ... Love one another, do good to those who despitefully use you, love thy neighbor as thyself.'[17] This set the tone for his public pronouncements from then on, although as the political crisis which the war had caused intensified, the political aspects of his religious message grew ever more urgent. 'The Labour movement, if it is to live and if this civilization is to be progressive, must adopt the spirit which Christ proclaimed: "He who would save his life must lose it."'[18] 'We must in humble lowly spirit range ourselves alongside the greatest and mightiest of all revolutionists, those who claimed for poor struggling humanity the right and duty of even still more sacrifice.'[19] 'After all,' he wrote in the *Herald* of December 1, 1917, 'Jesus was, and still is, the greatest social revolutionist.'

Here was the language of the religion of socialism at its most pristine. In Lansbury's case, actually, it was more pristine during and after World War I than it had been in 1892 when it had been more commonly employed and when, for example, he had used it to locate, for Bromley's Methodists, the origins of international conflict in the competitive values taught by capitalism.

We shall not get over the difficulties of today [1916], we shall not transfer the evils of militarism from our own backs or destroy the causes which make for war, until we have destroyed the spirit which is prevalent everywhere – that spirit which sends men and women out into the world merely to get something rather than to give ... The only thing that can save us is the practice of true religion –

> Cooperation, Brotherhood, Love and Care for one another ... [We
> must] fight against Mammon and greed, selfishness and lust of power,
> whether of individuals or nations ... The world will have peace when
> men and women are good enough to accept all the implications of the
> Gospel of Christ.[20]

Thus the war reconfirmed and strengthened Lansbury's prewar
conviction that peace, socialism and Christianity were indivisible.
What was new, however was the contention, which Lansbury
pressed with ever increasing fervor as the war continued, that
pacifism was inherent in Christianity and socialism both, that the
three were inseparable.

'All my life I have been more or less a pacifist,' he told an
interviewer for the *Christian Commonwealth* of August 11, 1915,

> but never an out and out pacifist until now ... In a sense I have gone
> back to a more definite acceptance of the Gospel teaching ... we can
> only overcome evil by good and ... to cast out an evil spirit is only
> possible by putting a better and nobler spirit in its place.

He had joined the Fellowship of Reconciliation, a Christian pacifist
group which grew out of a conference at Cambridge during the last
four days of 1914. The F.o.R. did not accept that there could be
'just' wars between nations – or even between classes, which, as
we will see in a moment, meant that Lansbury had altered his
outlook fundamentally when he joined the group. Nor did it argue
for pacifism on the basis of selective biblical texts. Rather, the
F.o.R. claimed that 'Love, as revealed and interpreted in the life
and death of Jesus Christ ... is the only power by which evil can
be overcome, and the only sufficient basis of human society.'[21]
Lansbury himself had arrived independently at the same position.
'The world is plunged in war,' he wrote in the December 1914
issue of the *Worker*, before the F.o.R. had been established, 'because
it refuses to literally accept the teachings of Christ.'

Membership of this organization held grave implications for

Lansbury's socialism. 'I see quite clearly now,' he told the interviewer,

> that the effort of any one class to impose its will upon the other classes by sheer force is bound to fail. After all the greatest force in the world is the force exerted by Christ, passive resistance to all wrong doing.

This was not to dismiss his early belief that class conflict was inherent under capitalism, but rather to reject the strategy he previously had thought would resolve it. Lansbury had come to believe that individual capitalists could never be coerced into socialism by trade unions or a political party, but that they might be reformed by the power of Christ-like example. He thought that World War I had put his old outlook to the test and found it wanting. Passive resistance to the outbreak of war would have been more effective in 1914 than such active resistance as had been mobilized, and more effective against capitalist employers during the prewar period than the confrontational tactics of even the mightiest trade unions. The starvation and violence which the workers of London and Liverpool had experienced during the strikes of 1911 and 1912 had led him to 'hate police and soldiers.' But Lansbury hated no longer. He had come to understand that

> soldiers and police in these struggles are the agents of Governments, who in turn are the agents of the monopolist possessing classes. I know now as I never knew before that force and violence are not the weapons we must use for securing happiness and well-being; that these can only come to us when brotherhood, love and cooperation are the guiding priciples of our life.[22]

These had been the guiding principles of Christ's life; they were the bases of socialism as Lansbury now understood it.

And, he believed, they could become the bases of political practice. During the summer of 1917 Lansbury attended a peace meeting which was broken up by jingo hooligans. He witnessed 'the worst struggle and violence' of the affray. The event had been made remarkable, however, not by this breach of civilized behavior, he maintained, but rather by what had occurred earlier. 'When the [jingo] crowd broke into the church,' Lansbury recorded,

> instead of rushing out, the audience sat calmly waiting to see what would happen. This exhibition of pacifism just nonplussed the invaders, who not being attacked, were quite unable to decide their course of action. An angry word and angry blow threw the whole place into disorder a little later on, but for a time practical pacifism triumphed, and I am sure it always would do so.[23]

Lansbury derived a not unexpected lesson from the debacle, 'we must go on with our work of education and propaganda.' This was a familiar exhortation from the original national organizer of the S.D.F., the advocate of a more democratic Labour Party, the champion of women's rights. But he had delivered it on behalf of a new crusade, perhaps the most difficult of his long career. As he had told the interviewer for the *Christian Commonwealth*, 'Whatever work remains for me to do in the world lies in trying to rouse an entirely different spirit, that recognises our common brotherhood and the unity of all life.'

For three grim years he devoted himself to this task, difficult enough in peacetime, nearly impossible of fulfilment one would have thought, during a national emergency. In season and out, no matter the opposition facing him (and it came not merely from his old enemies in the Liberal and Tory parties but from comrades in the labor and socialist movements as well), Lansbury could be found ranged on the side of the tiny minority who continued to insist that force was no remedy. He was prepared to cooperate, however, with practically anyone, including non-pacifists, who refused to accept unquestioningly the righteousness of the Allied cause, or the need to suspend socialist and other dissident activities until Germany had been defeated. Under his editorship the *Herald*, which during the Edwardian era had already become nationally famous, or infamous, as the organ of 'rebel' sentiment, cemented its reputation – and Lansbury's. In its columns he trumpeted his own message of pacifistic Christian socialism; and he opened its pages to nearly anyone wishing to express discontent with the political, social and economic conditions created by the war.

This put him in touch with a broad range of British 'troublemakers' as A.J.P. Taylor once called them. One organization to which he was instinctively drawn was the No Conscription Fellowship. Led by Clifford Allen, who before the war had been editor of the *Daily Citizen*, Labour's official newspaper, the N.C.F. campaigned first against government plans to introduce the draft and then, when Asquith instituted conscription anyway, on behalf of conscientious objectors to the war, many of whom had been imprisoned for their beliefs. C.O.s found defenders, too, in the Fellowship of Reconciliation, which Lansbury had joined. (In fact, the war spurred the formation of a number of pacifist groups.)

Most C.O.s objected to the war mainly on moral and religious grounds. Socialists in the I.L.P. refused to support the conflict on other grounds as well. 'Out of the darkness and depth we hail our working-class comrades of every land,' went one of the I.L.P.'s early anti-war manifestos. 'Across the roar of guns we send sympathy and greeting to the German Socialists ... They are no enemies of ours but faithful friends.'[24] Naturally Lansbury maintained his membership of this organization. He was in close contact, too, with anti-war members of the British Socialist Party, who finally succeeded in forcing out a patriotic old guard, including Hyndman, Thorne and Tillett.

And then there was the U.D.C., formed during the first days of the war by Trevelyan, Ramsay MacDonald, Arthur Ponsonby (a former Liberal with high connections at Court), and E.D. Morel, who was a publicist of genius. The U.D.C. hammered away, from the outset, against the notion that Germany was solely responsible for the war, and that the British Government could be trusted to fight for a fair peace, one without 'annexations or indemnities.' It demanded democratic control of foreign policy, arguing that aristocratic diplomats throughout Europe had maneuvered their governments into the war, and it maintained that a well-informed public would naturally oppose such machinations. U.D.C. propaganda had great effect, in part because its propagandists, Morel first of all, but also H.N. Brailsford and Norman Angell among others, were very good at what they did. And the U.D.C. supported the efforts of yet another committee with which Lansbury was involved, one demanding 'Peace by Negotiations' as opposed to the 'knock-out blow' for which the government stood after Lloyd George replaced Asquith as Prime Minister.

Over the years the brave efforts of these groups began to bear some fruit. This was largely due, of course, to hard work. But also, during a protracted war, public support of peace propaganda will grow in proportion to the suffering and hardship which the fighting has caused. After three years of unprecedented slaughter, hardly a family in Britain remained unscathed. By 1917, then, British dissidents, while still the object of hatred and abuse in some circles, were beginning to obtain a hearing among the public at large.

Lansbury remained always conscious of the tragedies which were the precondition to these first glimmerings of progressive revival, but he shared, too, the growing optimism of the British left. 'It is high time the Labour forces of Britain woke up,' he exhorted on March 17, 1917, in a *Herald* article in which hope, foreboding, resignation and outrage at the conduct of the government were mixed all together. He thought he discerned a portent of the awakening he desired in the 'very great deal of war weariness abroad,' and as it turned out he was right. War weariness alone might not have been enough, however, no matter how deftly the anti-war forces played upon it, but at this very moment news from Russia burst like a bombshell on British consciousness. The Tsar had fallen; his regime had been replaced by a liberal one which included, and would soon be led by, a moderate socialist, Alexander Kerensky. Labor and socialist movements the world over were transfixed. In Britain, a new political situation had been created.

By their very success, the Russian insurrectionists conferred a degree of plausibility upon British rebels of many different stripes, revolutionary socialists and conscientious objectors alike. 'I am not going to [cod?] myself the people are with us – yet,' B.S.P. organizer Alf Watts wrote to Lansbury in June 1917, 'but it is possible to do things now one couldn't do before.'[25] Lansbury agreed. It was as though a surge of electricity had galvanized him to renewed and redoubled effort. It was Lansbury who arranged the famous meeting at the Albert Hall to congratulate the men and women who had destroyed tsardom. He may have been the first Englishman to call for soldiers and workers councils ('soviets' the Russians termed them) as alternative loci of power to the official government in Westminster. 'If it is possible to overthrow the power of the Tsars of Russia,' he wrote in the *Herald* of April 14, 1917, 'it is certainly possible to overthrow every other form of autocracy or governmental tyranny which curses the world.'

One might have thought that the Russian Revolution, and especially the Bolshevik coup which threw out Kerensky's Government, would undermine Lansbury's new faith in non-violence and passive resistance. After all, the Russians had seemingly demonstrated the efficacy of force. Yet Lansbury did not waver for an instant. Although a pacifist, his commitment to 'a complete social and industrial revolution brought about by the organized Labour and Socialist movements' of Britain remained strong as ever, he asserted in the *Herald* for February 3, 1918. It was the means to the end which had changed. Lansbury was determined to make sure that the expected, indeed as he thought, inevitable, British revolution would not be brought about by violence.

Lansbury's line brought him into conflict with some of his closest allies of the 1914-18 period. Many of these were 'learning to speak Russian,' as the B.S.P. journal, the *Call*, put it; not literally, of course, but figuratively, by advocating what they thought to be Bolshevik methods. These most certainly did not include appeals to the common humanity of both the exploiting and exploited classes. Lansbury, a pacifist socialist, not a revolutionary socialist, continued to issue these and to warn against violence. 'Shall we strive to obtain power and in our turn use force to compel adherence and obedience to our principles?' he asked rhetorically on March 9, 1918, in the *Herald*, and answered himself,

> Surely not ... I fancy I can see a definite attempt to rest the Labour movement on force and violence. I want to urge our young people to build their faith on a surer and better foundation ... We must have not only a pure faith but pure methods.

Amidst the wave of industrial strife which began in early 1918, while the war was still being fought, and which did not crest until 1921 (1926 according to some labor historians), this was not necessarily a popular line.

Opposed on this issue by revolutionaries to his left, Lansbury had no dearth of enemies among Labourites to his right as well. The crudest among them, for example C.B. Stanton the miners' official who became an Independent M.P. for Merthyr Tydfil after Keir Hardie's death in 1915, were so enraged by his attitudes that, quite simply, they wanted him dead. Stanton wrote of Lansbury that he 'ought to be shot. These are strong words but I use them deliberately.'[26] Less bloodthirsty elements within the Labour Party likewise remained suspicious of the man who had called for establishing 'soviets' in Britain. Ramsay MacDonald, for example, kept Lansbury at arm's length even though, like the editor of the *Herald*, he had not supported Britain's entry into the war either. When, in 1924, MacDonald formed Labour's first government, he grudgingly offered Lansbury a minor post which did not include

Cabinet rank. Lansbury turned it down.

Yet it was precisely at this point, as the war was drawing to a close and Labour beginning to flex its muscles, that Lansbury may have attained his greatest influence on British politics and the hold upon British affections which he maintained for the rest of his life. For if his pacifism was absolute, so was his commitment to the socialist transformation of Britain. At a time when there was widespread hatred of both war *and* the capitalist system which many now believed to have produced it, a man of his views and character was particularly well situated.

3

Actually Lansbury's standing rose with that of the left in Britain as a whole. Labour reaped the political benefits which Lloyd George and his supporters had expected to gain from their role during the war. At first this was temporarily obscured by the 'Khaki Election,' which the Prime Minister called immediately after the armistice, and which resulted in a smashing victory for him (he was popularly known as 'the man who won the war') and for many candidates to whom he gave a 'coupon,' the imprimatur of his support. Lansbury himself went down to defeat in Bow and Bromley, by 8,190 votes to 7,248. But there were 33,486 electors in the district, many of them soldiers and sailors waiting to be demobilized, who were denied the opportunity to vote. Few of them still honored the men who had sent them to the inferno on the continent. Meanwhile, although Labour had 'done its bit' during the war, it could not be held responsible for the 'secret diplomacy' which, the U.D.C. taught with ever increasing success, had helped to cause it, or for the unsavoury bargaining between the Allies, in which they made plans for dividing up the colonies and other loot of their enemies. When the Bolsheviks had discovered the records of these 'Secret Treaties' in the Tsar's Winter Palace and released them to the public, in Britain it had been George Lansbury's *Herald* which first printed them.

With the return of the soldiers and sailors after the 'Khaki Election', the mood of the country veered sharply to the left. A political consequence was the Labour Party's rewritten Constitution whose famous Clause IV finally declared in favor of socialism. In the industrial arena, a series of strikes and threatened strikes by miners, railwaymen, transport workers and policemen among others, threw the country into greater turmoil than even during the prewar years 'of great unrest'. In Glasgow tanks were drawn up in the city center to overawe militant workers from the munitions factories and shipyards. There were many in Britain, not only on the left, who leaped to the conclusion that revolution was in the offing.

During this exciting period Lansbury performed a unique and vital service for the militant left. He could not have done it before the war; no one else could have done it at the time; I do not believe anyone in Britain has done it to the same extent since. What he did was to build a bridge between the Christian pacifist left and the Marxist revolutionary left by advocating, indeed by personifying, the transforming vision which both groups shared. He was capable of writing, 'There is no other way by which mankind can be saved but by love,'[27] and then, a little later,

> The class struggle will go on, must go on, till the causes which produce classes and class antagonisms are swept away ... It is too late in the day to deny [the] use [of direct action] to those of us who desire that the people in England shall cease to be divided into classes.[28]

The apparent contradiction between prosecuting the class war by 'direct action' and loving one's class enemies, seems to have bothered few on the left. This, after all was the period when the Miners' Federation could threaten a general strike partly on behalf of imprisoned conscientious objectors who had been denied the vote during the recent general election, and when pacifists in the I.L.P. could advocate membership in the (communist) Third International. It was a relatively shortlived moment in the history of the British left, but while it lasted only a few logicians questioned Lansbury's premise: that socialism meant love, and Christian pacifism meant love, and so there was more to unite pacifists and even the most militant socialists than there was to divide them.

In any event, Lansbury denied that 'direct action' would lead necessarily to violence. In 1921 the Poplar borough council was to conduct a political strike and term it passive resistance. As early as 1919 Lansbury was writing, 'the struggle of men and women on strike is passive resistance. History records the fact that this is the only effective weapon of the physically weak and those who lack material resources.'[29] Already he was working towards the strategy employed by Gandhi in South Africa and India, and Martin Luther King in America half a century later. Pacifist methods were not only morally superior to violent methods, under certain conditions they could be more effective. In 1921 the success of Poplarism seemed to demonstrate the truth of Lansbury's argument.

To those who objected that pacifism had been conspicuously absent during the Russian Revolution and would have failed abysmally had it been employed, Lansbury, responded, 'It is not approval of the methods ... of the Bolsheviks which makes me take my stand with those who cry: "Hands off Russia!" It is my faith that nations, like individuals, must work out their own salvation.'[30] In fact, there was more to it than that. Lansbury was disgusted by the hypocrisy of those who, willing themselves to use force in attaining their objects, recoiled in horror when workers threatened to gain their objects by force as well. 'Those men who for years past have taught the working class that might is right and force is the one and only remedy must not complain if those whom they have thus educated take them at their word.'[31] Lansbury did not wear his pacifism lightly. It had become part and parcel of the Christian socialism for which he lived. 'Nothing which comes to us by inflicting injustice, suffering and wrong on others can ever be of the least worth to anyone,' he exhorted readers of the *Herald* on March 9, 1918. But he knew where he stood. If it came to bloody conflict between the classes he would side with the workers.

Again, especially in historical retrospect, the contradiction seems obvious. It was not so at the time. Most of his audience took his fervent protestations as evidence of a transcendent integrity, of devotion to a cause and to the class whose cause it was. In advocating pacifism and revolutionary socialism at once Lansbury had squared the circle.

Lansbury was an articulate, determined, pacifist, socialist and internationalist with an important newspaper at his disposal. It would be hard to exaggerate his influence at this juncture or the respect he now commanded. Even Beatrice Webb, whose judgements on people were usually harsh, confided to her diary that Lansbury had become 'one of the most significant men of today, ranking in his unique position above either the leading trade unionists or the leaders of the I.L.P.'[32] The Transport Workers' leader, Robert Williams, who thought Lansbury had given the *Herald* a 'circulation that is equal to that of all the other Labour papers put together,' recommended that he should be included in the War Emergency Workers' National Committee, a watch-dog organization founded at the beginning of the war on labor's behalf.[33] Arthur Henderson believed Lansbury would have to be included in any government which replaced that of Lloyd George, although as noted above, in the event MacDonald disagreed.[34] Even Woodrow Wilson was willing to grant him an interview at Versailles while the peace negotiations were in progress, a real indication of the influence Lansbury was thought to wield. Nor, for that matter, was Lansbury shy in attempting to wield it. 'Central Europe, especially Germany, now lies at the mercy of the Allies,' he wrote privately to Lloyd George. 'You can now establish disarmament, abolish conscription and make the Council of the League of Nations the one power in the world for peace and war ... God grant you may be worthy of your opportunities.'[35] What the Prime Minister thought of such exhortations went unrecorded, but he directed his secretaries to keep an eye on the man who had written to him. Today the historian can track George Lansbury's postwar activities in the newspaper clippings collected for Lloyd George three-quarters of a century ago.

The best record of Lansbury's doings, however, remains the *Daily Herald*. In its pages Lansbury continued to assert the need for unity on the left and the natural affinity of pacifism and socialism, not excluding communism. A trip which he made to the Soviet Union early in 1920 vividly demonstrated the dual nature of his outlook and its appeal. His impressions of the revolutionary state were transmitted almost daily to Fleet Street (via the Foreign Office which had directed the Marconi Company to intercept Lansbury's telegrams). It was a tremendous coup for the *Daily Herald* and for Lansbury who addressed the Moscow soviet, interviewed Lenin and publicly invited Lloyd George to do the same. For our purposes, however, the trip seems most notable for illustrating the central tension and contradiction in Lansbury's thought. 'Arrived here today,' he cabled the *Daily Herald*, which printed his telegram on February 10. 'The Churches are all open, and people going in and out.' This was his first concern. In subsequent dispatches he dwelt upon the beneficent transformation of life envisioned and already partially achieved by the revolutionaries, his love and respect for them, and the difficulties they faced as a result of the Allied intervention on behalf of the counter-revolution. Upon leaving the Soviet Union twenty-four days later, he attempted to draw together the two threads, Christian pacifist and revolutionary socialist, which now bound up his world view. 'Religion is not a matter of churches or of words, it is a matter of deeds,' he wrote on March 18 for his newspaper. 'If it is possible to be a Christian and a soldier under orders from a government, it is also possible to be a Christian and a revolutionary when serving in an army commanded by Lenin and Trotsky.'

There is some evidence that Lansbury himself was troubled at times by the difficulties of this line of reasoning. He claimed that he had extracted from Lenin, during the famous interview, an admission that in Britain at any rate, it might be possible to achieve socialism without going through a bloody revolution. But six years later, during a second trip to Moscow, he found it hard to answer a young Bolshevik 'who lived a lingering death in Siberia and other prisons in order to make a revolution,' and who now would not 'sit down quietly with folded arms and see the fruits of victory taken away.' Returning home Lansbury asked 'which of my pacifist friends will write a 500 word reply to this comrade?' He himself had been forced by the discussion to 'realise how easy it is for people like me who are pacifists to ride our theories to death.'[36]

Such honesty, combined with his fearlessness and many talents, made him during the early aftermath of the war the indispensable man on the British left, perhaps the only person in the country respected at once by nearly all its disputatious and fissiparous elements. He stood with one foot in the camp of the revolutionaries and the other planted firmly among the men and women of religious faith and conscience. During so tumultuous a period this made him a man with which the rest of Labour, and even the government, had to reckon. Always a significant figure on the British left, his conversion to pacifism and rededication to Christianity made him something more. His millenarian outlook coincided with the popular mood of postwar Britain.

A national mood, especially one like that, however, is hard to sustain. During the spring of 1921, the miners waged the campaign referred to in Section I, against decontrol of the mines. The militant left hoped that the Triple Alliance, the very organization to which Lansbury had appealed for a general strike to avert World War I, would call one now on the Miners' behalf. On April 15, 1921, however, this mammoth combination again failed to act, even though the Miners had already downed tools in expectation of its support. 'Black Friday' was a crushing defeat for the left which was forced to realize that the British revolution was no longer imminent, if ever it really had been. Popular militancy had crested; ebb tide now set in (though the Poplar Labour councillors successfully fought it, and, indeed, five years later, during the general strike of 1926, it seemed for a moment as though things were flowing the other way again).

In retrospect, however, it is clear that 1921 was a climacteric. Amid changed circumstances Lansbury's standing on the left changed, too, although his message did not. It was no longer possible for him to successfully square the circle, as he had in the charged atmosphere of the immediate postwar period. His sympathy for the Soviets remained undiminished. He continued to support the advocates of direct action in Britain, including the Communists, although he proposed uniting with them not to make a violent revolution but rather, as he put it in the *Daily Herald* of August 27, 1921, 'to do the day's work nearest our hand.' Simultaneously he continued to advocate absolute pacifism based upon the teachings of Christ. Where previously he had been confident that the British people were with him, or soon would be, however, he had now to admit that his was the position of a decided minority. This was nothing new for Lansbury. He simply drew breath and went on arguing for what he believed in.

Although the wave of industrial unrest had broken, the popular mood it reflected had permanently altered the political landscape. Labour had become Britain's main anti-Conservative party. If not exactly poised to take power, its leaders were now considering what policies to implement when finally they formed the government. Lansbury remained deeply concerned with the viability of pacifism as a tactic of the workers in class struggle, but he also began attempting to make plain the international pacifist line which he thought a Labour Government should follow. His urgings prefigured the policy *he* would advocate ten years later as Labour Party leader.

In a nutshell his policy was the 'out and out pacifist position' of 'No armies and no armaments.' He wrote in the *Daily Herald* of July 14, 1923, 'When we are asked what will become of us if we are not armed and will not fight, ask those who put these questions what will happen to us if we do.' His own answer was that 'nothing that could happen could possibly be more terrible than what has happened to all who in the past or present have put their trust in that form of murder we call war.'[37] For this reason Lansbury was already advocating that Britain should disarm unilaterally. 'Some nation must start [disarming] and the one that does ... will, I am sure, not go down to destruction but, on the contrary, will become the greatest people the world has ever known.'

This was not a policy likely to commend itself to the rest of the party leadership who, although now publicly committed to socialism, were also determined to prove that Labour was 'fit to govern.' MacDonald, who had considered Lansbury a problematic colleague ever since the agitation for women's suffrage a decade earlier, passed him over when forming his first Cabinet early in 1924. A good deal of tongue wagging ensued, and five years later, when MacDonald put together his second administration, he dared not exclude the Member for Bow and Bromley.

And, of course, in the meantime Lansbury had hardly been idle. Disappointed by MacDonald, he had advised his readers (and himself) to 'possess our souls in patience and go on working in whatever way we can to create public opinion on behalf of our policy.'[38] In Parliament he actually proposed the abolition of the British Royal Navy (and received nineteen supporting votes, all from Labour Members). Outside he became active in the No More War Movement which was the British section of the War Resisters

International. In 1926 he was a prominent supporter of Lord Ponsonby's 'Peace Letter,' a declaration which would be imitated in 1935 by Canon Dick Sheppard to great effect (see below, pp. 178–80). Ponsonby's early effort read:

> We the undersigned, convinced that all disputes between Nations are capable of settlement either by diplomatic negotiations or by some form of international arbitration, hereby solemnly declare that we shall refuse to support or render war service to any Government which resorts to arms.[39]

In short Lansbury had returned to his familiar position as Labour's gadfly and left-wing conscience.

But he had, as never before, a national reputation. When, in 1929, Labour won office for the second time and MacDonald could not escape offering him a seat in the Cabinet as Minister of Works, Lansbury accepted. Although he could not know what was in the offing, he was on the verge of a momentous step. No sooner had the government taken office than it was confronted with the stock crash in New York City and the onset of global depression. In August 1931 Lansbury was one of those who led the fight from within the Cabinet against reducing benefits for Britain's unemployed as a budget-balancing measure. Such a move was favoured by MacDonald the Prime Minister, Snowden the Chancellor of the Exchequer, and J.H. Thomas, previously the Minister responsible for dealing with unemployment. When no compromise could be reached MacDonald requested the resignation of his Cabinet, received the king's commission to form a new government, brought Snowden and Thomas into it and also the leaders of the Conservative and Liberal Parties. He soon after called the general election of 1931 and campaigned against his former colleagues and the party with which he had been associated for nearly forty years. This resulted in a massive majority for the newly formed 'National' Government of which he was Prime Minister. It decimated Labour, whose representation in the House of Commons was reduced from 285 to 46 (plus 5 members of the I.L.P. and 1 independent who usually voted with them). Lansbury was one of the few senior Labour Members to survive. Amid the recriminations, backbiting and maneuvering which accompanied the disaster, his integrity and strength of purpose stood out all the more. Lansbury, now seventy-two years old, was still an absolute pacifist who believed that Communists and Labourites should cooperate with each other, but in the hour of its greatest need the Labour Party turned to him for leadership.

4

Lansbury was chairman of the Parliamentary Labour Party from 1931 to 1935. He also became leader of the party as a whole in the autumn of 1932, after Henderson's resignation from that post. His stint at the top coincided with a period of great tension and danger for the world as much as for Britain. Within a month of MacDonald's 'betrayal,' as Labour deemed it, and Lansbury's ascension to MacDonald's former position, Japanese soldiers had invaded Manchuria. Within a year and a half, Hitler had become the German Chancellor. In quick order he withdrew his country from disarmament talks and from the League of Nations, initiated a program of massive rearmament, reinstituted military conscription and began developing plans for *Anschluss* with Austria and re-occupation of the Rhineland. In Italy, Mussolini dreamt of Rome's former glory and laid covetous eyes upon Abysinnia. It was amid these circumstances that the shattered and demoralized Labour Party struggled to define its foreign policy. (We will not be considering its domestic program.) Labour's pacifist leader thought he knew what that foreign policy should be. And, unlikely though it might seem, and distant though the prospect was, he would become Prime Minister if Labour won the next general election.

Possession of the leadership did nothing to alter or moderate Lansbury's views. During 1931–35 he remained what he had been since 1918, an absolute pacifist and committed internationalist with a wealth of experience in Britain's labor and socialist movements. Thus, when confronted with the Japanese invasion of Manchuria, which began in 1931, or with the prospective Italian incursion into Abyssinia, in 1935, he looked almost instinctively for a collective, not a national, answer, one coordinated by the League of Nations, and limited to economic, not military, measures. Many in the Labour Party, however, were not pacifists and were not willing to restrict their options so severely. Thus, the seeds of the dispute which would drive him from the leadership four years later were present from the outset of Lansbury's period at the top of the Labour hierarchy.

History is rarely kind to losers and so, perhaps, it is not surprising that most assessments of Lansbury's stint as party leader have been negative. 'The Parliamentary Party is a poor little affair ... Attlee is Deputy Leader ... and he and [Stafford] Cripps ... sit in Lansbury's room at the House all day and all night and continually influence the old man.'[40] Scholars have tended to accept Hugh Dalton's contemporary judgement. Meanwhile, according to this standard accounting, Lansbury's pacifism was so manifestly incapable of meeting the fascist threat that little by little his position as party leader became untenable. At the Labour Party Annual Conference of 1935, Ernest Bevin, the bulldog leader of the Transport and General Workers' Union, finally dispatched him to the political wilderness with a brutal, but appropriate, speech. And, it is often said, Bevin destroyed not merely Lansbury and pacifism in that speech, but also the remaining reservations felt by Labour's left wing against giving weapons to a government led, since MacDonald's retirement from the Premiership, by reactionaries such as Baldwin and Neville Chamberlain. Thus, despite Lansbury, Labour finally endorsed the rearmament program which enabled

157

Britain to survive the inevitable Nazi onslaught which began four years later, or so the story goes.

That parts of this interpretation hold explanatory power no one would dispute, but the biographer of George Lansbury cannot accept it altogether. It seems more appropriate and more useful to view Lansbury's experience as party leader, and his defeat at Bevin's hands, in the context of his career as a whole. In that light it is easy, first of all, to dismiss Dalton's charge that the 'old man' was being manipulated by Attlee and Cripps. Throughout his long career, whether as a Liberal, or as a member of the S.D.F., or as an advocate of 'Votes for Women,' or, especially, as a pacifist (neither Attlee nor Cripps were pacifists), George Lansbury always was his own man. If anything, perhaps he was too much so; too prepared to tell the truth as he saw it regardless of the political consequences. Quite likely Dalton, who had lost his seat in the general election of 1931, was jealous of Labourites who remained at the center of things, and particularly of Cripps and Attlee who had been, like him, junior members of the second Labour Government, but who had survived the electoral débâcle. But, anyway, Dalton's charge is a relatively minor matter in a chapter devoted to Lansbury's pacifism. Much more significant is the broader indictment, by Bevin, of Lansbury's role and conduct, which so many historians have accepted more or less uncritically.

The point that needs stressing here is that it was *not* only a political difference, *not* only a question of what kind of sanctions Labour should support against Japanese and Italian aggression, which Bevin wished to resolve at the Labour Party Annual Conference of 1935. Those issues were paramount, no doubt, in the minds of assembled delegates and, indisputably, Bevin helped resolve them with a powerful speech. However, the debates over pacifism in the 1930s, including the debate over sanctions at Labour's Annual Conference of 1935, cannot be isolated from the debates, in which Lansbury had always taken a leading part, over such fundamental issues as the meaning of socialism and the ultimate goals of the Labour Party, which had divided the British left since the late nineteenth century. In his new position as party leader, Lansbury had to deal with many mundane, quotidian, problems, for instance maintaining the morale of his troops at Westminster, deputing and briefing Labour Members to speak, handling a mountain of correspondence, and so on, and (Hugh Dalton to the contrary notwithstanding) he proved to be very good at it;[41] but also, in his new role he continued, only with greater visibility and impact than ever before, to work for the religion of socialism as he understood it. During his term as party leader he sought to apply the lessons he had been learning all his life to the political situation of the 1930s. He had learned very radical lessons. This is what brought him up against Ernest Bevin in 1935. It was an entire world view, and an approach to international relations as a whole, which Bevin sought to crush at that fateful gathering. That was what made his speech there so important. That Bevin felt this task to be necessary suggests why Lansbury's stint as party leader was so significant.

The religion of socialism remained the foundation of Lansbury's outlook. He thought it 'blasphemous' that want and superabundance existed side by side in Britain. He exhorted voters to follow the biblical injunction to '"Love thy neighbor as thyself." This is what the world needs,' he wrote. 'Christ calls to us across the centuries, "Choose ye this day whom you will serve; you cannot serve God and Mammon!" … Socialism is the opposite of Mammon worship.'[42]

And he applied the same logic and style to foreign affairs and the empire. Lansbury was, probably, the most anti-imperialist leader Labour has ever had. We have already seen how, while still a Radical and a Liberal, he had condemned imperialism in generous, Gladstonian, terms, and how, following his conversion to socialism, he added to his original reasons for opposing imperialism his belief in international working-class brotherhood. After World War I he discovered yet another reason to oppose it. Imperialism was bad, he thought, not least because it rested upon force and domination. If Britain did away with her army and navy which, as a pacifist he now believed she should do, then she would never be able to maintain her empire. Thus, in renouncing force, Lansbury was renouncing imperialism as well. He thought this would have an added benefit: 'As to our enemies abroad,' he wrote in August 1926, 'if we gave up imperialism we should have none.'[43]

Five years later, although he was party leader and a potential prime minister, his point of view remained the same. Lansbury still opposed British imperialism on humanitarian, socialist and pacifist grounds. He wrote,

> Our people must give up all *right* to hold any other country, must renounce all imperialism and stand unarmed before the world. [Great Britain] will then become the strongest nation in the world fully armed by justice and love ... Socialism, which is religion, is the one road which will lead to salvation.[44]

Barely into the leadership he was already working towards the policy which enraged the 'realists' like Bevin and for which eventually he was driven from the top post of his party. Perhaps it *is* naive for a political leader to advocate unilateral renunciation of anything; but the position at which Lansbury finally arrived was the culmination of his conversion to the religion of socialism some fifty years before.

Here it is necessary to work into the analysis Lansbury's approach to Germany during the 1930s. He had known almost since the ink was dry on the Treaty of Versailles that it had sown the seeds of a terrible reckoning for the peoples of Europe. Therefore he had been an appeaser from 1919 on, in the sense that he wished to appease what he considered to be Germany's justified complaints against the peace treaty by altering its most punitive provisions. For example, he supported Germany's demand for equality of armaments with the victorious powers, arguing not that Germany should be permitted to rearm to French and British levels, of course, but rather that the victors should disarm to the level permitted Germany. Nor did he believe Germany should be forced to pay reparations to the Allies. Rather he held that 'they had to wipe the slate of reparations both inside and outside this country.'[45]

Lansbury never held any illusions about the character of fascism. As he put it in Hyde Park, at the May Day rally of 1933, 'fascism with all its nonsensical talk about nationalism ... [is] the gospel of decadence and despair.'[46] It was, he charged some months later, 'the greatest of all enemies to human progress.'[47] And, of course, it hardly needs saying, he had no time at all for anti-Semitism.[48] He did not believe, however, that Hitler's seizure of power affected the injustices done at Versailles or the need for revising the treaty concluded there. In fact, as Lansbury saw it, the 'best way of strengthening Fascism is to treat Germany stupidly by giving Germans the impression that she is not regarded as on an equality with other nations.'[49] In particular Lansbury accepted the German complaint, which did not originate with Hitler but which the Führer made much of, that Versailles had created in Europe a great dichotomy between the 'have' powers which had won the war, and the 'have not' powers which had lost it. The latter were suffering greatly from economic scarcity and were determined to improve their lot. This was one of the primary sources of tension in the world. 'The war spirit abroad is the direct outcome of economic nationalism, fostered and developed by the brutal, cynical, peace treaties,' Lansbury told a meeting at Exeter.[50]

Lansbury's desire to appease the legitimate demands of such 'have not' powers as Germany, his anti-imperialism, and his unilateralism, were fused during his period as Labour Party leader. 'What is the cause of war?' he asked a meeting in Bow. 'It is the need for expansion; the desire for that which other countries have – raw materials and markets. But why should countries fight for these objectives? Why not get together and pool the resources?' After all, Lansbury explained, there were 'plenty of raw materials and markets for everybody ... We Britons could give the lead and offer to other countries a share of the products.'[51] 'Our nation is the greatest imperialist power in the world,' he wrote in the *Daily Herald* of September 10, 1935.

> The same call which Christ gave to the rich young man is calling to us. We are given the opportunity to place our all on the altar of common service. We must be prepared to share the natural sources of wealth which are ours with the rest of mankind. [This] ... is the only road to peace and security. The British nation which leads the world so far as possessions go, must hammer out a scheme which can be placed before a world conference.

For Lansbury, then, Britain's ideal role in the world was clear and his attempt to guide his country towards it nothing but the expression of his unwavering faith in the religion of socialism.

The 'scheme' he had in mind was undoubtedly the most audacious ever contemplated by a modern major party leader in Britain.

> All narrow and other waterways, such as the Straits of Dover, Gibraltar, the Suez Canal, coaling and other stations would be handed over to the League of Nations for international instead of national control ... all Air Stations or Air Ports under our control should be dealt with in the same manner ... [T]he enormous territories of raw materials under the control of Great Britain would ... be transferred to international authority created through and by the League of Nations. India and Egypt would be given absolute freedom to choose their own representatives to the League of Nations ...[52]

Some would think giving up so much a heavy price to pay, Lansbury acknowledged, but it was 'only heavy to those who count life by the amount of material wealth they possess.' Lansbury knew that the religion of socialism did not accept that arithmetic and that Labour should not accept it either.

Always an optimist, Lansbury believed that if Great Britain took the steps he advocated other nations would follow her lead. Referring to Germany in a letter to Cripps, he wrote 'no nation can stand out against the public opinion of the world,'[53] but, in fact, the conduct of other nations was immaterial to him. His whole point was that Britain must renounce imperialism and war unilaterally. 'Somewhere a start must be made,' he averred. 'There is no nation so well placed as we are to throw down this challenge to the world.'

Again, let it be said, that while Lansbury's plan seemed outrageous to many, it represented nothing more than an attempt to put into practice the ideals which British socialists had been advocating for nearly half a century. For Lansbury this meant pacifism too, which led to much private murmuring at party headquarters and elsewhere. But few among the movement's leaders were willing to dispute him publicly because, pacifism aside, he was manifestly insisting only that Labour live up to its own anti-imperialist rhetoric. Thus Lansbury received consistent votes of support from the Parliamentary Labour Party and the National Executive Committee.

Lansbury made it hard, even, for politicians entirely outside Labour's ambit to criticize him. He was, after all, an experienced and effective agitator, which was one reason why Bevin's attack when it finally came had to be so savage. Lansbury wanted the British Government to ask the League of Nations to convene the conference where the 'have not' nations could state their grievances and discuss methods for assuaging them with the 'haves.' The government, however, had no intention of carrying out Lansbury's wishes. So, on August 19, 1935, Lansbury wrote a letter to *The Times*, calling upon Baldwin to take the initiative he desired. But it was not only an economic conference he wanted now. He suggested, too, that Britain's archbishops 'appeal to his Holiness the Pope to join in and call a solemn convocation or congress representative of every phase of Christian and other religious thought ... to meet in the Holy Land at Jerusalem ... and bid the war spirit rest.' To Baldwin, or anyone else who might think such an appeal foolish and sentimental Lansbury's response was simplicity itself. It was 'the foolishness of the Gospel which has taught me that the law of God is love and the application of that law is sharing.' Which politician would want to tangle with that?

In seeking to place Lansbury's Christian, socialist, pacifist, outlook of 1931–35 into historical perspective I do not wish to romanticize it. I have tried to show only that his efforts, which have most commonly been denigrated as shortsighted at best, in fact were based upon a much longer view of politics than his critics were willing to admit. Lansbury was attempting to make the Labour Party live up to its own ideals as he understood them after nearly half a century of active involvement in their formulation, and to force Labour's political opponents to take them into account. But was his plan a realistic alternative to the policies actually carried out by the Conservative Governments?

It should be mentioned first of all in attempting to answer such a question that neither Stanley Baldwin nor Neville Chamberlain, who followed Baldwin as Prime Minister, dealt well at all with the fascist leaders during this period. They consistently underrated the fascist threat and so ill prepared their country to meet it that, despite the rearmament program they belatedly and half-heartedly instituted, when war finally came Britain nearly lost it. It is hard to imagine that things could have been much worse in 1940 had Lansbury been Prime Minister for the past five years, than they actually were after half a decade of Baldwin and Chamberlain. It is not, then, as though we can compare Lansbury's plan for dealing with the fascists against one that actually worked.

Most historians, however, have held that Baldwin and Chamberlain should have listened not to Lansbury but to Winston Churchill who, from the backbenches to which he had been banished for previous indiscretions was, like Lansbury, offering his own alternative approach to the Nazis. This was, in essence, a much vaster program of rearmament than the government was willing to contemplate. Had his recommendations been followed, it is generally held, the 'have not' countries would have been afraid to attack Great Britain, or could have been more expeditiously defeated when they did attack.

As with Lansbury's approach to fascism, however, so Churchill's must be placed in historical perspective. His prescient warnings about the Nazi peril stemmed, in part, from his desire to maintain the British empire and Britain's world role. He was much more worried about the Nazis in Germany than the fascists in Italy, because the Germans threatened British pre-eminence and the Italians did not. In fact, he found it possible on occasion to speak well of Mussolini and of fascists elsewhere, for example in Spain. But, of course, Lansbury did not accept Churchill's assumptions. He wanted to break up the British empire, not to maintain it; to transform Britain's world role, not to ensure its continuation along present lines. He surveyed the scene from atop a foundation built of socialism, Christianity, and pacifism; Churchill stood upon 'Rule Britannia' and 'the White Man's Burden.' Lansbury's proposals were meant to achieve very different goals from Churchill's and therefore should not be measured against them either.

Given that Lansbury and Churchill envisioned different futures for their country, the question is not whether Britain would have prevailed against Germany in World War II had Lansbury been Prime Minister during the 1930s, but rather whether it would have had to. Could pacifist tactics have contained Hitler's Germany, or was the only answer to him a 'fortress Britain,' as Churchill maintained? Or was war inevitable once Hitler had taken power, regardless of who was Britain's Prime Minister?

Pacifism can be an effective political force under certain circumstances, as Gandhi and Martin Luther King have proved, and as Lansbury himself demonstrated in Poplar in 1921. But British soldiers in India, segregationists in America, the opponents of Poplar's Labour councillors in London, were all accountable to elected governments which depended upon a public opinion that had to be courted, not commanded, and for whose support the apostles of non-violence also competed. In other words, pacifist methods worked against authorities in England and America and even subject India; and might conceivably have found some purchase in a Germany led by Chancellor Stresemann or Bruning; but were they feasible when authority was represented by Adolf Hitler and his henchmen?

As we have seen, Lansbury's answer to this question was dictated by his understanding of the religion of socialism. War between England and Germany, even Germany governed by the Nazis, was not inevitable, he argued, because revising the Treaty of Versailles, as simple justice demanded, would both deprive the Nazis of their main excuse for war preparations and simulataneously weaken their grip on power. War *could* be deterred without rearmament, in other words, by 'sharing,' by Christian socialism – that is to say, by assuaging the economic demands of the 'have not' powers. And to those who might object that essentially the appeasers *did* attempt assuaging Germany at Munich in 1938, a pacifist Christian Socialist would have answered that by then the economic appeasement Lansbury had envisioned was at least three years out of date and, moreover, that the gathering for which Lansbury had called was not one where representatives of the major powers dictated to the smaller powers, as at Munich, but rather one where the rest of the world divided the possessions of the major powers into more equal shares. At such a meeting Britain would have lost much territory and Germany gained some; but the entire process would have been democratically carried out.

Perhaps Lansbury's 'scheme' was more mistimed than anything else. Had it been applied during the 1920s before Nazism was a significant force in Germany, many calamities might have been avoided. Had Lansbury been Prime Minister early in the 1930s before Hitler took power, perhaps it still was not too late. Perhaps, although here I remain unconvinced, even during the first two years of Hitler's dictatorship it remained possible to so ameliorate world conditions that aggressive war would have been unpalatable to the people of Germany. It is at least arguable that Lansbury's approach was more principled and could, therefore, have been more effective than the program of appeasement actually followed by Baldwin and Chamberlain, and that it was no more risky than the alternative broached by Churchill whose only certain effect would have been to better prepare Britain for war. But history cannot be written in the speculative mode and the historian can pursue a counter-factual argument only so far. The fact is that once Hitler took power Lansbury could not convince even his own party, let alone the country or subsequent generations of historians, that the practice of international socialism by pacifist methods could contain and eventually overthrow German or Italian or Japanese fascism. All sectors of the labor movement, the T.U.C., P.L.P., and constituency parties, favored the use of sanctions organized by the League of Nations against aggressors, even if they led to military confrontation.

Thus Lansbury was leader of a party whose vast majority rejected a fundamental aspect of his outlook. Could he maintain his integrity and his position simultaneously? Arthur Ponsonby, one of the founders of the old U.D.C., author of the 'Peace Letter' of 1926, and now leader of the Labour Group in the House of Lords, thought no pacifist could reconcile his beliefs with Labour's official policy. He resigned the leadership of the Labour Lords and pressed Lansbury to quit leading in the Commons. Lansbury resisted. He remembered 1912, when he had resigned his parliamentary seat

167

and entered the political wilderness because Labour did not support 'Votes for Women' with sufficient vigor. From that episode, he often said, he had learned an important lesson: 'Never Resign!' If he had believed that when he rejoined the Labour Party after World War I, say, or in 1929 when he became a member of the Labour Government with whose policies he often disagreed, how much more so did he believe it in 1934 and 1935 when, as party leader and potential Prime Minister, he thought he might soon have a chance to save the world from catastrophe? So Lansbury compromised. During this difficult period, when he spoke as leader of the Parliamentary Labour Party or of the national Labour Party, he carefully made plain that he was representing not his own views, but those of the movement. It was only when he spoke for himself that he advocated pacifism. But how long could so anomolous a position continue?

As the international situation deteriorated, the pressures on Lansbury to advocate forcible resistance to fascism increased. Still he held fast. Testimony to Lansbury's persuasive powers, he even managed, against all odds, to pull the movement halfway with him. At Labour's Annual Conference of 1935, the motion (which provided the occasion for Bevin's withering attack) demanding sanctions against Italy, including if necessary the use of force, actually ended up reiterating Lansbury's appeal for the British Government

> to urge the League of Nations to summon a World Economic Conference, and to place upon its Agenda the international control of the sources and supply of raw materials with the application of the principle of economic equality of opportunity for all nations in the underdeveloped regions of the earth.[54]

And, irony of ironies, Hugh Dalton in moving the resolution for the N.E.C. paid tribute to the 'two men who, more than any others in this country, have put this economic aspect of the case upon the map,' George Lansbury – and Ernest Bevin! But the delegates could not agree with Lansbury that such a conference was all that was required either to appease the 'have not' powers or to avert a war. For the latter armed force might be necessary, too. They voted for the motion; Lansbury opposed it unavailingly. This was the defeat which forced him, finally, to resign the leadership.

Again, although it was not generally perceived at the time, there was more at stake during this momentous debate than Lansbury's leadership, more than whether Labour should endorse 'economic' or 'military' sanctions. In part Lansbury was arguing for, and many of his opponents were arguing, in part, against the religion of socialism. For this reason the debate was one of the most important in Labour Party history.

Lansbury entered the debate at a grave disadvantage, precisely because the question was so bound up with, and muddled by, international complications. Labour's small pacifist contingent would follow him practically anywhere, and certainly into the 'Noes' lobby when it came time to vote; however, the Labour left, his most natural constituency, might not. It was deeply divided – not over the religion of socialism which most of its members understood in the same way that Lansbury did, but over the proper response to aggressive dictators. Many on the Labour left were not pacifists and would not rule out the use of force against the fascists. As it transpired, aside from the pacifists, only those on the extreme left of the party voted against the motion. They did so because they did not trust the government, or the League of Nations, to deploy justly or wisely British troops which would be drawn primarily from the working class. As William Mellor, a prominent member of the Socialist League, put it in a speech opposing the motion, 'Our enemy is here.'

So divisive was the issue of sanctions and what they entailed, that it drove a wedge between Lansbury and many old friends. Even the original members of the U.D.C. found themselves opposing one another. Thus Ponsonby supported Lansbury on pacifist grounds, while Charles Trevelyan supported sanctions in order to uphold the principle of international law. Seeing these two old comrades arrayed against one another at a Labour Party Annual Conference, listening to Trevelyan attacking his own position, for that matter, must have have been difficult for the party leader.

Worse still, while the left was fragmented, Labour's big guns were unitedly opposed to Lansbury's position. In this sense the conference of 1935 presaged the line up which ten years later would dominate the party. Hugh Dalton introduced the resolution, Herbert Morrison, Lansbury's foe of 1921, wound up for it, Clement Attlee supported it with a pithy, unassailably logical speech, and Ernest Bevin, speaking with the weight of the trade-union movement behind him, carried the biggest stick of all. What could Lansbury counterpose against this formidable combination except his own idealism and strength of conviction?

The speech he finally delivered was characteristically straightforward, humble, and unyielding. He explained first the 'Dr. Jekyll and Mr. Hyde position' he had been in as spokesman for a policy with which he disagreed, and his reasons for finally making his disaffection public. 'I want everyone to understand,' he said at the beginning,

> that it is difficult for me to stand here today and publicly repudiate a big fundamental piece of policy. If I were in any doubt about that policy, I am sure that I should not take the line I am taking, but I ask Conference to believe me when I say that I have never been more convinced that I am right, and that the Movement is making a terrible mistake, than I am today.[55]

He spelled out his commonsense objections to rearmament and his pacifist conviction that 'force never has and never will bring permanent peace and permanent goodwill in the world.' Then he reiterated his famous 'scheme,' for British unilateral action.

> If I had the power to go to Geneva backed by our people ... I would
> say ... that Great Britain ... was finished with imperialism, that we
> were willing that all the peoples under our flag, wherever you can
> establish Government, should be free to establish their own Govern-
> ments, that there should be no such thing as domination ... but that
> we would be willing that the whole of the resources which are under
> our control should be pooled for the service of all mankind. Not
> handed out here and there to individual nations to exploit, but put
> under the positive control of an International Commission. And I
> would say further that ... we would be willing to become disarmed
> unilaterally.

Here the argument was in secular language, but Lansbury employed
the rhetoric of 'the religion of socialism' as well. 'This Christianity,' he asserted at one point during the speech,

> is the realist principle of life because it says 'We are willing that you
> shall carry out the doctrine of those who are strongest helping with
> the strength of their brain and their power the weak ...' This is no
> mere ideal; it is no greater [as an] international ideal than the national
> ideal of common service for each other ... We have got somewhere
> to begin, and I want our people to begin. And that is the message that
> somehow I must put to the world wherever people will hear me.

He knew that his was the position of a minority in the Labour Party
and, as he said, that he might never again address the conference
as party leader, at which point according to the record of
proceedings, cries of 'No', rang through the hall. But 'the only
thing worth while for old men to do is to at least say the thing they
believe.' Accordingly, he concluded,

> If mine was the only voice in this Conference, I would say in the name
> of the faith I hold, the belief I have that God intended us to live
> peaceably and quietly with one another, if some people do not allow
> us to do so, I am ready to stand as the early Christians did, and say,
> 'This is our faith, this is where we stand, and if necessary, this is where
> we will die.'[56]

171

It was, as always with Lansbury, an effective effort. Perhaps for a moment it even seemed as though he had captured the sentiment of the conference, if not a majority of its votes. But then, 'as the applause died away and the wave of emotion subsided ... [Ernest] Bevin was seen to rise to his feet and without hurrying make his way to the platform.'[57]

Bevin's crushing rejoinder to Lansbury reads somewhat strangely half a century later. It is long on emotion and short on substance, an unexpected realization for the historian who always thought that Lansbury was the sentimentalist and Bevin the realist. Bevin's main point was that Lansbury, and all who opposed League of Nations sanctions against fascist aggression, were disloyal to a party policy that had been democratically hammered out over the years by majorities on the N.E.C., T.U.C. and Labour's Joint Council. Now pacifists who wished to place their personal scruples above party policy were guilty of the same sin that Ramsay MacDonald had committed in 1931. After all, MacDonald, too, had insisted upon going his own way without reference, especially, to the T.U.C. Trade-union leaders, who had responsibilities to their membership, understood the meaning of loyalty. They must see to it that the Labour Party stood by its commitments, regardless of middle-class parliamentarians like MacDonald – and George Lansbury.

Really that was the essence of the speech. Bevin did not defend sanctions as a tool of foreign policy, and hardly mentioned the issues which Lansbury had raised. For example, with regard to unilateral disarmament Bevin merely said, 'I do not remember – and I have a good memory – a single member of the Parliamentary Labour Party, including the Leader ... ever suggesting that we should put unilateral disarmament in [Labour's position paper, *For Socialism and Peace*].' On the empire Bevin was only slightly more detailed. 'If we go on being merely anti-imperial where does it lead?' he asked. 'It leads to a scramble in the world. It will lead to wars all over the world.' He advocated, therefore, that imperial territories be jointly controlled by their current occupier and the League of Nations.

What set Bevin's speech apart, then, and what gave it an undeniable force, was not its substance but rather its tone and the style of its delivery. The leader of the Transport and General Workers' Union was an imposing figure, squat and powerful. No doubt his very demeanor played a role. More, his speech gave the impression of being a weighty pronouncement, a point by point refutation not so much of Lansbury's pacifist position, as of his claims to self-doubt and discomfort at leading a movement with which he disagreed. Bevin posed as a practical man dismissing the inconsequential musings of a saint.

He was vehement, self-righteous, and intensely personal. 'I am a democrat and I feel we have been betrayed,' he cried at the outset, because Lansbury had not stuck to the policies outlined in *For Socialism and Peace*. 'It was cowardly to stab us in the back,' by opposing sanctions after Labour's Joint Council had endorsed them, he charged towards the end of his tirade, a phrase he would use again to great effect twelve years later when demolishing his left-wing opponents in the Labour Party at another annual conference. For Lansbury's biblical references, and thus for the religion of socialism, Bevin displayed the deepest contempt. 'There is one quotation from the Scriptures which George Lansbury has quoted today which I think he ought to apply to himself – "Do unto others,"' meaning that Lansbury was not treating Labour's leaders as he, in turn, would wish to be treated. And again, later in the speech, '"Do unto others as you would they should do unto you," he [Lansbury] said. I wish that had been applied by him to the rest of the members of the National Joint Council.' But the phrase for which the speech is best remembered came in response to an offer Lansbury had made to step down from the leadership, or not to step down, depending on the vote of the Parliamentary Labour Party or of the Conference itself if it wished to intervene. Bevin thought Lansbury should make that decision by himself. 'It is placing the Executive and the Movement in an absolutely false position to be taking your conscience round from body to body asking to be told what you ought to do with it.' At that, apparently, the delegates grew restive, for Bevin had to shout, 'It is all very well to cheer somebody you like and interrupt somebody you do not like, but I ask you to hear the arguments.'

And yet the arguments were unfair, based largely upon half-truths and untruths. It was absurd to compare Lansbury to MacDonald, as Bevin did, or to accuse him of being less a democrat than the trade-union leaders were. 'MacDonaldism' in the Labour Party, by which was meant an undemocratic approach to politics, had encountered no more constant foe than George Lansbury. Throughout his career, in fact, Lansbury's aim had been to make the Labour Party *more* democratic, not less. It was the trade unions, Ernest Bevin's enormous Transport and General Workers' Union not least of all, which dominated Labour conferences by means of an undemocratic bloc vote, as was well known, if forgotten in the heat of the moment. Moreover, Lansbury was not disloyally announcing his opposition to sanctions at the eleventh hour, as Bevin charged. He had been in hospital when *For Peace and Socialism* was drafted and had sent in written objections at the time. Since then he had made clear his opposition to portions of the document, but privately, so as not to embarrass the movement. He had only gone public, as he said at the outset of his speech, because of the gravity of the issue at hand, and, even so, he would 'not consider an expression of opinion hostile to my continuance as Leader as anything more than natural and perfectly friendly.'

Why, then, the ferocity of Bevin's speech? Conference's verdict on sanctions was never in doubt. Even if the section of the party most likely to oppose sanctions, the Labour left, had not been visibly divided on the issue and even if Labour's pacifists had not represented so tiny a fraction of the movement as a whole, the trade-union bloc vote ensured the outcome. When it came time to vote, the supporters of sanctions defeated the opponents by an overwhelming majority, 2,168,000 to 102,000. So it cannot have been the fear that Labour would oppose sanctions which inspired Bevin's venom.

Nor, in all likelihood was it the calculation that Lansbury's pacifism would cost Labour precious votes at the next general election. For, although there can be no gainsaying that Lansbury's attitude *was* awkward for the party and movement as a whole, it had not been *so* awkward as to preclude their recovery since 1931. In September 1935, in fact (and this is real testimony to Lansbury's skills as a practical party leader), Labour was just beginning to believe in its power to upset the Conservatives in the next contest against them. But only two weeks after Bevin destroyed Lansbury, plunging Labour into disarray once again and, inadvertently, placing the unknown Clement Attlee into the leadership position, Baldwin drew his own conclusion and suddenly called the general election, and won it in a walkover. So, if Bevin was attempting to protect Labour's electoral prospects by demolishing Lansbury he entirely failed to do so. And Bevin rarely failed to gain what he sought.

The conclusion must be, then, that Bevin was looking far beyond the next round with the Conservatives or the vote on sanctions. It was Lansbury's approach to foreign affairs as a whole that he wished to demolish. He knew that the Parliamentary Labour Party and the N.E.C. had voted several times during the past few years for Lansbury to continue in the leadership position, despite his pacifism and opposition to sanctions. Thus Bevin must have objected to Lansbury requesting the 'expression of opinion' regarding his leadership not because 'it was putting the movement in a false position,' as he demagogically claimed, so much as because he feared that the movement would vote for Lansbury to stay on. It was that which Bevin feared most.

175

Again the argument must be counter-factual to a degree. But it is worth remembering that Bevin became Foreign Minister only ten years after the demolition job he performed on Lansbury. Under his aegis 'continuity of foreign policy' became the watchword. And the policy he continued was precisely the one Lansbury had intended to break up. Lansbury had wanted to deconstruct the British empire; Bevin (as much as Winston Churchill) was one of its last great defenders. Lansbury opposed rearmament because, in his opinion, rearmament would not avert war but better prepare Britain to fight one; Bevin supported rearmament, as Churchill did at the time, because he wanted to defend Britain's place in the world. Lansbury's defeat, in 1935, should be seen in this perspective. It was one of many, and one of the most decisive defeats, which advocates of the religion of socialism sustained in their long battle to make the Labour Party live up to its original ideals.

Lansbury, for one, recognized this. He resigned his leadership position almost immediately. He was seventy-six years old. But, like another grand old man of politics, William Gladstone, Lansbury too was 'terrible on the rebound.' Within months he had launched his last, and greatest, crusade.

5

'Send me to Parliament with a mandate to call the nation to one great supreme effort for peace,' Lansbury appealed during the general election of 1935, his final, and most successful, electoral campaign. (Although Labour badly lost the general election, Bow and Bromley voted by 19,064 to 5,707 in his favor.) For the next five years, which were the last five years of his life, Lansbury himself certainly made the supreme effort. He travelled the world on behalf of peace; met with world leaders to discuss how peace could be best maintained; helped to build a massive and important British peace movement into a political factor which the Conservative Government dared not ignore. The energy, stamina, strength of purpose and political effectiveness which he displayed were astonishing for a man of his age. Towards the end, however, with the world situation growing ever more desperate, he displayed, too, a narrowed focus, a kind of tunnel vision. He became, finally, a man possessed, one who held an *idée fixe*. Then nothing could divert him, not even reality.

At first, however, it seemed almost as though relinquishing leadership of the Labour Party had given him a new lease on life. He wasted little time, if any, on self-pity. 'I really do not need any sympathy or thanks,' he told the Christian Pacifist Movement at an Armistice Day rally six weeks after the Labour Party Conference. 'When it comes to a downright question of principle, we all have to make up our mind and take our stands accordingly ... If you do what you think you ought to do, well, in the doing that is the thanks.' He was back, now, where he almost always had been and where, doubtless, he was most comfortable, on street corners and in meeting halls, speaking to the faithful, and to potential converts, organizing with great skill a movement to shake the powerful. To Vera Brittain, who once shared a platform with him during this period, he appreared 'shrewd and benign, sturdily erect in his black alpaca coat.'[58] He continued to hammer at old themes: 'It is no use thinking that just by saying "We want peace" we shall get it,' he warned his audience,

> We must *will* the means to peace ... [R]emember that in our country we, the common ordinary people, have got it within our power whenever we have the will, to say 'Our country shall turn its back on that bestial business [war] once and for all.'

Thus the man Ernest Bevin had accused of defying democratic principles within the Labour Party based his last great crusade upon his own faith that democratic practices could save the world.

Lansbury's goal remained what it had been while he was still leader of the Labour Party, a world conference to solve the economic problems which otherwise would lead to war. His tools for achieving the goal, however, were different. The Labour Party had broken in his hands. As a result, 'I think my work for the party is finished,' he acknowledged sadly, in June 1936, in a letter to Cripps.[59] There still were in Britain, however, peace groups and pacifist organizations left over from World War I. It was to these groups that he now turned. They, he decided, would have to generate the irresistible pressure for a world conference which Labour had failed to exert. He still belonged to the Fellowship of Reconciliation, which, in 1935, had a membership of approximately 3,300.[60] He still belonged, too, to the British section of the War Resisters International, the No More War Movement, which was even smaller than the F.o.R. Lansbury really was in the political wilderness again. These were the tiny building blocks at his disposal.

He was not without important allies, however. Of these, the most significant was Canon H.L.R. 'Dick' Sheppard with whom he had been in touch since 1912. Sheppard was presently Canon of St. Paul's Cathedral; previously he had been Vicar of St. Martin-in-the Fields Church and, before that, the Dean of Canterbury. An organizer of exceptional ability, Sheppard had converted to pacifism in 1927, but did not devote himself entirely to the pacifist cause until seven years later, when the rise of Hitler and growing likelihood of another world war concentrated his mind. Then, on October 16, 1934, he published in the press a letter asking readers to send him a postcard supporting the following resolution: 'We renounce war and never again, directly or indirectly, will we support or sanction another.' And now it became apparent that anti-war sentiment in Britain was stronger than the membership lists of pacifist organizations seemed to indicate. World War I had inspired among many the determination that another international conflict must never occur. During the 1920s and early 1930s, pacifist ideals had surfaced at the universities, most famously in 1933 when the Oxford Union declared: 'This House will in no circumstances fight for King and Country'; during by-elections, of which John Wilmot's victory for Labour at East Fulham in 1933 created the greatest stir; in films, plays, novels and poems. The response to Sheppard's inquiry in the newspapers, however, was unlike anything seen in Britain before. Two-and-a-half thousand cards arrived within a couple of days; fifty thousand arrived in all. In July 1935, worried about the Italian–Abyssinian crisis, Sheppard announced a meeting at the Albert Hall to which signatories of the postcard would be invited. Seven thousand attended. And Sheppard now took up Lansbury's call for a world economic conference. On September 13, both men attended a rally on behalf of this proposal at Central Hall, Westminster, which was packed to overflowing, with fifteen hundred disappointed supporters having to be turned away for lack of room.

Some months after that meeting, and shortly after Lansbury stepped down from leading the Labour Party, Sheppard organized the Peace Pledge Union. This became the main pacifist body in Britain before World War II. Membership of other pacifist groups had never reached five figures. P.P.U. membership reached six figures within a few months. Its twenty original 'Sponsors,' according to one historian, 'comprised perhaps the most intellectually distinguished committee ever assembled by a controversial British pressure group.'[61] Lansbury was the most prominent, of course, but among others there were important clerics, such as the Anglican Canons Stuart Morris and Charles Raven, and the Methodist Minister, Donald Soper; and Labour Party figures such as Ellen Wilkinson, James Hudson, and Lord Ponsonby; and intellectuals, academics and publicists, for example Bertrand Russell, Aldous Huxley, Vera Brittain, Rose Macaulay and Siegfried Sassoon. The P.P.U. was so successful that the N.M.W.M. ended its own independent existence and joined as a body (except for the Birmingham branch). When Sheppard died suddenly and unexpectedly in October 1937, Lansbury was elected to be its president.

So, when Lansbury stepped down from his position of leadership in the Labour Party, he was simultaneously stepping across to another movement, albeit a movement that had been waiting to happen, a movement in embryo, as it were, until called into existence by Sheppard's enquiry in the newspapers. Now Sheppard became its main organizer; Lansbury its chief propagandist. Together they helped to mobilize the largest peace movement Britain had yet seen.

The years had done nothing to dull Lansbury's skills as an agitator or his shrewdness as a political operator. He was a world figure, a man who, when leader of the Labour Party, had been potentially the next Prime Minister of Great Britain. As such he had been in touch with other world leaders and potential world leaders and still could gain entrance into ministries, palaces and buildings of state where less well-known figures would be unwelcome. This world status was his chief asset to the peace movement, and he was determined to make the most of it. No other convert to the cause could do what Lansbury now set out to accomplish, which was to rally not merely British but world opinion behind his crusade for peace. During the spring of 1936 he undertook a tour of the United States, speaking in twenty-seven cities, and broadcasting over the radio ten times including, on April 21, a speech heard nationwide in which he called, once again, for the world conference and for his listeners to 'take the Gospel message at its face value.' The most significant moment of the trip and the main reason for which it had been organized, however, came when he conferred with the American Secretary of State, Cordell Hull, the Secretary of Labor, Frances Perkins, and most importantly, with President Franklin Roosevelt himself. From Roosevelt he appears to have extracted a pledge to seriously consider calling the world conference once the elections of November 1936 had taken place, if there was evidence that the major European powers would attend. 'I will get it for you,' Lansbury promised.[62]

Thus mobilizing support for the conference among other heads of state became his primary task and really, it almost seems, his main reason for being. No sooner had he returned from America than he was off again, this time to France, where he met with Leon Blum, leader of the Popular Front Government. The socialist, Blum, would have seemed a natural ally, and apparently he was one, for he promised to 'talk with the American Ambassador, and I know he has done so from a friend in London,' Lansbury reported to the F.o.R., which had sponsored this second international trip. Lansbury himself seemed heartened, for 'I ... feel sure he, Blum, is strengthened in support of our view.' From France he continued to Belgium where he conferred with the King, and then on to Scandinavia, where he met with the Prime Ministers and Foreign Secretaries of Norway, Sweden, and Denmark.

'I am not stupid enough to think that anything I may have said has immediately influenced any policy,' he admitted to *Peace News* on October 3, 1936. On the other hand, probably no proselytizing pacifist had ever captured Britain's attention so well, or commanded so effectively the newspaper headlines and radio waves. 'George Lansbury is doing more for real peace than all the official politicians of all the camps put together,' enthused his friend and admirer, the pacifist Labour M.P. for Bermondsey, Alfred Salter.[63] The War Resisters International made him their president. Dick Sheppard called him 'Public Pacifist Number 1.' He was, at this stage, quite literally indefatigable. For he was not only criss-crossing Europe and America, but in between these international jaunts he was traversing Britain too, in an old-fashioned revivalist campaign, enrolling countless thousands into the pacifist army. 'I had ten great meetings in Scotland last week,' he reported typically in *Peace News* for February 13, 1937.

Political histories of the period tend to discount these efforts. Nevertheless, it is true that Lansbury and the others had conjured up, almost out of the ground, a new factor in British affairs. The raw sentiment had been there waiting, as noted previously. But it needed the organizational skills of Dick Sheppard and the old agitator, George Lansbury, among others, to transform inchoate sentiment into a political force. That they had done this, and almost overnight, seems evident. During part of 1936 the P.P.U. was expanding by 4,500 per week. It paid a staff of thirty officials. It published a weekly newspaper, *Peace News*, with a steady circulation of about 20,000.[64] It organized great pacifist conventions throughout England's major cities. The first, in Manchester, attracted over 900 delegates from 332 organizations. A national conference in London was attended by 1,100 delegates representing more than 400 peace, religious, Labour, trade-union and cooperative groups. One 'Sponsor,' Canon Stuart Morris, enthusiastically suggested at this point 'that one hundred candidates should be put up for the next General Election.' Lansbury successfully opposed this overly optimistic proposal, but that it could have been advanced at all gives some indication of the heady exhilaration which important members of the organization were feeling. And then Cordell Hull confirmed publicly Roosevelt's private commitment to Lansbury that the U.S. would arrange the famous economic conference if other European powers would participate. By now it was apparent that Ernest Bevin had been wrong in thinking that pushing Lansbury from the Labour leadership would silence him or render him politically ineffective.

Yet the pacifists were working against time, working against odds, and Lansbury knew it. In the year since he had lost his post with Labour, Mussolini had invaded, and conquered, Abysinnia. The League of Nations had all but died. Hitler's rearmament program had continued apace and, now, Britain had begun rearming too. In Spain, Franco had begun the civil war and, already, the Germans and Italians had intervened on Franco's side, and the Russians on the side of the Loyalists. Spain could become in 1936 what Serbia had been in 1914, the powder keg whose explosion ignited Europe and the world. 'We are on the brink of an abyss,' Lansbury reported to another great peace gathering, at Caxton Hall in London.[65] There was nothing for it but to redouble his efforts.

It is at this point that one may begin to sense a change in George Lansbury. He never hesitated to follow his star, even when it led him away from friends and colleagues, for example in 1892, out of the Liberal Party and into the socialist movement or, twenty years later, out of the House of Commons and into the movement of the suffragettes. Yet he had always retained a shrewd political sense of what was possible and, more importantly, a firm grasp of the greater reality into which his own strivings must fit. It was this sense of perspective which, at age seventy-seven, Lansbury finally began to lose. Also, when Lansbury had joined them, the socialist and womens' movements contained leaders of a stature equal to, or greater than, his own. Ever since then, in any discussion of strategy, tactics or goals, Lansbury always had to contend with views advanced by men and women as forceful, experienced and savvy as he. With Sheppard's premature death, however, the same could no longer be said of the pacifist movement. In it, Lansbury was pre-eminent, an undesirable situation given his state of mind.

In this sense only, perhaps Bevin had succeeded after all. When he cut Lansbury off from a leading role in the Labour Party he cut him off, too, from the main current moving the Labour left during the 1930s. It happened to be a current which Bevin opposed equally with pacifism, the agitation for a 'popular front' against fascism, but this is by the way. The point is that Lansbury focussed on the P.P.U. to the exclusion of all else, to his own detriment. He was so appalled by what World War I had wrought, so horrified by the prospect of another conflict in which combatants would wield weapons even more destuctive, that he could not imagine anything worse, although something worse was incubating in Nazi Germany, as many a Popular Fronter could have told him. He was so certain that he understood how to avert another war, that he could imagine no other way than his own, although again the advocates of a Popular Front knew something he did not.

Lansbury remained a man of the left. He was shortly to compose a pamphlet, *Why Pacifists Should Be Socialists*, which repeated arguments he had been making ever since 1914: that capitalism was based upon competition which led to class conflict at home and to war abroad; and that pacifists did not get to the root of matters unless they condemned the economic system which bore such bloody fruit. The pamphlet's title notwithstanding, however, Lansbury was now less interested in making pacifists into socialists than in making socialists into pacifists. And thus he was cut off from, indeed was often at odds with, his most natural constituency and accustomed allies.

Previously the demand for a world economic conference had reflected in equal proportions his pacifism and his anti-imperialism; now, however, it reflected mainly his loathing of war. He insisted, against all the evidence, that the legitimate complaints of the 'have not' powers still could be satisfied, that Hitler's fangs still could be drawn, through economic appeasement. If only the Germans would indicate their willingness to sit down at the conference table, Lansbury reasoned, then perhaps Roosevelt, backed by Blum and the leaders of the other nations he had visited, would convene the great meeting. In fact, the time for the conference had passed, if ever since 1933 it truly had existed. All Lansbury could see, however was that he needed additional endorsements of the conference from world leaders and from Adolf Hitler most of all. So Lansbury decided to undertake another journey.

Is it possible that he arranged these 'Embassies of Reconciliation,' as he now was calling them, because he missed the trappings of power to which he had become accustomed while leader of the

Labour Party? Did they in some way satisfy his ego and make him feel important? I think not. Lansbury was sincerely humble throughout his life, as any review of his personal papers (held at the British Library of Political and Economic Sciences) will attest. Giving up position and place was routine for him; he did it periodically throughout his career. Lansbury's desire now to meet with Hitler testifies not to his longing for the limelight, but rather to his willingness to undertake anything, literally anything, which he thought might help to keep the peace.

On January 15, 1937, the British pacifist paid a call upon Anthony Eden at the Foreign Office. He had received an invitation from some Lutheran friends to visit Berlin. He intended to accept and hoped to see Hitler while he was there. Of course, if the interview did take place, he would make clear that he was speaking in a purely personal capacity. He would then explain to the Chancellor that

> while himself a pacifist the overwhelming majority of Labour opinion in this country did not share his view, that therefore if Germany thought that by force she would gain her way ... she was wrong ... [and] that since Hitler could get nothing by force of arms he should come to a conference for the purpose of arms limitation and economic cooperation.

Eden concluded in his report to one of Britain's diplomats in Berlin, Sir Eric Phipps, that 'I am myself reluctant to put a veto on Mr. Lansbury's visit, and even see some advantage to it if he speaks on the lines he suggests.'[66]

What that advantage could have been is difficult to imagine. Perhaps the men conducting Britan's foreign policy, including even anti-appeasers like Eden, were no less full of illusions than George Lansbury. In fact, all concerned in this affair – on the British side, at any rate – seem slightly out of focus. Hitler sent word in March that he would grant Lansbury an audience on Monday, April 19.

The man who, with brutal thoroughness, had crushed all opposition in Germany was to host Britain's apostle of non-violence, Christianity and international cooperation. This was incongruous enough. Perhaps even more so was the P.P.U.'s response. On April 17, *Peace News* exhorted its readers to send a postcard to Hitler conveying 'the hopes and wishes of many thousand young English people for a favourable outcome' to the meeting with Lansbury. Thoughtfully the editors supplied a German translation of this message which they had crafted to soften Hitler's heart.

Lansbury's tunnel vision seems now to have taken over completely. He prepared a memorandum for Hitler to read before their meeting. It began, 'Many millions of people are daily working, longing and praying for peace, a peace based on the great saying of Jesus Christ, "Do unto others as you would that they should do unto you.I come to you with the same message."'

Biblical injunctions aside, the memorandum might have made sense five, or possibly even two, years earlier. By 1937, however, it was hopelessly outdated. It condemned the 'penal clauses' of the Treaty of Versailles, as if simple revision was any longer the main issue at hand. It called again for the conference 'at which all nations must be represented and all attend as equals,' although the time for such a meeting was gone, predicted that Roosevelt would convene such a gathering 'if he could expect a response from the other great powers,' although this manifestly was no longer the case, argued that the first task of the meeting would be to declare a truce in the armaments race but that its 'main business ... would be to consider how to deal with the causes of war,' and proposed that in essence 'the "Haves" must share with the "Have-nots." ... An effort must be made,' Lansbury argued, 'to treat the world as an economic unity, all nations understanding that the prosperity of each means the prosperity of all.' He was preaching international socialism to Adolph Hitler!

'You will have gathered,' Lansbury continued in the memorandum, 'that my desire is that you should give a public pledge that, if such a conference is summoned, Germany shall be represented and her statesmen shall direct their best thought and energy towards finding a peaceful settlement of all outstanding questions.' He hoped, too, that the proposed conference would help to settle peacefully the civil war in Spain and finally, that out of the conference 'there would be evolved a real League of Nations.' In his concluding paragraphs Lansbury argued that the fears between nations could be overcome by 'perfect love'; and he wound up repeating the phrase with which he had begun: "Do unto others as you would that they should do to you." '[67]

Hitler's genuine response to this document may be supposed. When it came to hosting the elderly pacifist from Britain, however, he appeared a model of sympathy and courtesy. 'It was not anything like people said it would be,' Lansbury gushed immediately afterwards.

> There was no long speech from him. It was a real conversation. We discussed the whole gamut of subjects over two hours and a quarter. The whole talk was as satisfactory as those with Blum and Roosevelt. Hitler treated the interview very seriously. I think he really wants peace.

The two men had argued back and forth over whether rearmament made the world safer or more dangerous. They discussed the conflict in Spain, which Hitler blamed entirely on 'the Bolsheviks.' Hitler claimed that 'Germany wanted only Germans in the Empire, and did not want to impose the Nazi regime on other countries.' He declined, himself, to host the world conference because, Lansbury reported him saying, 'nobody trusted him and if he attempted to take the initiative it would spoil the chances,' but he promised to attend if Roosevelt or another statesman convened one. This was what Lansbury wanted. 'The task now,' he concluded in the report he sent back to the F.o.R., 'is to get our own Government to move.'[68]

To some it almost appeared that Lansbury was better satisfied with Hitler than with his own country's leaders or, even, with the present leaders of the Labour Party. 'People thought George Lansbury was an admirer of Fascism and Nazism and the editor of the *Daily Mail*' (a pro-appeasement newspaper) warned a member of the F.o.R., even before the trip to Berlin took place. In retrospect the distinction between Lansbury's views and those of the 'appeasers' seems clear enough, yet Lansbury himself could not help seeing that former allies and friends were becoming alienated. Returning to Britain, he offered a defense of his conduct to a socialist newspaper, the Glasgow *Forward* on May 8. It was revealing, sadly, of the loss of perspective that now characterized his activities and strategy. 'I know, of course, about German prisons and German Concentration Camps,' he admitted.

> But because we are opposed to Herr Hitler's dictatorship and its methods is it right for us to refuse to ... do all in our power to prevent a war which will be a ghastly tragedy for Britons and Germans alike? ... We cannot destroy their system of government; only the German people can do that ... I am pleading that no matter how much we may dislike the[ir] form of government ... or their persecutions or imprisonments, we should do our utmost to prevent the youth of today from becoming victims in another great war.

This statement glossed over the extent of Nazi barbarity, as if imprisonment was the worst form of punishment Hitler meted out to dissidents, and as if persecution meant, say, merely systematically declining to make purchases in Jewish-owned shops. Lansbury's approach to the Nazis was based upon a failure of imagination. He thought Hitler was the Kaiser again, and could be dealt with as, perhaps, the Kaiser should have been dealt with in 1914, when Germany was also demanding her 'place in the sun.' Economic appeasement might have averted World War I. Now, he believed, it could avert World War II.

The meeting with Hitler had only compounded this misunderstanding. 'Mr Lansbury was really delighted with his conversation and readily admitted that he had fallen a victim to the Chancellor's charm,' the diplomat, Ivone Kirkpatrick, reported to William Strang at the Foreign Office. Lansbury put it somewhat differently in a private letter to Clifford Allen, the World War I pacifist and founder of the N.C.F., whom the Führer had also entertained some time earlier. Hitler 'is a very lonely man and has no spiritual background to fall back upon.' Such a figure, although 'ruthless and quite cynical with everything that seems to stand in his way,' sincerely wanted to avoid war, or so Lansbury assured Allen. But, then, British rearmament really was unnecessary; and the economic conference all the more justified.

It does not seem to have occurred to Lansbury that Hitler risked nothing meeting with him, since while Lansbury could not influence the rigidly controlled German public, the Führer, through Lansbury, might influence the British; and that in agreeing to attend a conference he was, anyway, committing himself to nothing, since it was unlikely that the conference would ever take place and, even if it did, that it would succeed. In any event, as a 'have-not' power, Germany had little to lose at such a conference. It should have given Lansbury pause, too, that the pacifist cause in Britain had received a filip from the German leader who hoped to breed a race of warriors. But Lansbury was looking in one direction only. The conference was almost within his grasp. 'I got from Herr Hitler what I wanted to get from him,' he commented with obvious satisfaction shortly after the meeting had concluded.[69] Nothing else mattered.

Home in late April he plunged again into pacifist propaganda, speaking at Friends House in London, to the Thornbury Divisional Labour Party, to the Annual Conference of Welsh Congregationalists. And then, in July, he was off to the continent yet again, this time to Rome where he met with Mussolini, who told him that it

189

was a privilege to greet so sincere a harbinger of peace. 'The cynics might say that Signor Mussolini's assurance was only to "cod" a silly old man,' Lansbury admitted upon his return, 'but he preferred to take people at their face value.'[70] A few months later he was back in central Europe, visiting in succession Austria, Poland and Czechoslovakia and meeting with their leaders. The pace was whirlwind, the message always the same. Convene the conference before the next war, not afterwards when it would be too late. 'Another great war will mean the collapse of civilisation,' he warned in the F.o.R. publication *Reconciliation* in January 1938. 'The practice of pacifism does not bring about anything worse than the collapse of civilisation.' In fact, it would save it, if only the statesmen would agree to attend the conference, if only, although this was an even more remote possibility, at the conference Britain would provide inspiration by a grand, unilateral, gesture of renunciation.

The war clouds were massing on the horizon and Lansbury could see them clearly, perhaps more clearly than the statesmen who all encouraged him with polite phrases but would not act as he wished them to. The only thing he could do about it was to go on agitating. There was something almost frantic about his crusade now. In Bristol, Manchester, York, Taunton, Liverpool, London, wherever opponents of war were gathered, there, too, was he. He was nearly seventy-nine, an 'old man in a hurry' if ever there was one. Then, in September 1938, came the penultimate crisis. Hitler was determined to end the independent existence of Czechoslovakia, a nation possessing an efficient army, advanced industry, and defense pacts with Russia and France. The German leader coached a Czech fascist, Henlein, to demand that German-speaking Czechs in the Sudetenland be incorporated into the Reich. This would have meant the disintegration of Czechoslovakia which, naturally, Czech officials and patriots opposed. They looked to their allies for support. Russia was willing to back them and France might have been, but the French were connected by treaty to the British, and the British Prime Minister, Neville Chamberlain, did not want to help the French support the Czechs. He did not want war with Germany any more than George Lansbury did, although he was far from being a pacifist. On September 15 he flew to Berchtesgaden, Hitler's country retreat, to confer with the Führer, and really in search of a way to give him what he desired. The world held its breath. Everyone believed that peace or war hung in the balance.

The Czech crisis, finally 'resolved' at Munich when the British and French forced Czechoslovakia to accede to all Hitler's demands, revealed Lansbury's tragic deterioration. He had become, finally, an advocate of peace at any price. And yet, singleminded as he was, he was not a simple apologist of the Chamberlain brand of appeasement. Because Lansbury wanted peace he supported the Munich 'settlement,' but only up to a point. His solution to the crisis would have been substantially different from the one Chamberlain found.

From the beginning of the crisis Lansbury was determined that it must not lead to war. He told a conference of the International F.o.R. meeting in Holland, before Chamberlain's flight to Berchtesgaden, that of course Germany must not annex Czechoslovakia, but 'whatever the theory of government on this side of the frontier or on that, our interest is the maintenance of the peace of Europe.' As always, he emphasized the economic bases of world tensions. The Czech crisis could be resolved, Lansbury argued, if trade and investment in the region were increased. 'The British Government ought to be willing in the interests of peace and prosperity for all to take the lead in helping to make available the international finance necessary for developments of this kind.' He believed, inevitably, that a conference to arrange these economic matters should be convened as soon as possible.[71]

As the crisis developed, so Lansbury's search for a solution that would not involve recourse to arms evolved. On September 21 he explained his views to his constituents in Bow and Bromley. Chamberlain's mission to Hitler, undertaken the previous week, had been 'courageous,' Lansbury thought. It could even be the first move towards the meeting of world statesmen he so desired. He did not know what the two leaders were arranging. (Chamberlain wound up suggesting the transfer to Germany of all Czech districts containing 50 percent or more German speakers. This would mean the end of Czechoslovakia as an independent state.) Lansbury thought, however, that 'we in Britain, whatever our opinions may be, who at the moment are living in safety, dare not advise any small people to accept war as an alternative to proposals now being considered.' Yet he was far from endorsing Chamberlain's approach to world politics generally, or to Czechoslovakia specifically.

> Everybody who believes in right and truth and justice must and does sympathise with small nations when they are oppressed. Many of us have given our sympathy to the people of Ireland, India and elsewhere. But always we declared our faith, 'force cannot outlaw force, evil cannot conquer evil' ... We pacifists hate persecution, tyranny and the mailed fist by whomsoever it is used. We are, however, convinced that if the present crisis ends in universal war our last state will be worse than the first. It is not fear of our own lives, but the horrible fact that when the slaughter is over nothing is gained – everything is lost.[72]

Thus the original socialist agitator still may be perceived, however dimly, within the elderly pacifist he had become. Where sympathy for subject peoples once had shaped his world view, however, in 1938 it was secondary. Simple loathing of war determined his outlook and conduct.

Lansbury had ruled out forcible resistance to the Nazis. How did his approach differ, then, from that of Chamberlain and other appeasers? The answer was provided next day, September 22, when the 'Sponsors' of the P.P.U. convened in emergency session and hammered out a statement which Lansbury and several others delivered immediately to Downing Street and the Foreign Office. This document encapsulates Lansbury's world view at the end of his life; its phraseology and emphasis bear his unmistakable imprint.

The P.P.U. declaration began by situating the present crisis within an historical context. The Sudeten agitation, the German demands, stemmed from the injustices and failures of the vengeful Treaty of Versailles. Thus Germany was no more to blame for the current dangerous situation than any other great power. Then came the clear delineation between Lansbury's pacifist and socialist approach to world affairs and that of the appeasers.

> We believe that we have no moral right to demand concessions from Czechoslovakia without being ready to make sacrifices ourselves. We therefore urge that our Government should at once invite the representatives of all nations to meet in Conference with the immediate object of revising existing Treaties. Such a Conference can succeed only if the Government of this country goes into it prepared to regard the question of colonial possessions and our own economic policy as open to drastic revision.[73]

This had been the essence of Lansbury's outlook ever since he had comprehended and repudiated the Treaty of Versailles. It was basically the program he had unsuccessfully attempted to sell to the Labour Party during his period as its leader and for which he had been campaigning ever since. Farsighted and generous though the outlook had been a decade, or even half a decade ago, however, in 1938 it reflected Lansbury's myopia – or even blindness, to the facts of life. No such conference would or could take place now, for a myriad of reasons.

Nevertheless, once again the venerable agitator helped to organize a great campaign. The P.P.U. declaration travelled far beyond 10 Downing Street and the Foreign Office. Three thousand huge placards bearing its message were posted in Paris. It was published, in translation, in Finland, Denmark, Belgium and Norway.

It appeared throughout the British and Irish press. P.P.U. groups were supplied with 150,000 copies.[74] To these public efforts Lansbury added his own form of private diplomacy, the saddest aspect of his response to the crisis in my opinion. During his trip to Prague the previous spring he had met the Czech President, Edouard Benes. Now Benes was under irresistible pressure, exerted by Chamberlain, Daladier of France, Mussolini and, of course, Hitler, to acquiesce in the destruction of his country. To the unholy chorus of voices urging him to knuckle under, Lansbury added his own. He cabled to 'My Dear Dr. Benes,'

> The world's peace may now depend upon your accepting further sacrifices and giving way before the further demands, backed by the threat of force, thus letting force appear to win the victory. This is the sacrifice Christ made, an unconditional sacrifice ... Not law, now, but only grace is strong enough ... My friends and I here, who cannot share this sacrifice with you, would ourselves wish to meet all tyranny in this spirit, and if war came to meet all its sufferings in a like way.[75]

The missive was characteristic in a sense: when Lansbury had determined he was right, then no force on earth could keep him from throwing every ounce of his strength into battle. On the other hand, pressuring Benes, a bottom dog if ever there was one, to kneel before an imperialist conqueror was also absolutely incompatible with the values Lansbury had fought for and, indeed, embodied, during most of his life.

In the aftermath of Munich, many in Britain felt ashamed of Chamberlain's conduct, especially when Hitler invaded Czechoslovakia despite having won all his demands at the conference. As a result, they began reconsidering, and rejecting, appeasement. This was the beginning of the public change of heart which led, finally, to Chamberlain's downfall. Lansbury, however, did not share in it. He remained determined to spend his all attempting to avert the war that was coming, not helping to better prepare for it as most of Britain and the world now was doing. He thought that perhaps the smaller European nations could prevail upon one of the great powers to convene the famous conference (Belgium seemed the most likely candidate), and so he planned another series of continental journeys and actually travelled briefly to Brussells where he spoke with the Prime Minister, Pierlot, and with the King of the Belgians. He appealed in a public letter, for the Pope to convene a peace conference on the Mount of Olives on Easter Sunday. And he continued to agitate for the P.P.U. in Britain.

But he was eighty years old and finally his strength had begun to ebb. For most of his life his health had been robust. Now he had to contend with physical infirmities. Perhaps, too, he was becoming discouraged. 'It may be that I have been too believing; that I should be more skeptical,' he wrote in *Reconciliation* for November 1938, although he added defiantly immediately afterwards, but 'I am not built that way.' At any rate, in April 1939, he conveyed to the P.P.U. his desire to step down both as President and Sponsor, and only agreed to stay on when the positions were made purely honorary.[76]

When the war finally came, he opposed it on the usual grounds. 'I am more a Pacifist than ever, if this is possible,' he wrote to Cripps.[77] But he was prepared, finally, to let it rest. His son-in-law writes that Lansbury realised now that his life was drawing to a close. He was not bitter or defeated, but 'As a man who is waiting may do, he spent a good deal of his time tidying up.'[78] On May 17, 1940, while the German armies were racing towards Paris, George Lansbury died.

4 Conclusion

George Lansbury was politically active for more than half a century, from the mid-1880s to the late 1930s. During that time Britain was transformed. Lansbury had something to do with that transformation; it should be clear by now that he deserves a place among the pantheon of Labour pioneers, if not quite at the very front with Keir Hardie, Ramsay MacDonald and Arthur Henderson, then certainly in the next rank with, say, Philip Snowden, Beatrice and Sidney Webb, and Bruce Glasier. After 1918 his personal following surpassed anything that Snowden, Glasier or the Webbs ever attained.

This volume has not attempted to provide a complete biography but rather has highlighted Lansbury's contributions to the socialist, women's and peace movements. Let us review them very briefly and in doing so attempt to draw together the several threads I have advanced.

Lansbury's feminism was grounded in his instinctive sympathy for the 'bottom dog.' In its earliest manifestation, when he acted as campaign manager for Jane Cobden in 1888, his feminism was reflected in his Radical politics. He thought that 'Votes for Women' must be a component of any democratic political system, and that a franchise based upon universal suffrage would be more Radical than one limited to men only. He did not question the existence of separate spheres for the two sexes, wishing merely to enlarge the sphere in which women operated so that it might include the political realm. This approach was well intentioned but limited; it has outlasted George Lansbury, I think. But Lansbury himself, who was already on the verge of transcending it even in 1888, did so with a vengeance during the Edwardian era. By then he understood that 'Votes for Women' meant much more than a democratic, or even Radical, electorate. He believed that the enfranchisement of women was a necessary step towards the liberation of half the human race. He condemned the very concept of separate spheres and believed that possession of the franchise would help women to eradicate it. At the same time he believed that women could only realize their full human potential in a socialist society. In the by-election of 1912 he attempted to link the women's and socialist movements, while insisting upon the distinctiveness of each.

Lansbury was not, perhaps, indispensable to the women's movement, but he played a major role during a crucial epoch in its history, one which only this study has examined in any detail. His experiences cast light upon a broad conceptual or theoretical issue, the relationship between feminism and socialism. Moreover, they suggest new ways of regarding certain historical problems. For instance, Sandra Holton has suggested recently that feminists played an important part in helping to establish Labour as a significant political force during 'the years of great unrest.' This in itself represented a significant revision of previous interpretations, which discounted the feminist role. Lansbury's associations during the two years before the outbreak of World War I, however, suggest that a further refinement may be necessary. They seem to indicate that feminists were involved not merely in Labour's attempts to enlarge the franchise as Holton argued, but in Lansbury's own efforts to unify the myriad of left-wing groups and individuals dissatisfied with the policies advanced by Labour's leaders. The suffragette role in Lansbury's crusade requires more research before it can be established, but the part of Section II that deals with the Edwardian era tentatively poses a new way of regarding some of the political struggles which marked it.

Or consider the origins of the Labour Party. Historians have emphasized diverse factors to help explain how, in the 1880s and 1890s, Labour began its rise to power. They have mentioned increased class consciousness among the workers, the snobbery of local Liberal parties, Gladstone's obsession with Ireland, and so on. No scholar has suggested that feminists played a significant role during this early period. In Lansbury's case, however, it seems clear that they did. His commitment to 'Votes for Women' helped him to pinpoint Liberal deficiencies. In 1892 he joined the S.D.F., in part because he was disgusted by the luke-warm support Liberal leaders offered Jane Cobden in her campaign for the first London County Council. Even Raymond Postgate failed to mention this, yet clearly it was critical (and if to Lansbury then, possibly, to the comrades he brought with him from the Bow and Bromley Liberal and Radical Association into the S.D.F.). Thus again the career of George Lansbury seems to suggest that the relationship between feminists and Labourites was more symbiotic, more complex, and of longer standing than historians have realized.

Lansbury's connection with the pacifists, while well known, has been virtually ignored by historians of post-1914 Britain, perhaps because at first glance it appears relatively unproblematic. Lansbury is usually held to have been a saint-like figure, not wise in the ways of the world, and manifestly unfit to lead a major political party. He played his role to perfection during World War I, according to this view of his life, when he bravely championed international and Christian principles against a tide of chauvinism and martial ardor. During the period when he led the Labour Party, however, he was out of his depth, or so this version of events would have it. Had Bevin not dispatched him to the political wilderness in 1935, it would have been necessary for someone else to do so.

Examining Lansbury's pacifism has led me to different conclusions, however. I have tried to show that his pacifist ideals were linked, inextricably, with his socialism; and that his defeat at the hands of Ernest Bevin should be viewed in a wider context than historians usually have brought to bear upon that famous confrontation. This does seem to suggest a new way of viewing the period and its political struggles. Lansbury was not so much out of his depth during 1931-35, as he was out of touch with majority sentiment in the labor movement. He was fighting a rearguard battle in which the chance of success was extremely slight. At Labour's Annual Conference in 1935, according to this way of viewing things, Bevin vanquished not merely opposition to sanctions but also a vision, of socialism and of what the Labour Party should be, whose roots stretched back at least to the 1880s. Lansbury embodied that alternative understanding.

If 1931-35 was most important for defining the wideranging nature of Lansbury's pacifism, however, 1918-21 was when he first had demonstrated that it was more than a beautiful, impractical theory. During the postwar period, he linked pacifism with class struggle. Lansbury maintained that workers who refrained from violence while they were on strike were engaged in a form of passive resistance. Thus 'direct action,' as revolutionaries of the period termed it, and passive resistance as Lansbury understood it, were not mutually exclusive tactics between which Labourites must choose. Rather they could be combined in a single strategy for attaining socialism. In 1921 the Poplar councillors demonstrated the truth and effectiveness of Lansbury's approach, at least under certain historical conditions.

Lansbury was not an original thinker or important theorist. His speeches and writings hardly demonstrate a sophisticated understanding of socialist principles. He held that competitive capitalism was inherently unfair to workers, that socialism represented a higher stage of human existence than capitalism because it would be based upon cooperation and sharing, that class struggle could never be resolved in a capitalist society, that the state was dominated by a ruling class which, under capitalism, was the

George Lansbury

bourgeoisie, and that the workers must have their own political party so that they could capture state power for themselves. These were his ABCs and he never relinquished them.

Eventually, however, they were overlaid by Christian pacifist ideals. We have seen how his merging of Christ and Marx during and immediately after World War I brought him to a pinnacle of popularity and influence.

Twenty years later, when he sent the telegram to Benes advising him to turn the other cheek to Hitler, and when he supported Chamberlain at Munich, they brought him, ironically, to the nadir of his career. Nevertheless, if Lansbury did have an original and lasting contribution to make to the theoretical underpinnings of the British labor and socialist movements it was in this area. The argument that socialism, Christianity and pacifism could not be disentangled, that each implied the others, has characterized the outlook of an important section of the Labour Party ever since. Lansbury held that socialism meant religion and that religion meant pacifism. Those equations still echo at Labour Party conferences fifty years after Lansbury's death.

Yet he was not a dreamy sentimentalist who was content merely to mouth idealistic phrases, nor was he a crank. It would be unfair to associate him with the sandal-wearing vegetarians George Orwell excoriated with macho elan in *The Road to Wigan Pier*. Rather, from the beginning of his career until its very end, he was a canny, hard-working, politician. During the 1880s the Liberals valued his efforts in their behalf so highly that they offered to find him a seat in Parliament; during the 1890s the Social Democrats discovered him to be the best organizer they ever had. During the first decades of the twentieth century when he was a Poor Law guardian and county councillor, he built the socialist movement of Bow and Bromley, and of the East End more generally, into a powerful, democratic, political machine. Eventually the former saw-mill laborer became a Cabinet Minister and leader of the

Labour Party. During1935–39 he helped to mount and direct a massive peace campaign. This, and it is only a partial listing of his accomplishments, testifies not only to his willingness to work hard, but to his talent for the nuts and bolts of political organizing' which are prerequisites for any successful political career. His many successes indicate, too, that he must have been a master negotiator, someone who well understood the give-and-take in which all politicians must engage.

Yet he was stubborn. When he became convinced that he was right, then nothing and no one could change his mind. Over the course of fifty years this proved both a strength and a weakness. Lansbury never feared to face the wilderness. In fact, at times he seemed positively to relish it. On the one hand this is not surprising. Why should a man who had seen a band of street-corner agitators and visionaries build a party to replace the Liberals within twenty-five years fear the political wilderness? Lansbury may have said that he learned from the by-election of 1912 to 'Never Resign,' but he seems also to have learned that resigning would not necessarily keep him on the political sidelines forever. Adhering to principle could pay political dividends in the long run. Was this not, eventually, the lesson of 1892 when he left the Liberals, of 1912 when he forced the by-election, of 1914-18 when he was an unpopular pacifist, of 1921 when he was leader of the rebel Poplar councillors? As a result of his actions during those years he gained a reputation for integrity and generosity which still endures.

On the other hand, stubborness can be a form of selfishness; adherence to principle, on some occasions, can be a demonstration of pride or of an unwillingness to face facts. During his last years Lansbury's refusal to acknowledge the futility of the campaign for a world economic conference meant that he had become blind to reality. His meetings with Hitler and Mussolini testified, no doubt, to his principled opposition to war; but they testified, too, to a sad lessening of his critical faculties. Where once he had put principle above pride of place, at the end, just possibly, he had placed his pride above his principles.

His stubborness only let him down towards the end of his last decade. By then there was something almost anachronistic about him. During the 1930s George Lansbury, a Victorian who lived almost long enough to learn of Dachau, was out of place and time. He belonged to Keir Hardie's generation, not to Clement Attlee's. He was a true exponent, I have tried to show, of the religion of socialism. But, during the last years of his life, he was preaching to deaf ears. Lansbury had had trouble enough with unbelievers such as Webb, MacDonald, and the other Labourist pioneers at the turn of the century and during the Edwardian era. The new generation of movement leaders, Bevin, Attlee, Dalton and Morrison, were even less amenable. They were adherents of Keynes more than of Marx, of Sidney Webb more than of Keir Hardie. Can one imagine Keir Hardie leading Labour in the 1930s? That was the unlikely role in which the Labour figure who most bears comparison to Hardie found himself at the end of his career. George Lansbury served as leader of the Labour Party during a crucial moment of transition, but he would not transit with it. He was a true representative of a dissident strand which has been present throughout Labour's history, one which I hope this book has helped to illuminate.

Chronology of Lansbury's life

2.21.1859   Birth of George Lansbury in Suffolk.

1868   Family moves to East London.

1875   Death of Lansbury's father. Lansbury meets his future wife, Elizabeth Jane Brine.

Under the influence of Reverend J. Fenwick Kitto, Vicar of Whitechapel, he becomes religious.

1.29.1880   He marries Bessie.

1881   Death of Lansbury's mother.

1884   Emigrates to Australia with wife, three children and a younger brother.

1885   Returns to London.

1886   Organizes anti-emigration conference impressing Samuel Montagu.

Becomes a ward secretary of Bow and Bromley Radical and Liberal Association.

Successfully organizes Montagu's campaign during general election.

Accepts invitation of J. A. Murray MacDonald to become his election agent.

Promoted to general secretary of Bow and Bromley Radical and Liberal Association.

1888   Appointed Jane Cobden's election agent.

1.13.1889   Cobden wins election to first London County Council.

Lansbury helps establish monthly review, *Coming Times*.

He aids London dockers in their famous strike.

12.4.1889   Ruled out of order at Manchester Conference of National Liberal Federation.

1890   Loses religion.

Lansbury actively involved in campaign to change law excluding women from county councils.

1891   Cobden finally ruled ineligible to serve on L.C.C.

Coming Times suspends publication.

1892 Successfully manages Murray MacDonald's parliamentary campaign in general election.

Resigns from Liberal Party and joins Social Democratic Federation.

A candidate of the S.D.F., he is elected to Poplar Board of Guardians.

1893 I.L.P. is established. Lansbury does not join it.

1895 Lansbury stands as S.D.F. candidate at parliamentary by-election in Walworth. Among other socialist luminaries, Emmeline and Richard Pankhurst campaign in his behalf. He gets 347 votes.

Stands for Walworth again in general election. This time he gets 203 votes.

Appointed national organizer of S.D.F.

1896 Gives up post as S.D.F. national organizer upon death of father-in-law.

1900 Labour Representation Committee, direct forerunner of the Labour Party, is established. The S.D.F. affiliated to it.

During the general election Lansbury stands for Bow and Bromley sponsored jointly by the L.R.C. and the S.D.F. He opposes the Boer War, an unpopular position. But this time he gets 2,558 votes against 4,403 for the Conservative.

1903 Probably the year that Lansbury leaves the S.D.F. for the I.L.P.

Women's Social and Political Union established by Emmeline Pankhurst.

1904 Lansbury meets Joseph Fels.

3.5.1904 At Lansbury's urging Poplar Board of Guardians takes over Laindon Farm, recently purchased by Fels.

Fels also purchases Hollesley Bay Agricultural College to be used as a farm colony by committee appointed by Walter Long, Conservative President of the Local Government Board.

1905 Conservative Government establishes Royal Commission on the Poor Law. Lansbury appointed to it.

1906 Massive victory of Liberal Party during general election.

Entrance of Parliamentary Labour Party onto historical stage.

Lansbury stands for Parliament as an independent Labour Candidate at Middlesbrough. Loses badly to J. Havelock Wilson, Lib-Lab leader of Seamen's and Firemen's Union. But he becomes friends with Marion Coates Hansen who recruits him as a chief male supporter of the W.S.P.U.

6.7.1906   First session of inquiry, chaired by James Davy and set up by John Burns now President of Local Government Board, into Laindon Farm Colony and procedures of Poplar Board of Guardians.

1907   Victor Grayson elected to parliament for Colne Valley as an 'Independent Socialist.' This serves as precedent for Lansbury's Bow and Bromley by-election campaign five years later.

1909   Poor Law Commission recommends abolition of the Poor Law. Minority Report, signed by Lansbury, recommends much more.

1910   Lansbury elected to L.C.C.

Elected to Parliament in second general election of the year.

Green Manifesto, written by I.L.P. militants, questions their party's adherance to Labour Party. Lansbury disapproves. Supports position of MacDonald reaffirming the worth of affiliation.

Conciliation Bill passed by House of Commons seems to indicate that government will accept some measure of female enfranchisement soon.

1911   Asquith abandons Conciliation Bill in favor of Adult Suffrage Bill. Suffragettes resume militant agitation.

Establishment of *Daily Herald*.

5.26.1911   Lansbury demands 'relentless oppostion' to the government until it falls or enacts women's suffrage, a position which MacDonald will not accept.

Lansbury stands for chairmanship of I.L.P. Defeated by W.C. Anderson, 185 votes to 112.

6.25.1912   Lansbury accuses Asquith of being 'beneath contempt' during session of House of Commons.

11.11.1912   Resigns parliamentary seat in order to force a by-election on issue of women's suffrage.

11.26.1912   Loses the by-election.

7.29.1913   Lansbury sent to prison for inciting criminal acts, i.e., militant ones, on behalf of women's suffrage. Released after hunger strike of three days' duration.

Daily Herald, under Lansbury's direction, supports all rebel tendancies everywhere.

8.2.1914   Lansbury organizes famous anti-war demonstration at Trafalgar Square.

8.4.1914 Britain declares war.

Formation of Fellowship of Reconciliation, which Lansbury joins.

1915 Death of Keir Hardie.

Asquith establishes his first Coalition Government.

1916 Lloyd George kicks out Asquith and establishes a second Coalition Government.

1917 First Russian Revolution.

Leeds conference advises British people to establish 'Workers' and Soldiers' Councils' on the Russian model. Lansbury, unable to attend due to illness, agrees wholeheartedly.

Bolshevik Revolution.

11.4.1918 Armistice.

'Khaki Election' results in massive victory for Conservatives and Lloyd George-sponsored candidates. Labour Party, reorganized by Henderson and Webb and now with a socialist constitution, returns 59 representatives as opposed to less than 30 Asquithians. But Lansbury loses once again in Bow and Bromley. This time the count is: Lansbury 7,240, Blair (Conservative) 8,190.

1919 Treaty of Versailles made public. Lansbury immediately criticizes it as punitive and likely to lead to a second world war.

Daily Herald, under Lansbury's direction, supports 'direct action,' i.e., strikes for political purposes, which Labourists fear as revolutionary.

Lansbury elected Mayor of Poplar

2.5.1920 Lansbury becomes first British editor to visit Russia. Meets Lenin: impression positive. Lansbury declares 'Hands Off Russia!'

British 'Council of Action' threatens general strike if Lloyd George supports Poles in war against Russia. No such war takes place.

4.15.1921 'Black Friday' results in disintegration of Triple Alliance.

Unemployment reaches two million.

Poplarism results in 'equalisation of the poor rate.'

1922 Conservatives withdraw from Lloyd George's Government, forcing a general election which they win. Bonar Law becomes Prime Minister.

Lansbury re-elected to Parliament, this time in a landslide,

15,402 to 8,626 for the Conservative candidate, Duveen. Labour has now 142 M.P.s.

Lansbury elected to Labour Party Executive. Supports membership of Communists in Labour Party.

He gives up editorship of *Daily Herald*, which Labour Party now takes over.

1923   Baldwin calls another general election. Labour, with Liberal backing, has parliamentary majority. Lansbury again re-elected for Bow and Bromley in a landslide. MacDonald forms the first Labour Government. Offers Lansbury Ministry of Transport, a minor post which Lansbury declines.

1924   Liberals withdraw support and Labour government falls.

1926   General strike.

1929   Formation of second Labour Government. MacDonald, again Prime Minister, brings Lansbury into Cabinet as First Commissioner of Works.

Wall Street Crash, world depression, unemployment in Britain.

MacDonald appoints Lansbury to Unemployment Committee headed by J.H. Thomas, the Lord Privy Seal. Its two other members are Oswald Mosley and Tom Johnston.

1930   Depression worsens, Thomas fails to devise a constructive program for dealing with it, Mosley drafts memorandum, supported by Lansbury and Johnston, advocating proto-Keynesian solutions to unemployment. Chancellor of Exchequer Philip Snowden will not accept increased government expenditure. Mosley resigns.

1931   Unemployment rises nearly to three million. May Committee of Inquiry into government economic policies demands massive cutback in government expenditures. Meanwhile banks collapse throughout Europe. Run on Bank of England follows. American banks offer loan if British Government makes cutbacks recommended by May Committee. Nine Cabinet Ministers, including Lansbury, oppose cutting unemployment benefits. Hopelessly divided, the entire Cabinet resigns. MacDonald accepts resignations and, retaining his own position as Prime Minister, forms a Coalition Government with Conservatives and Liberals. Invites three former Labour Ministers, including Snowden, to stay on.

MacDonald calls general election, appealing for a 'Doctor's

Mandate' to support his 'National' Government. Wins in a landslide. Labour decimated. Old party leaders swept away, except for George Lansbury who now becomes party leader.

Japanese invade Manchuria.

1932   I.L.P. secedes from Labour Party.

1933   Hitler takes power in Germany.

Germany withdraws from disarmament talks at League of Nations.

Lansbury opposes fascism, but supports appeasement of powers victimized by Treaty of Versailles.

Lansbury's wife, Bessie, dies.

1934   Lansbury developing scheme for Britain of unilateral renunciation of empire and unilateral disarmament.

Canon Dick Sheppard sends letter to press which leads to establishment of Peace Pledge Union.

1935   Italian invasion of Abysinnia.

Lansbury driven from leadership of Labour Party.

Lansbury launches his last campaign – to avert a second world war.

1936   Lansbury tours U.S. in peace crusade. Meets with President Roosevelt.

He travels to France, Belgium, Scandinavia, on same quest.

Outbreak of civil war in Spain.

1937   Hoping to drum up support for the world economic conference, Lansbury meets with Hitler.

Lansbury meets with Mussolini.

Lansbury meets with leaders of Czechoslovakia, Poland and Austria.

1938   Lansbury meets with leaders of Romania, Yugoslavia, Hungary, Bulgaria.

German *anschluss* with Austria.

Munich Agreement truncates Czechoslovakia. Lansbury supports it because war would lead to worse things.

1939   Hitler siezes the rest of Czechoslovakia.

Lansbury, hoping against hope, continues meeting with various leaders of European countries in desperate search for support of the world economic conference.

Germany invades Poland.

Britain and France declare war on Germany.

5.17.1940   Death of George Lansbury.

Notes

Introduction

1 *Daily Herald*, May 21, 1921.

2 *Daily Herald*, August 27, 1921.

3 Ivan Maisky, *Journey Into the Past* (London), 1962, p. 134.

4 Raymond Postgate, *George Lansbury* (London), 1951, pp.289-90.

1 Lansbury and socialism

1 Postgate, *George Lansbury*, p. 31.

2 For Britain's great depression see S.B. Saul, *The Myth of the Great Depression* (London) 1969; for East London during this period see especially Gareth Stedman Jones, *Outcast London* (Oxford), 1971; for the I.L.P. during its pioneering days see David Howell, *British Workers and the Independent Labour Party 1886–1906* (Manchester), 1983.

3 For Liberalism in Britain as a whole during this period see H.V. Emy, *Liberals, Radicals and Social Politics, 1892-1914* (Cambridge), 1973; for Liberals in London see Paul Thompson, *Socialists, Liberals and Labour, The Struggle for London, 1885-1914* (London), 1967.

4 The flyer, dated February 1886, is preserved in the George Lansbury Collection, B.L.P.E.S., Vol. 1.

5 *Liberal Year Book*, 1886.

6 See below, pp. 68-86.

7 Quoted in *Coming Times*, January 1891.

8 Lansbury, however, went home from Trafalgar Square.

9 See, for example, Cobden Unwin Collection, Bristol University Library, Lansbury to Cobden, December 29, 1888.

10 *Ibid.*, June 2, 1891.

11 *Ibid.*, January 1, 1890.

12 *Coming Times*, August 1889; see also *Reynolds's Newspaper*, July 21, 1889.

13 Cobden Unwin Collection. See, for example, Lansbury's letters to her of December 29, 1888, August 17, 1889, April 20, 1890, May 1, 1890, May 5, 1890.

14 Lansbury Collection, for example, J.A.M. MacDonald to Lansbury, February 17, 1890; see also, *Coming Times*, November 1889.

15 Cobden Unwin Collection, Lansbury to Cobden, May 14, 1890.

16 Lansbury Collection, see MacDonald's reply of June 18, 1892 to Lansbury's letter, 'I don't think this fear operates to any important extent.'

17 The classic account of Labour's rise is Henry Pelling, *The Origins of the Labour Party* (London), 1955.

18 Cobden Unwin Collection, see Lansbury to Cobden January 13, 1889.

19 *Coming Times*, December 1890.

20 For the London meeting see *ibid.*, August 1889.

21 Postgate, *George Lansbury*, p. 36.

22 Cobden Unwin Collection, Lansbury to Cobden, June 2, 1891.

23 *Coming Times*, December 1890.

24 *Ibid.*

25 Cobden Unwin Collection, Lansbury to Cobden, August 17, 1891.

26 *Ibid.*, 1891.

27 *Daily Herald*, January 21, 1922.

28 *Ibid.*, October 3, 1921.

29 *Labour Leader*, May 17, 1912.

30 *Coming Times*, February 1890.

31 Lansbury explaining 'Why I left the Radicals and joined the S.D.F.' to the Walworth Liberal and Radical Club and Institute, Justice, July 21, 1894.

32 *Labour Leader*, May 17, 1912.

33 Rather like bird droppings piled up to make a nest MacDonald said, if I remember correctly.

34 *Daily Herald*, October 3, 1921.

35 John Saville, 'The Ideology of Labourism', in *Knowledge and Belief in Politics: the Problem of Ideology*, Robert Benwick, R.N.Berki and Bhikhu Parekh (eds.) (London), 1973, pp. 213-26.

36 Lansbury's *Labour Weekly*, July 16, 1927.

37 *Justice*, April 22, 1893.

38 Edward Thompson, 'The Peculiarities of the English', *Socialist Register 1965*, pp. 311-62; Stephen Yeo, 'The Religion of Socialism', *History Workshop Journal* 4

(Autumn 1977), pp. 5-56.

39 See Lansbury's *The Principles of the English Poor Law: Being a paper read at the Central Poor Law Conference held at the Guildhall 1897*, 1897, in which this notion is implicit throughout.

40 *Ibid.*, p. 6; *Justice*, May 11, 1895.

41 Lansbury, *Principles of English Poor Law*, p. 11.

42 *Ibid.*, p. 13.

43 Lansbury's by-election address, February, 1894, and general election address, May 1895, both preserved in Lansbury Collection, vol 30.

44 *The Arbitrator*, May 1892. Speech delivered April 13, 1892.

45 February 1894 is the date given on hand-written notes of an address by Lansbury. Lansbury's 'Message to the Electors of Walworth', *Justice*, May 11, 1895.

46 *Daily Herald*, January 14, 1913.

47 George Haw, (ed.) *The Religious Doubts of Democracy* (London), 1904, p. 8.

48 *Social Democrat*, January, 1900, p. 5.

49 *Justice*, March 14, 1896.

50 *Labour Leader*, May 17, 1912.

51 Postgate, *George Lansbury*, p. 32.

52 Quoted in *ibid.*, p. 44.

53 *Justice*, February 8, 1896.

54 *Report of the Sixteenth Annual Conference of the S.D.F.*, August 2-3, 1896, p. 1. Lansbury was chairman of the conference and these remarks were part of his chairman's address.

55 *Daily Herald*, October 2, 1920.

56 *Justice*, November 3, 1894.

57 *Ibid.*, March 19, 1898.

58 *Ibid.*, April 28, 1894.

59 *Ibid.*, February 17, 1900.

60 *Social Democrat*, January 1897, p. 18.

61 *Justice*, October 27, 1894.

62 Postgate, *George Lansbury*, p. 33.

63 *Social Democrat*, January, 1900, p. 16.

64 *Justice*, October 13, 1894.

65 Postgate, *George Lansbury*, p. 71.

66 George Lansbury, *Unemployment, the Next Step* (n.d.), p. 6.

67 George Lansbury, *My Life,*, 1928, p. 141.

68 For more on the Poor Law Commission and Minority Report see, especially, Beatrice Webb, *Our Partnership* (London), 1948, chapter 7.

69 For a more complete description of the inquiry see Postgate, *George Lansbury*, pp. 77-8, on which my own account is largely based. For more on Burns see W. G. R. Kent, *John Burns, Labour's Lost Leader* (London), 1950.

70 Lansbury wrote to the *Labour Leader* of November 16, 1906, 'the London press, both Liberal and Tory ... forgot to print the returns from my ward'.

71 *Labour Leader*, February 1, 1907.

72 *Bow and Bromley Worker*, October 1910.

73 *Labour Leader*, October 18, 1907.

74 *Ibid.*, July 9, 1909.

75 *Ibid.*, January 7, 1910.

76 Keir Hardie is much less easily defined.

77 For more on Labour Party attitudes to unemployment during this period see Kenneth D. Brown, 'The Labour Party and the Unemployed Question, 1906-1910', *Historical Journal*, XIV, 3 (1971), pp. 599-616, and José Harris, *Unemployment and Politics: a Study in English Social Policy, 1886-1914* (Oxford), 1972.

78 Lansbury, *My Life*, p. 155. Eventually the Metropolitan Water Board was also included on this list.

79 Noreen Branson, *George Lansbury and the Councillors' Revolt: Poplarism, 1919-25* (London), 1979, is the indispensable source for this episode.

80 *Daily Herald*, September 26, 1921.

81 *Labour Monthly*, June 1922, 'Poplar and the Labour Party' by George Lansbury, p. 388.

82 *Daily Herald*, October 29, 1921.

83 *Ibid.*, September 26, 1921.

84 *Ibid.*, July 16, 1921.

85 *Ibid.*, September 2, 1921, also quoted in Branson, *George Lansbury and the Councillor's Revolt*, p. 50.

86 *Ibid.*, October 14, 1921.

87 *Ibid.*, July 29, 1921.

88 *Ibid.*, August 6, 1921.

89 *Ibid.*, September 1, 1921.

90 *Ibid.*, September 12, 1921.

91 It was not, however. See, for instance, James Hinton, *Protests and Visions: Peace Politics in 20th Century Britain*, 1989, pp. 83-4.

92 *Herald*, September 1, 1917.

93 *The Times*, January 9, 1924.

94 *Daily Herald*, September 13, 1919.

95 *Ibid.*, March 27, 1920.

96 *Ibid.*, April 3, 1920.

97 *Ibid.*, January 31, 1921.

98 *Ibid.*, March 21, 1921.

99 *Ibid.*, July 30, 1921.

100 *Labour Monthly*, June 1922, pp. 390-1.

101 *Daily Herald*, March 23, 1921.

102 *Ibid.*, August 17, 1921.

103 *Ibid.*, October 11, 1921.

2 Lansbury and feminism

1 See *Pall Mall Gazette*, November 19, 1888, for a more detailed description of this meeting.

2 See Constance Rover, *Women's Suffrage and Party Politics in Britain, 1866-1914* (London), 1967, pp. 102-43.

3 A little-known sidelight: Lansbury opposed Besant in this contest, working instead for the Liberal candidate, the Reverend J.F.Porter. See *Social Democrat*, January 1900, p. 5.

4 Cobden Unwin Collection, Lansbury to Cobden, July 1, 1890.

5 *Ibid.*, December 9, 1888.

6 *Ibid.*, undated.

7 *Ibid.*, December 14, 1888.

8 *Star*, December 29, 1888.

9 *Ibid.*

10 *East London Observer*, January 6, 1889.

11 Cobden Unwin Collection, Lansbury to Cobden, December 21, 1888.

12 Ibid., December 20, 1888.

13 *Pall Mall Gazette*, January 24, 1889.

14 *The Times*, May 15, 1889.

15 *Ibid.*, May 20, 1889.

16 Cobden Unwin Collection, Lansbury to Cobden, May 21, 1889.

17 *Ibid.*

18 *Ibid.*, August 17, 1889.

19 *Ibid.*, October 25, 1889.

20 *Ibid.*, January 7, 1890.

21 See *Pall Mall Gazette* for March 5 and March 10, 1890.

22 Cobden Unwin Collection, Lansbury to Cobden, April 20, 1890.

23 *Ibid.*, Lansbury to Miss Browne, February 28, 1890.

24 *Ibid.*, Lansbury to Cobden, April 28, 1890.

25 *Ibid.*, May 26,1891.

26 *The Times*, April 17, 1891.

27 See Erna Reiss, *Rights and Duties of Englishwomen* (Manchester), 1934, p. 206.

28 Cobden Unwin Collection, Lansbury to Cobden, July 1, 1890.

29 *Ibid.*, June 2, 1891.

30 *Ibid.*

31 *Votes for Women*, April 25, 1913.

32 Sandra Holton, *Feminism and Democracy, Women's Suffrage and Reform Politics in Britain, 1900-1918* (Cambridge), 1986.

33 Cobden Unwin Collection, Lansbury to Cobden, June 2, 1891.

34 See his letters to Ramsay MacDonald, in the MacDonald Collection at the Public Record Office, PRO30/69/1149.

35 On this see, among many, David Coates, *The Labour Party and the Struggle for Socialism* (Cambridge), 1975.

36 *Labour Leader*, April 28, 1911.

37 Lansbury Collection, Marion Coates Hansen to Lansbury, May 24, 1906.

38 *Ibid.*, Emmeline Pethick Lawrence to Lansbury, June 25, 1906.

39 Passfield Collection,B.L.P.E.S.,11/4/e/21, Lansbury, to Beatrice Webb, July 28, 1911.

40 *Votes for Women*, November 24, 1911.

41 *Labour Leader*, October 20, 1911.

42 *Daily Herald*, May 20, 1912.

43 *Votes for Women*, March 15, 1912.

44 *Ibid.*, May 10, 1912.

45 Independent Labour Party Collection, B.L.P.E.S., N.A.C., 1/6.

46 I.L.P. Collection, Correspondence Box 27, Lansbury to Hardie, March 8, 1912.

47 See the *Daily Herald*, June 26, 1912, and *Votes for Women*, June 28, 1912, upon which my description of the event is based.

48 *Votes for Women*, October 4, 1912.

49 *Ibid.*, October 18, 1912.

50 *Daily Herald*, November 28, 1912.

51 *Labour Leader*, December 15, 1912.

52 *Daily Herald*, October 19, 1912.

53 *Labour Leader*, December 5, 1912.

54 *Daily Herald*, November 4, 1912.

55 *Votes for Women*, November 22, 1912.

56 *Daily Herald*, November 28, 1912.

57 *Ibid.*, November 21, 1912.

58 *Ibid.*, November 19, 1912.

59 Lansbury Collection, J. Scotney to Lansbury, November 17, 1912.

60 *Daily Herald*, November 28, 1912.

61 *Ibid.*, November 20, 1912.

62 *Votes for Women*, November 22, 1912.

63 *Suffragette*, November 29, 1912.

64 Lansbury Collection, G. Saunders Jacobs to Lansbury, November 27, 1912.

65 *Votes for Women*, July 5, 1912.

66 *Suffragette*, November 29, 1912.

67 *Daily Herald*, December 17, 1912.

68 *Suffragette*, October 25, 1912.

69 *Votes for Women*, November 22, 1912.

70 *Suffragette*, November 22, 1912.

71 For descriptions see *Votes for Women*, November 29, 1912, *Suffragette*, November 29, 1912, and *Daily Herald*, November 26, 1912, from which all quotes are drawn.

72 E. Sylvia Pankhurst, *The Suffragette Movement* (London), 1931, p. 426; see pp. 424-7 for a scathing account of the campaign.

73 *Daily Herald*, November 27, 1912.

74 *Labour Leader*, November 28, 1912.

75 *Daily Herald*, November 27, 1912.

76 *Votes for Women*, April 18, 1912.

77 *Daily Herald*, May 5, 1913.

78 George Dangerfield, *The Strange Death of Liberal England* (London), 1935.

79 See Holton, *Feminism and Democracy*, p. 124.

80 *Daily Herald*, September 22, 1913.

81 Lansbury Collection, undated lecture entitled 'Our Wives', tentatively dated 1899 by Lansbury's executor, Raymond Postgate.

82 George Lansbury, *Socialism for the Poor*, 'Pass on Pamphlets, no. 12', 1909, p. 19.

83 Lansbury Collection, Lansbury to Marion Coates Hansen, October 31, 1912.

84 *Daily Herald*, May 5, 1913.

85 *Suffragette*, June 20, 1913.

86 Lansbury Collection, Burrows to Lansbury, November 27, 1912.

87 On this issue see, especially, Jill Liddington and Jill Norris, *One Hand Tied Behind Us, The Rise of the Women's Suffrage Movement* (London), 1978.

88 David Howell, *British Social Democracy* (London), 1976, Stanley Pierson, *British Socialists, the Journey from Fantasy to Politics* (Cambridge, Mass.), 1978.

3 Lansbury and pacifism

1 *Reconciliation*, October 1935.

2 *Arbitrator*, May 1892.

3 *Ibid.*

4 'George Lansbury's Election Address,' printed in *Justice*, September 29, 1900.

5 *Ibid.*, January 19, 1901.

6 *Report of I.L.P. Annual Conference*, 1910, pp. 66-7, quoted in Douglas Newton, *British Labour, European Socialism and the Struggle for Peace* (Oxford), 1985, p. 254.

7 *Herald*, May 15, 1915.

8 I.L.P. Collection, Correspondence Files, Box 30, Lansbury to Hardie, n.d., but from internal evidence probably July 31, 1914.

9 Beatrice Webb, *Beatrice Webb's Diaries, 1912-24*, 1952, p. 25.

10 *Daily Herald*, August 3, 1914.

11 C.P. Trevelyan Collection, University of Newcastle Library, CPT 73, Lansbury to Trevelyan, September 2, 1914.

12 Lansbury Collection, Minutes of *Daily Herald* Management Committee, August 25, 1914; John Burns Collection, British Library, Add. Ms. 46303/f.5, Lansbury to Burns, August 4, 1914.

13 George Lansbury, *Jesus and Labour*, 1924, p. 1.

14 Violet Markham Collection, B.L.P.E.S., 25/49, Lansbury to Markham, June 7, 1916.

15 *Herald*, June 1, 1918.

16 *Daily Herald*, May 8, 1912, for example: 'Christianity means first the bettering of the individual, secondly the improvement of the family, and thirdly and consequently, the progress of society towards Socialism.'

17 *Worker*, December 1914.

18 *Herald*, September 18, 1915.

19 *Ibid.*, March 9, 1918.

20 *Ibid.*, September 16, 1916.

21 Martin Ceadel, *Pacifism in Britain, 1914-45* (London), 1978, p. 36.

22 *Herald*, May 15, 1915.

23 *Ibid.*, August 4, 1917.

24 I.L.P. Manifesto, August 13, 1914, quoted in *The Left and the War, The British Labour Party and World War I*, Peter Stansky (ed.) (Oxford), 1969, p. 80.

25 Lansbury Collection, Watts to Lansbury, June 15, 1917.

26 *Daily Express*, January 18, 1916.

27 *Daily Herald*, May 17, 1919.

28 *Ibid.*, July 26, 1919.

29 *Ibid.*, October 4, 1919.

30 *Ibid.*, September 13, 1919.

31 *Herald*, September 1, 1917.

32 *Beatrice Webb's Diary*, vol. 3, February 24, 1920, p. 356.

33 Labour Party Collection, Walworth Road, WNC 19/2/392, Robert Williams to J. S. Middleton, February 13, 1918.

34 See *Beatrice Webb's Diary*, April 25, 1918, vol. 3.

35 Lloyd George Collection, Records Office, House of Lords, F/95/1/12-13, Lansbury to Lloyd George, July 2, 1919.

36 *Lansbury's Labour Weekly*, August 28, 1926.

37 *Ibid.*, March 15, 1924.

38 *Daily Herald*, July 14, 1923. He was being patient about something else, but the logic was the same.

39 Public Records Office, H045/24834.

40 *Hugh Dalton's Diary*, Ben Pimlott (ed.) (London), 1987, October 8, 1932, p. 169. For a rare example of the contrary view see Michael Foot, *Aneurin Bevan* (vol 1) (London), 1975, p. 167.

41 Actually, Postgate in *George Lansbury* makes this point too.

42 George Lansbury, *The Futility of the National Government*, n.d., p. 8.

43 *Lansbury's Labour Weekly*, August 28, 1926.

44 James and Lucy Middleton Collection, Ruskin College, Lansbury to James Middleton, September 8,1934. (Photocopy of this letter at Labour Party Headquarters.)

45 *New Chronicle*, January 29, 1932.

46 *Daily Herald*, May 8, 1933.

47 *Manchester Guardian*, July 31, 1933.

48 See, for example, his short pamphlet, *Anti-semitism in the East End*, n.d.

49 *Daily Herald*, October 20, 1933.

50 *Birmingham Post*, September 9, 1933.

51 *Daily Herald*, September 9, 1933.

52 *Reconciliation*, October 1935, but Lansbury delivered this speech on September 13, while still Labour Party leader.

53 Lansbury Collection, Lansbury to Cripps, January 1, 1934.

54 *Report of Labour Party Annual Conference*, 1935, pp. 153-4.

55 *Ibid.*, p. 175.

56 *Ibid.*, 175-7.

57 Alan Bullock, *The Life and Times of Ernest Bevin* (London), vol. 1, 1960, p. 567.

58 Vera Britain, *Testament of Experience* (London), 1957, p. 165.

59 Lansbury Collection, vol. 28, Lansbury to Cripps, June 20, 1936.

60 Ceadel, *Pacifism in Britain*, p. 317.

61 *Ibid.*, p. 223.

62 Fenner Brockway, *Bermondsey Story, The Life of Alfred Salter* (London), 1949, p. 198.

63 *Ibid.*, p. 199.

64 Ceadel, *Pacifism in Britain*, pp. 262-4.

65 *Peace News*, August 22, 1936.

66 Public Record Office, F.O. 371/20745/387, Eden to Phipps, January 15, 1937.

67 *Ibid.*

68 Lansbury Collection, vol. 16, 'Notes on George Lansbury's Interview with Hitler', April 19, 1937.

69 *Peace News*, April 24, 1937.

70 *Manchester Guardian*, July, 19, 1937.

71 *Reconciliation*, September 1938.

72 *Daily Herald*, September 21, 1938. Lansbury's papers, vol. 16, contain a fuller account of this meeting, but they are incorrectly dated September 28.

73 Peace Pledge Union Collection, Dick Sheppard House, 'Emergency Sponsors' Meeting', September 22, 1938.

74 P.P.U. Collection, Chairman's Report, October 6, 1938.

75 Lansbury Collection, vol. 16, Lansbury to Benes, September 26, 1938.

76 P.P.U. Collection, Minutes, April 20, 1939.

77 Lansbury Collection, vol. 17, Lansbury to Cripps, April 22, 1940.

78 Postgate, *George Lansbury*, p. 321.

Bibliography

1 Papers of individuals

Jane Cobden Unwin Collection, University Library, University of Bristol.
George Lansbury Collection, British Library of Political and Economic Science.
Passfield Collection, B.L.P.E.S.
Violet Markham Collection, B.L.P.E.S.
Lord Ponsonby Collection, Bodleian Library, Oxford.
Lloyd George Papers, Records Office, House of Lords.
Herbert Samuel Papers, Records Office, House of Lords.
C.P. Trevelyan Collection, Library, University of Newcastle-upon-Tyne.
John Burns Collections, British Library.
James and Lucy Middleton Collection, Ruskin College, Oxford.
James Ramsey MacDonald Papers, Public Record Office, Kew.
Sir Normal Angell Collection, University Library, Ball State University.

2 Papers of organizations

Independent Labour Party Collection, B.L.P.E.S.
Fellowship of Reconciliation, B.L.P.E.S.
Labour Party Collection, Walworth Road, London.
Social Democratic Federation Collection, Marx Memorial Library, London.
Peace Pledge Union, Dick Sheppard House, London.

3 Government papers

Foreign Office files, P.R.O., Kew.
Home Office files, P.R.O., Kew.

4 Newspapers and journals

Daily Herald
Lansbury's Labour Weekly
Justice
Labour Leader

Bibliography

Coming Times
Pall Mall Gazette
Star
East London Observer
Votes for Women
Suffragette
Peace News
Reconciliation
Social Democrat
Socialist Review

5 Books by Lansbury

My Life, 1928.
Looking Backwards and Forwards, 1935.
Your Part in Poverty, 1918.
These Things Shall Be, 1919.
My England, 1934.
Why Pacifists Should Be Socialists, 1937.
What I Saw in Russia, 1920.
My Quest for Peace, 1938.

6 Pamphlets by Lansbury

The Principles of the English Poor Law, 1897.
London for Labour, 1909.
Unemployment: The Next Step, 1909.
Socialism for the Poor: the End of Pauperism, 1909.
My Impressions of Soviet Russia, 1920.
Jesus and Labour, 1924.
The Futility of the National Government, n.d.
Anti-semitism in the East End, n.d.

7 Articles by Lansbury

'Hollesley Bay', *Socialist Review*, I (May 1908) pp. 220-33.
'Poplar and the Labour Party: a defence of Poplarism', *Labour Monthly*, 2 (June 1922) pp. 383-9.

For secondary sources consulted please see endnotes.

Index

Index

Index